# The Challenge of School Change

∞

*A Collection
of Articles*

Edited by
Michael Fullan

**CORWIN PRESS**
A SAGE Publications Company
Thousand Oaks, California

*For information:*

Corwin Press
A Sage Publications Company
2455 Teller Road
Thousand Oaks, California 91320
www.corwinpress.com

Sage Publications Ltd.
1 Oliver's Yard
55 City Road
London EC1Y 1SP
United Kingdom

Sage Publications India Pvt. Ltd.
B-42, Panchsheel Enclave
New Delhi 110 017   India

Printed in the United States of America

ISBN 1-57517-039-6
LCCCN: 97-070719

This book is printed on acid-free paper.

05   06   07   08   09   10   9   8   7   6   5   4   3   2   1

| *Illustration and Cover Designer:* | David Stockman |
| *Book Designer:* | Heidi Ra |

# Contents

# Introduction

# The Challenge of School Change

In this collection of articles, we see the richness of analysis and insight that can be generated by altering the way we think about change. The technical-rational approach to reform gives way to a more balanced approach, which retains technical knowledge, but adds new concepts that relate more accurately to the dynamics of nonlinear change, and the emotional and moral purposes of educational reform. The struggles of change and the patterns of breakthrough become much more accessible with this more grounded analysis.

The articles in this book take recent developments to new levels of detail. They provide greater critical analysis and powerful empirical and theoretical observations about successful school change. Section 1 establishes some of the new theories of change. Section 2 takes a critical approach to examining new forms of leadership for change among educators, whether they be administrators or teacher leaders. Section 3 consists of a closer analysis of the school and community levels, drawing on some excellent recent empirical work.

In the final section, we step back from the fray by introducing two powerful new concepts—emotion and hope—arguing that the future of reform must embody these deeper personal and human characteristics in the never-ending journey of educational reform.

# Section 1

# Theories of Change

My colleague Andy Hargreaves and I have argued in our *What's Worth Fighting For* trilogy that we must combine a deeper analysis and understanding of the key concepts of change with a commitment and set of ideas for action (Fullan 1997, Fullan and Hargreaves 1996, Hargreaves and Fullan 1997). We have argued that teachers and principals must take the initiative if they are to break the vicious cycle of always being on the receiving end of reform. They must regroup internally and reframe their relationships with their colleagues and others inside and outside the school. They must, we said, go both deeper and wider if they are to have any change of healthy survival. Section 1 lays some of the groundwork for this line of thinking and action.

The article on complexity of change establishes the foundation for understanding the reality of non-linear change (Fullan 1993). Drawing on both theoretical and empirical evidence from business and educational literature, eight key lessons are formulated. These lessons, taken together, form a new mindset for understanding change. They introduce fresh insights about the dynamics of change—insights that, once articulated, make greater sense. Thinking about change in this new way opens up whole areas of pursuit and understanding.

In the subsequent articles, Andy Hargreaves takes us further down the path of complexity. He makes the case that the context of reform has fundamentally changed with schools to operate in very diverse and transparent ways. In "Cultures of Teaching," he presents the theoretical case that cultures of schools, as well as the culture of the entire teaching profession, must develop away from relative isolation and segmentation into collaborative cultures. Both Hargreaves and I have claimed that schools and the profession must "reculture" (see Section 3) as well as "restructure." Indeed, the rest of this book is about the many dimensions of reculturing.

## REFERENCES

Fullan, M. 1993. *Change forces: Probing the depths of educational reform.* Bristol, Penn.: Palmer Press.

———. 1997. *What's worth fighting for in the principalship.* 2nd ed. New York: Teachers College Press; Toronto: Ontario Public School Teachers' Federation.

Fullan, M., and A. Hargreaves. 1997. *What's worth fighting for in your school.* New York: Teachers College Press; Toronto: Ontario Public School Teachers' Federation.

Hargreaves, A., and M. Fullan. 1997. *What's worth fighting for out there.* New York: Teachers College Press; Toronto: Ontario Public School Teachers' Federation.

Senge, P. 1990. *The fifth discipline.* New York: Doubleday.

# Rethinking Educational Change

by Andy Hargreaves

## INTRODUCTION

A few years ago, in *What's Worth Fighting For In Your School,* Michael Fullan and I argued for a new approach to educational change (Fullan & Hargreaves, 1991). In the face of global tendencies to force educational change through externally imposed restructuring and reform, we emphasized the parallel and often greater importance of improving the internal interactions and relationships of schooling. We talked less about *restructuring* schools than *reculturing* them. We were concerned not with how teachers should commit to other people's changes but with how we might make schools into the kinds of places that stimulate and support teachers to make changes themselves. How teachers work with teachers, we showed, affects how well they work with their students. It was clear to us, therefore, that cultures of teaching should be a prime focus for educational change.

A central task in creating cultures of educational change is how to develop more collaborative working relationships between principals and teachers, and among teachers themselves. We pointed to the need for teachers to collaborate with each other, with trust, candor, openness, risk-taking, and commitment to continuous improvement. This article extends this argument further. It endorses the value of professional collaboration among teachers within the walls of schools, but argues that we now need to extend this collaboration beyond the school walls as well.

From *Rethinking Educational Change with Heart and Mind,* 1997 ASCD Yearbook, pp. 1–26. © 1997 by the Association for Supervision and Curriculum Development. Reprinted with permission.

Teachers' professional communities can easily turn into incestuous and protectionist ones. Teachers who work with other teachers are sometimes less inclined to work with anyone else. Collaboration can include the school professionals but exclude the wider community. New and innovative secondary schools, for example, typically falter because their leading edge, enthusiastic professionals fail to consult and involve the surrounding communities from which their students will be drawn (Sarason, 1971). If we are going to work together successfully for positive educational change, teachers now need to move beyond their own communities of fellow colleagues. Our change efforts need to go wider, beyond the school, if we are going to make significant improvements in what goes on within it.

**Teachers who work with other teachers are sometimes less inclined to work with anyone else.**

Why is it necessary to broaden our approach to educational change and school improvement? Many teachers are already overwhelmed by pressures for change *within* their own schools and classrooms. Don't they have enough to deal with already, without having to attend to yet more demands—demands that will now require teachers to extend their work beyond the school into homes, communities and workplaces? Aren't we in danger of making schools into dumping grounds for social and economic problems that are really other people's responsibility? Are teachers to be at the beck and call of every pushy parent and pressure group that has a bee in its bonnet or an ax to grind? Surely the last thing we need is yet more diversion of teachers' efforts and energies away from working with children in their own classrooms. Put more money in the classroom and leave teachers alone to do a professional job— isn't that a better solution? Who needs all this other stuff anyway?

I sympathize with these objections and reservations. It is true that many specious changes have been brought about under the banner of creating better partnerships between schools and other organizations. All too often, partnerships with industry have led to corporate dollars driving the curriculum in dubious directions; partnerships with faculties of education have come down to school teachers carrying the university staff's supervision load for them; and partnerships with parents have amounted to little more than cosmetic committee work, or to appeasing the demands of a pushy minority. It is also true that teachers have become increasingly and unreasonably buffeted by the single-issue demands of multiple interest groups and by the capricious policy whims of successive governments who have made education their altar of change and sacrificed teachers upon it. Partnerships are not always benevolent and pressure groups outside the school frequently have more than the children's interests at heart.

> **Schools can no longer pretend that their walls will keep the outside world at bay.**

So why should teachers and principals work with others outside the school for better teaching and learning within it when so many outside demands are politically suspect or bureaucratically time-consuming? What's the problem here?

## WHAT ARE THE PROBLEMS?

There are several reasons why schools need to make conscious and constructive connections with the wider world beyond them. These are:

1. schools cannot shut their gates and leave the outside world on the doorstep
2. schools are losing their monopoly on learning
3. schools are one of our last hopes for rescuing and reinventing community
4. teachers need a lot more help
5. market competition, parental choice and individual self-management are already redefining how schools relate to their wider environments
6. schools can no longer be indifferent to the working lives that await their students when they move into the adult world

More than ever today, *schools cannot shut their gates and leave the troubles of the outside world on the doorstep.* Schools can no longer pretend that their walls will keep the outside world at bay. They have become porous and permeable institutions (Elkind, 1993). Increased poverty creates hungry children who cannot learn and tired ones who cannot concentrate. Fractured, blended and lone parent families fill teachers' classes with children who are often troubled, present teachers with parents' nights of labyrinthine complexity, and leave them with outdated curriculum materials where families with two parents and their own children are presented as the cultural norm. In the face of mounting social problems, schools have often been made the sole public response, at the very same time that wider social support and intervention has been trimmed back (Barlow & Robertson, 1994). Although opinion polls indicate that most parents are not really dissatisfied with their children's education (Livingstone, 1993), business and the media are trying to inveigh parents into being critics and consumers of their children's schools: exercising choices, asking questions, making demands in the interest of trying to insure their offspring against uncertain economic futures (Grace, 1995).

Increased rates and changing patterns of global migration coupled with continuing low levels of teacher recruitment from visible minorities, also mean that teachers are often teaching "other people's children" whose backgrounds are unfamiliar to them and whose learning needs are unknown (Delpit, 1988). In some of the large urban school districts with which we have worked, over 50% of the students are classified as English as a second language and over 70 languages are spoken in the schools. For teachers, what's "out there" beyond their school is not an academic abstraction or a futuristic projection. It stares back at them everyday through the eyes of the children they teach. The reality of "what's out there" is therefore inescapable. It is something that teachers already deal with every day of their working lives. Teachers' interactions and responsibilities are becoming more extended. What matters, is not *whether* teachers connect with what's "out there" beyond their school, but how effectively they do so.

*Schools are losing their monopoly on learning.* One in three young people now have access to a personal computer at home (Hargreaves & Goodson, 1992). Many more make extensive use of television, video and the music culture of the streets. For the youth of today, the geography of learning stretches far beyond the physical space of the school. New technologies enable many students to reach out and connect with other students, other teachers, other worlds: to surf the Internet and ride the information superhighway without the teacher's immediate monitoring, support and intervention. Learning can often take place as easily at home as at school. Schooling is now available in cyberspace. Indeed, home-schooling is enjoying a spectacular rise in popularity. Children may know more about technology than their teachers and be able to access learning more easily through it. Unless teachers get up to speed in using technology in their classrooms, the hold they have on their students will weaken. Equally, however, in their rush to compete with the computer age and to keep their children's attention, teachers run the risk of reducing education to entertainment and losing sight of their larger purposes as a result (Postman, 1992; Stoll, 1995). The computer age is chipping away at the walls of schooling and at the autonomy and authority of teachers within them. Indeed, by permitting worldwide communication at the tap of a keyboard, computer technology dissolves the distinction between "what's out there" and "what's in here" altogether.

In fundamental and far reaching ways, new technologies are starting to redefine the social geography of schooling. Internally, they are challenging the spatial segregation of schooling into separate subjects and classes. Externally, students' capacity to access knowledge and information independently and to communicate with other children and adults internationally, is starting to dissolve the boundaries between community and school, making curriculum "relevance" a global and not merely an immediate and spatially "local" matter. Similarly, professional development networks for teachers challenge the spatial conventions of professional development as either school-based or university-based, and raise status issues about who controls such development by being able to define and distribute where it takes place. Teachers should not capitulate unthinkingly to new technology but they clearly cannot turn away from it either. Their students will not let them.

> **New technologies are starting to redefine the social geography of schooling.**

Across much of the developed world, *people are experiencing a crisis of community and schools provide one of our last and greatest hopes for resolving it.* Science and technology, rational planning and modernization have eroded tradition and eliminated the places where community once thrived (Giddens, 1995). The friendly clutter of the corner store has been replaced by the sleek lines and anonymity of the pedestrian precinct and the shopping mall. Many of the middle classes have deserted the city for the safety of the suburbs where neighbors care more for their lawns than they do for each other. Affiliation with major Christian churches is in decline, as is attendance at religious services (Hargreaves & Goodson, 1992). Only on the television program "Cheers," it seems, can most people find a bar where "everybody knows your name." The price of consumer affluence has been anonymity and alienation. And the heaviest price has been paid by those too poor to participate in the consumer society at all, eking out their existence in the dislocation and desolation of the old inner cities which modernization has left behind (Baumann, 1992).

Recently, there are signs that people are struggling to recreate a sense of community and the meaning and support that are to be found there. They are looking for fellowship, searching for a sense of place. This can be

**The struggle for community should not create enclaves for the elite.**

seen in the self-help and support groups that are springing up everywhere (Giddens, 1990), in the resurgence of religious fundamentalism (Ignatieff, 1992), in the talk groups and virtual communities that are being established on the Internet (Rheingold, 1993), in the simulated reconstructions of tradition in downtown restorations and waterfront developments (Harvey, 1989; Shields, 1994) and (most ominously) in the trend towards upscale housing developments being constructed and presented as secure "communities" within walled boundaries that keep the barbarian underclass beyond their gates (Soja, 1989).

The struggle for community should not create enclaves for the elite. It should not divide us from one another but benefit us all. Etzioni (1993) believes that if the moral infrastructure of our communities is to be restored, schools will have to step in where other institutions such as the church and the welfare state have failed. Sergiovanni (1994) argues that schools must play a much more vital and central role in community building; in providing care, developing relationships, creating common purpose and fostering a sense of attachment among people to something greater than themselves. Because of its geographical convenience and its connection to the lives of many families, the neighborhood school is the most obvious focus for these community-building efforts. How schools can serve communities, build community and be communities is something I explore later.

*Teachers need a lot more help.* The point about community is not just that schools can serve their wider communities better, but that these communities can also be an active source of support for teachers in school. And teachers can certainly do with the help. More and more social work and paperwork is getting in the way of classroom work with children (Hargreaves, 1994). Scarcely a week goes by without schools being confronted by more imposition of endless change. My earlier research, and that of many others', has shown how working more closely with colleagues can reduce duplication, share the burden, provide moral support and give teachers the collective strength to set priorities among all the demands that are placed upon them (Hargreaves, 1994; Johnson, 1990; Rosenholtz, 1989). But even this is no longer enough. The pressure for teachers to change their classroom practice towards more intensive work with individuals and small groups so as to accommodate the multiple intelligences and varied learning styles of culturally diverse students, means that teachers need help inside the classroom as well as collegial support outside it. This means bringing the community into the school and into the classroom in volunteer and paid positions, to offer clerical support, help in preparing materials, supervision of needy students, and assistance with children's reading. All these kinds of support already have a strong record of success in many schools though, as paid positions, they are often the very items that are most vulnerable to budget cuts. More radical is the idea of locating social work and youth services in the school so that teachers and social workers can work on the children's welfare together. More radical still is the notion that community members might even take over some of the less complex instructional aspects of teaching, releasing teachers to work on more demanding things. This already occurs in areas such as sports coaching, but can also be extended to more specialized areas of support such as computer instruction, and even to teaching students routine operations like the practice and consolidation of basic skills.

The coming years will likely see an extension and reinvention of what it means to be a teacher's assistant or a teacher's aide (Mortimore & Mortimore, 1994). Teachers may welcome this support in some ways but will also be threatened by it in others.

What will it mean to give up some parts of their teaching to people who are not qualified teachers? How will it affect their sense of autonomy and professionalism? Should teachers martyr themselves to menial work just to protect this sense of autonomy and professional control? Or can they share out some of their work in ways that enhance their professional authority instead of undermining it? At the same time, how can we guard against risks of exploitation, of governments using cheaper assistants to *replace* teachers and to deprofessionalize the work of teaching instead of supporting teachers to reach the higher levels of skills and competence that the changing social world requires? Bringing the community into the school and classroom means that teachers will not only have to redefine their relationships with other adults, but rethink what it means to be professional and to belong to a wider profession as well (Hargreaves & Goodson, 1996).

*Market competition, parental choice and individual self-management are redefining how schools relate to their surrounding environments.* Although schooling is becoming more centralized in some respects, through the proliferation of common curriculum targets, learning outcomes and standardized achievement tests, their day-to-day management and responsibility for meeting quality standards and performance goals is increasingly a matter for individual school determination. Schools are having to become more market conscious, more competitive for "clients," more preoccupied with image and public relations (Caldwell & Spinks, 1992). School councils or parent councils have been widely legislated as one way to push schools in this direction of market consciousness and client responsiveness. It is clear that such councils are turning teachers and principals outwards toward wider publics as they plan, present and defend what they teach. The benefits of all this symbolic busywork for students are much less clear, however.

While market competition and school self-management may make teachers more diligent in courting parental support and involvement, and while they may even urge teachers to work more closely with their immediate colleagues to ensure the success and survival of their own school, this kind of institutional competitiveness tends to divide schools and their teachers from one another. Decentralization can sweep away bureaucracy, but it often removes local professional support as well. Teachers have little incentive to work with and learn from colleagues in other schools when their schools are in competition for clients. So professional development tends to become more school-based, home grown, parochial and mediocre (Day et al., 1993). An unintended consequence of the self-managing school movement is that it is creating huge vacuums of professional development at the local level (Hargreaves, 1994). Filling this vacuum means searching for new and better ways to enable teachers to learn from their colleagues in other schools (even in a world of self-management); to belong in a real sense to a wider profession, with all the wisdom and learning it has to offer.

> **The way we package work into discrete, well-defined, lifelong bundles called jobs, is itself a fading phenomenon.**

*Schools can no longer be indifferent to the working lives that await their students when they move into the adult world,* or to the organizations which have the power to shape their student's futures. When students leave school or even university, there is no work for many of them anymore, or the work is very different that it used to be. The economies of the developed world are in turmoil. Restructuring and downsizing and pervasive. Bridges (1994:5) comments that after the U.S. recession of the late 1980s and early 1990s, only 18% of the lost jobs had returned. In other recessions, the jobs eventually came back. This time, he says, the message is clear, "jobs are going away, not just until times improve but for good." More than this, he observes, the way we package work into discrete, well-defined, lifelong bundles called jobs, is itself a fading phenomenon.

Part-time work, temporary work and contracting out are the new ingredients of corporate flexibility. Their rapid growth is challenging our traditional conceptions of what work is and how it is organized, along with our relationships to employers, and the importance we attach to paid work within our wider lives. Handy (1994) notes that for more and more young people, paid permanent work will start later in their lives and finish sooner, compared to their parents' generation.

So it seems very likely that work will have a difference prominence and provenance in the future lives of the young people we now educate than it has had for us. Just what that work will look like, how skilled it will be, and how we should prepare young people for it is widely disputed, however. Indeed, writers like Wynn (1994:111) argue that "the perspective informing educational restructuring has a narrow approach, representing the interests of employers and business. This perspective sees young people only in terms of what they can offer a restructuring economy," and not in terms of their interests in a broader and secure livelihood in which finding love, forging relationships, forming a family and getting one's own apartment and independence are all seen as important.

**Some want schools to wash their hands of the business connection because it corrupts the curriculum.**

Employer organizations like the Conference Board of Canada (1992) see the new workplace as being high-tech and high skilled, and want schools to prepare students with "employability" skills in communication, cooperation, taking initiative and such like, that they see as appropriate to this corporate future. Schlechty (1990) sees the American economy shifting from manual work to knowledge work and argues that the task of schools should be to produce the kinds of knowledge workers who will have the skills and qualities necessary to operate in an information-based society.

Others contend that most Western economies are becoming pear-shaped with only very few high-skill opportunities being available for small technical and symbolic elites at the top (Menzies, 1989; Lash & Urry, 1994). Barlow and Robertson (1994:61) put it the most provocatively: "While it is easy to find many examples of business criticizing education's 'failures,'" they say, "it is much more difficult to find concrete promises of real jobs by the corporate community." We have a job crisis in our society, they argue, not because schools are failing to turn out students with the requisite skills, but because transitional corporations are moving the jobs to other countries with weaker environmental controls and cheaper, more docile labor.

What are schools and teachers to make of all this? Some want schools to wash their hands of the business connection because it corrupts the curriculum. Instead, they argue, schools should return to a liberal curriculum which educates children in traditional civic virtues (Emberley & Newell, 1994). While these critics may be right about the dangers of schooling being driven by business values, adopting the ostrich position towards economic change makes no sense. Students are as aware as anyone of the changing economic realities. They know that pieces of paper no longer provide automatic passports to security or success. The job lights are dimming at the end of the educational tunnel and this is leading students to question their work ethic and the relevance of what their schools offer them (Hargreaves, Earl & Ryan, 1996). What's out there in the changing economy is also inside students' heads; in their anxieties and aspirations. There is a crisis of motivation in our secondary schools and the changing economy is very much at the root of it (Hargreaves, 1989). We should certainly critique these changing work realities as we connect with them, but we can't turn back the clock to simpler schooling for simpler times and act as if they are not there.

Many other people respond to the changing realities of employment by arguing for closer connections between schooling and work. They advocate partnerships with industry, corporate investment in education, business involvement in the curriculum, more student placements on work experience, putting more emphasis in schools on the skills that business requires, and restructuring the management and organization of schooling along similar lines to the restructuring that has taken place elsewhere. These kinds of connections can provide a treasure chest of stimuli for learning. Or they can be a Pandora's box of corporate "hype" and financial expendicy which threaten the moral purpose of what schools should do (Calvert & Kuehn, 1994; Hoggart, 1995:32). The real challenge in connecting schools with the world of work, therefore, is not just to build partnerships with business, but to create partnerships that are morally defensible and educationally worthwhile (and to ensure they stay like that).

## THE CHALLENGE

Schools can no longer be castles in their communities. Nor can teachers equate professional status with absolute autonomy. The forces of change are already making themselves felt within countless classrooms, in the characteristics of the children, in the problems they bring to school and in the ways they approach their school work. Within the challenges and complexities of these postmodern times, teachers must find more and better ways to work with others in the interests of the children they know best. They must reinvent their sense of professionalism so that it does not place them above or set them apart from parents and the wider public, but gives them the courage and confidence to engage openly and authoritatively with others who also have the children's interests at heart (and even with those who don't).

This does not and should not mean teachers running themselves into the ground with extra work beyond the responsibilities they already have within it. An evaluation of the Advanced Skills Teaching Initiative in Australia has shown that overburdened teacher leaders are likely to "live off past preparation" when teaching their own students in order to accommodate the additional leadership responsibilities that are supposed to benefit those very students (Ingvarrson et al., 1994)!

But when teachers work more closely with those outside the school for the benefit of their students within it, not any kind of partnership will do. Partnerships should be meaningful and moral; not cosmetic and superficial.

**Partnerships should be meaningful and moral; not cosmetic and superficial.**

Professionalism should not mean being condescending to others when we work in partnership with them. Partnerships should not be seen as missionary work, where teachers minister to the needs of the unenlightened and the less fortunate. Some of England's first self-conscious community schools—Henry Morris's village colleges—made this very mistake when they assumed that professional teachers trained in the culture of the city, would be the ideal people to recreate and uplift the rural communities in which they would do their work (Morris, 1925). Nor should "partnerships" open up teachers' lives to endless inspection by the prying eyes of parents or other community members in the way that was once true of many schools in the 1930s, and is still true of many rural areas today (Waller, 1932). Work with others beyond the school to bring about positive change within it will require emotional maturity, openness, and assertiveness. It will need to rest on a firm moral platform where the children's needs are paramount.

What this means is that if our attempts to go *wider* in our change efforts are to be educationally productive, we must also go *deeper* and examine the moral grounds and emotional texture of our practice, of what it means to be a teacher. To twist the words of a popular song, in a world where the walls of schooling are breaking down, successful change needs to be river deep, prairie wide. Otherwise, we will lose sight of what all this other work beyond the school is for. Rethinking educational change means giving it greater depth as well as breadth. I now want to explore what it means to go deeper in this way.

## THE EMOTIONS OF EDUCATIONAL CHANGE

If our understandings of the theory and practice of educational change need to extend beyond the school, they also need to probe deeper into the heart of what teaching is, and into what moves teachers to do their work well. Good teaching is not just a matter of being efficient, developing competence, mastering technique and possessing the right kind of knowledge. Good teaching also involves emotional work. It is infused with desire: with pleasure, passion, creativity, challenge and joy (Hargreaves, 1995). It is in Fried's (1995) terms, a passionate vocation. English primary teachers interviewed by Jennifer Nias (1988) spoke of their relation-

> **Increasing numbers of women in the principalship are becoming the emotional middle-managers of educational change.**

ships to the children they taught in terms of care, affection and even love. The "creative" primary teachers studies by Woods and Jeffrey (1996) tried to generate classroom relationships that featured "interest, enthusiasm, inquiry, excitement, discovery, risk-taking and fun." Their cognitive scaffolding was "held together with emotional bonds" (p. 71). Noddings (1992) argues that educational reform efforts too often elevate cognition above care as a priority for improvement. Care for persons, things, and even ideas, become marginalized as a result. In Australia, Blackmore (1995) has described how increasing numbers of women in the principalship are becoming the emotional middle-managers of educational change, using what liberal feminists call women's ways of organizing and knowing (Gilligan, 1982; Belenky et. al., 1986) to smooth the process of organizational development and change. As a sign of our changing times, Tabin and Coleman (1991) have found that younger, new-generation women principals are more likely to acknowledge these gendered aspects of their leadership style than their older, more experienced female counterparts.

In a study of 32 Grade 7 and 8 teachers identified by system administrators as having a serious and sustained commitment to implementing common learning outcomes, integrated curriculum and alternative forms of assessment and reporting in their classes, my colleagues and I are also finding that teachers do not plan their courses or units of work in a linear way that starts with the outcomes first, then identifies the methods and materials which might lead to those outcomes being realized afterwards (Hargreaves, 1997). Rather, teachers start with knowledge and feelings about their students, with their intuitive understanding about what is likely to excite and engage those students, and with their own passions and enthusiasm about ideas, topics, materials and methods that they can picture working with their classes. Often, they brainstorm these ideas with their colleagues, "sparking off" one another in planning sessions of great creativity and emotional intensity. Only much later, as the course of study starts to take shape, do they then go to the list of prescribed outcomes, to check whether they missed anything and to ensure that their curriculum is balanced. The rational planning process implied by outcomes-based education is sharply at odds with the emotionally charged way that good teachers plan in practice.

Teaching and leading are therefore profoundly emotional activities. You would not guess this from much of the educational change and reform literature, however. One of the dominant discourses within this literature concentrates on issues like strategic planning, cognitive leadership, problem-solving and, more recently, organizational learning (e.g., Senge, 1990) as proper focal points for change. As I have argued elsewhere, by focusing on knowledge, skill, cognition, decision-making and reflection, those aspects of educational change and teacher development that are rational, calculative, masculine and managerial in nature are the ones that are given prominence in this discourse (Hargreaves, 1995).

A second discourse of educational change that has gathered strength in recent years does give considerable credit to the place of the non-rational, emotional aspects of educational change. Much of Fullan's definitive writing in this area is dedicated to acknowledging the subjective meaning that educational change has for individuals (Fullan, 1991) and to advising people how to deal with the forces of educational change that operate in an essentially non-rational environment (Fullan, 1993). The affective aspects of educational change that are embedded in trust, collaboration, shared meaning and moral support are directly addressed within this discourse, one to which I have actively contributed (Fullan & Hargreaves, 1991).

This evolving interest in the emotions of educational change has been spurred in the wider culture by a disillusionment with rationality and science. Increasing awareness of the imminent possibilities of environmental catastrophe on a global scale has seriously undermined faith in technology as a way of reliably predicting and controlling our world in the rational pursuit of progress (Harvey, 1989). And as these metanarratives of knowing have been questioned, other voices, other forms of understanding have come to be granted growing recognition—among them, feminist thought and women's way of knowing. Significantly, attention to the emotional aspects of human experience is a growth area in philosophy (e.g., Gordon, 1987) and social psychology (Oatley, 1992) alike.

Within education, the interior turn towards feelings, emotions and the self within the literature and practice of educational change has been prompted by growing frustration with the repeated and increasingly predictable failure of educational reform (Sarason, 1990), by the obstinate problem of teachers' resistance to imposed change and by awareness that change efforts therefore need to address teachers' varying personal, career and life stage concerns (Huberman, 1993), and by the equity agendas that have brought more women into middle management and school leadership along with distinctively gendered orientations to change and development that many such women offer (Acker, 1995). The acceleration and global diffusion of imposed reform and restructuring has made these problems of resistance to change and the need for new approaches to leadership all the more pressing.

Important as these new directions in educational change are for engaging with the emotional life of teachers and leaders and deepening our understanding of educational change, in three important respects, I believe, they have not yet gone far enough.

First, the feelings and emotion acknowledged in the educational change and development literature appear to be safer ones of trust, supportiveness, satisfaction and the like. More intense emotions tend to be excluded from discussions of ownership and involvement in change, collaboration and teamwork, and so on. Indeed, Nias (1989) sees intense emotion as a source of dangerous volatility in the safe places that classroom and schools should otherwise be. It is as if there is a fear of the furies, of unbridled irrationality run rampant among the education of the young. Excesses of emotion, it is felt, can interfere with measured judgment. Admittedly, the danger of this is very real. For as William James argued, "when any strong emotional state whatever is upon us, the tendency is for no images but such as are congruous with it to come up." Where reasonable ideas are concerned, James continued, "passion's cue . . . is always and everywhere to prevent their still small voice from being heard at all" (James, 1917:70). Along with emotional expression, we all need what Goleman (1995) calls "emotional intelligence": the capacity not only to be aware of and able to express our emotions, but to manage and moderate them effectively too. Emotional intelligence is what prevents anger turning into rage or sadness into dispair. Balanced leaders and teachers are ones who are both cognitively and emotionally intelligent, able to draw deeply on both parts of their psyche (Deal & Peterson, 1994).

Yet, not all passions are dangerously unruly and truly great teaching and leading often come about when there is exhilaration, experiences of creativity and breakthrough, cathartic connections to real purposes and real lives. Such are the peak experiences, the critical events in teaching and learning that connect with the passions and purposes of those who undergo them (Woods, 1993). As Farber (1996) argues, "our most important affairs—marriage, child-rearing, education, leadership—do best when there is occasional *loss* of control and an increase in personal vulnerability, times when we do not know what to do" (p. 38). For it is then that people learn they are dealing with a genuine person, without facade, pretense or defensiveness, not someone who is "managing" them (p. 39).

Sergiovanni (1992:130) goes even further than this and advocates what he calls "leadership as moral outrage" where "it is the leader's responsibility to be outraged when empowerment is abused and when purposes are ignored." Sergiovanni develops his position by arguing that

> Leadership by outrage and the practice of kindling outrage in others, challenge the conventional wisdom that leaders should be pokerfaced, play their cards close to their chest, avoid emotion and otherwise hide what they believe and feel.

When there are "shortcomings in what we do and impediments to what we want to do," it seems natural to react not in ways that are cool and dispassionate but with rightful moral outrage.

Intense passions such as this do carry elements of risk and unpredictability, however, and therefore threaten the control interests of those wishing to impose their will through educational change. This is perhaps why the emotions of educational change which are most commonly addressed are ones that help defuse so-called "resistance" to change by encouraging trust, support, openness, involvement, commitment to teamwork and willingness to experiment. It is emotionally malleable satisfaction not impassioned and critical engagement or critique that the merchants of imposed change most usually want to foster.

> **Our judgments concerning the worth of things, big or little, depend on the feelings the things arouse in us.**

Second, the literature and practice of educational change tend to treat emotional states as accomplishments to rationality, not as integral to reason itself. Some writers partially acknowledge the relevance of emotions to leadership and change, but treat them in behaviorist ways as physiological responses of emotional arousal to situational stimuli in relation to goal-directed behavior. This psychologically reductionist approach denudes the emotions of their human value and subjective meaning (e.g., Leithwood et al., 1993). Such writers may be somewhat attentive to educator's emotional lives, but this is largely in terms of their contribution to collaboration, climate-setting and management of the organization's culture. They are interested in the emotions only insofar as this might help them understand the "moods" that accompany problem-solving (e.g., Leithwood, 1993). It is still rationality, problem-solving and organizational learning that appear to prevail in the research and practical priorities of educational leadership.

Emotions, however, cannot be separated from reason, nor can judgment be set aside from feelings. William James put this point exceptionally well.

> Our judgments concerning the worth of things, big or little, depend on the *feelings* the things arouse in us. Where we judge a thing to be precious in consequence of the *idea* we frame of it, this is only because the idea is itself associated already with a feeling. If we were radically feelingless, and if ideas were the only things our mind could entertain, we should lose all our likes and dislikes at a stroke, and be

> unable to point to any one situation or experience in life as more valu-
> able or significant than any other. (James, 1917:229)

More recently, Damasio (1994) and Sacks (1994) have shown how
individuals who are brain-damaged in ways that make them emotionally flat, maintain intelligence in the abstract sense, but lose their
capacity for practical reason, for making judgments of human value.
This is because they have lost the feelings, the in-built biases that
narrow down the scope of potential judgments into a manageable
range. Although, Damasio argues, "we usually conceive of emotion
as a supernumary mental faculty; an unsolicited nature-ordained
accompaniment to our rational thinking" (Damasio, 1994:52), in
reality, reason and willpower, emotion and feeling go together.
Rationality results from their concerted activity (p. 128).

If feelings help make cognitive judgments manageable, considerable intellectual work also often precedes our experience of emotions. These processes are evident in:

> . . . what Othello goes through in his mind before he develops jeal-
> ously and anger; what Hamlet broods about after exciting his body
> into what he will perceive as disgust; . . . the twisted reasons why
> Lady Macbeth should experience ecstasy as she leads her husband
> into a murderous rampage. (Damasio, 1994:110)

As Hochschild (1983) notes, when women appear dangerously irrational in the eyes of men, they have often worked very hard to get
that way!

Our approaches to educational change need to recognize that
emotion is integral to reason, not a subordinate "handmaiden"
accompaniment to it. However, the reluctance of change theorists
and practitioners to accept the integral role of emotions in successful
change efforts, perhaps "reflects masculine illusions of separateness
and masculine fears of loss of control more than the universal traits
of human reason" (Ferguson, 1984:199). In this way, proposers of
top-down educational reform may simply fear that they have too
much to lose embracing the emotional foundations of educational
change efforts.

Third, caring occupations like teaching which involve commitment to the well-being of others, do not merely imply emotional
states of satisfaction or dissatisfaction, that are entailed in any kind

of work. Caring occupational also require active *emotional labor.* In her classic text on the subject, Hochschild (1983:7) writes:

> This labor requires one to induce or suppress feelings in order to sustain the outward countenance that produces the proper state of mind in others. . . . This kind of labor calls for a coordination of mind and feeling, and it sometimes draws on a source of self that we honor as deep and integral to our personality.

Teaching involves immense amounts of emotional labor—not just in terms of "acting out" feelings superficially, but also in terms of consciously working oneself into experiencing the necessary feelings required to perform one's job well—be these feelings of anger or enthusiasm, coolness or concern. In many respects, this emotional labor is a positive aspect of teaching. Classrooms would be (and sometimes are) barren and boring places

**Teaching involves immense amounts of emotional labor.**

without it. But emotional labor also exposes teachers, making their selves vulnerable when the conditions of and demands on their work make it hard for them to do their "emotion work" properly (Ben-Peretz, 1996).

Describing what happens when the work of flight attendants is speeded up so they no longer feel able to care for their passengers as they would like, Hochschild (1983:189) concludes that:

> The more often "tips" about how to see, feel and seem are issued from above and the more effectively the conditions of the stage are kept out of the hands of the actor, the less she can influence her entrances and exits and the nature of her acting in between. The less influence she has, the more likely it is that . . . either she will overextend herself into the job and burn out, or she will remove herself (physically or psychologically—AH) from the job and feel bad about it.

My own studies of teachers' work have indicated that when it is similarly speeded up or intensified and teachers are overwhelmed by change demands, those who invest their selves most heavily in the emotional labor of the work are likely to become racked by guilt, feeling that they are hurting those for whom they care (Hargreaves, 1994). Similarly, in England, Campbell & Neill (1994) have found that primary teachers trying to cope with a detailed and rapidly introduced National Curriculum often became crippled by their own

conscientiousness; by their determination to make the best of unreasonably imposed demands for the sake of the children they taught.
The costs of such intense emotional labor when the conditions of
teaching do not support it are that teachers overextend themselves,
burn out, separate themselves from their feelings (by insisting they
are teachers, not social workers, for example!), become cynical or
leave the profession altogether (Hargreaves, 1994).

Sometimes, emotional labor is itself the subject of managed
change efforts. In an incisive paper, Blackmore (1995) argues that
women leaders who are entering the principalship in growing numbers in many parts of the world are, in effect, becoming the "emotional managers" of educational reform. They take "soft" human
relations decisions as malleable middle-managers, while the top
(largely male) executives and financial managers take the "hard"
decisions that circumscribe the scope of self-determination for individual schools in which the middle managers work. Women principals, in this view, seem to be both the objects and the agents of the
"managed heart." Men, in the main, mandate system-wide changes.
They are largely the ones who cut jobs, shrink budgets, impose testing requirements, erect league tables of performance and demand
detailed paperwork for administrative accountability. Under the
aegis of empowerment, meanwhile, women use emotional management to offset resistance to the changes and stimulate the desire to
make them work.

If educational reformers and change agents ignore the emotional dimensions of educational change, emotions and feelings will
only re-enter the change process by the back door. Festering resent-
ment will undermine and overturn rationally-made decisions; committee work will be poisoned by members with unresolved grudges
and grievances; passive-aggressive leadership that masquerades as
rationality and reasonableness, will engender frustration among
followers who are exposed to it; and pedagogical changes will fail
because they have not engaged with the passions of the classroom.

Conversely, the emotions of educational change may be
acknowledged in change processes, but in ways that either sedate
into safer forms, or incorporate them into the purposes of emotional
management at that school level, so as to accommodate teachers to
the non-negotiable mandates of imposed reform.

Taking our improvement efforts deeper into the emotions of
educational change is therefore no easy matter. It means getting in

touch with our feelings, or acknowledging women's distinctive contributions to educational leadership. Going deeper, rather, means understanding how to create workplaces for teachers that promote positive, even passionate emotional relationships to teaching, learning and improvement. It also means protecting teachers from over-extending themselves through their emotional labor and from becoming burnt out or cynical as a result. It means reviewing and revising educational reform agendas and the ways in which they are implemented, so they do not impact negatively on the emotional labor and rewards of teachers' work.

## AN EXAMPLE

I want to take one example of what it might mean to redefine our educational change strategies by simultaneously turning outwards beyond the school and also inwards to embrace the emotional aspects of teaching and leadership. There are many eligible examples to choose from such as the relationship between education and enterprise, or between schools and technology. My colleague Michael Fullan and I devote space to these issues elsewhere (Hargreaves & Fullan, 1996). Here I want to explore what it might mean to go deeper and wider in educational change in terms of the relationship between schools and their surrounding communities. Building on a framework of three of school development planning described by Logan, Sachs and Dempster (1994), there are, it seems to me, four broad types of relationships between parents and schools: market-based, managerial, personal and cultural.

*Market-based relationships* treat parents as clients and consumers who can send their children to the schools of their choice (Ball, 1993). The connection here is a contractual one which tends to individualize and fracture collective social relationships between schools and their communities (Blackmore, 1995). Parental advocates of school choice tend to be articulate, white and well-organized members of the middle-class, prompted to exercise choice and to influence schools to move towards traditional curricula and the basics so that they can gain marginal advantages for their children in an increasingly perilous economy (Dehli, 1995). Such parents are small fractions but highly organized fractions of the wider parental community. They exert a disproportionate influence on the direction of school change in ways that connect to the interests and experiences of their own section of the community, but marginalize the experiences and interests of other less fortunate ones. The market is an inequitable device for articulating school to community (Wells, 1993). Better and deeper solutions need to be found for forging school-community relationships in ways that benefit all parents and their children, not just the favored few.

**The managerial approach is better at creating committees than at building communities.**

*Managerial relationships* presume that schools are rational organizations within a decentralized system. "Goals and priorities are set centrally for local interpretation and implementation. Decision-making is viewed as a logical, problem-solving process" (Logan, Sachs & Dempster, 1994:10). In its establishment of parent councils, school councils and school development planning, the managerial approach is better at creating committees than at building communities. Managerialism is a poor solution for the permeable school. It grants untoward influence to atypical parents, diverts teachers' and principals' energies to procedural accountability more than to personal and emotional responsiveness, and has as yet shown no demonstrable benefits for student outcomes (Fullan, 1993).

*Personal relationships* between teachers and parents, by contrast, concentrate on the most important interest that parents have in school; the achievement and well-being of their own children. This is where the emotional connection between school and community is strongest. Few parents wait anxiously for the new school development plan to arrive in the mail. But they are extremely keen to see reports about their own individual children. Yet the quality of information passed between school and home is often extremely poor. When we brought together teachers in our current project who had a serious and sustained interest in implementing educational reform, including alternative systems of assessment and reporting, they complained extensively to one another that they have to be evasive and euphemistic, or use precoded commands rather than words of their own? Why could they not tell the truth, the whole truth, in plain language, rather than in what Woods (1979) calls the "professionalism" of school reports. School reports often read more like insurance policies against potential parental criticism rather than means of strengthening home-school communication.

Parents' nights also have their communicative limitations. If a martian were to drop in on many parents' nights, it would assume that their purpose was for parents and teachers to conspire against the absent child—discovering extra details, revealing hidden truths that the child had managed to keep separately contained in the insulated biospheres of home and school.

One of our project teachers challenged the prevailing practice of parents' night by organizing it so as to open up communication and understanding between teacher, parent and child. The children in his class ran the parents' night themselves. Having been trained in interviewing skills, they brought a portfolio of work they had collected to share with their parents as a basis for dialogue. In this multicultural school, interviews could be conducted in the language of the home if preferred. The shortest of these Grade 8 interviews took 45 minutes; the longest 1 ½ hours. As in many cooperative learning settings, the teacher circulated around the interviews, advising, extending, supporting and commenting wherever necessary or desired. This intriguing example illustrates what it means to go deeper in parent-teacher relationships: bringing the principles of openness, trust, risk-taking and collaboration that are commonly advocated for collegial relationships among teachers to relationships between teachers, children and their parents.

> **Teachers and principals often fear washing their "dirty linen" in public for fear it will occasion criticism and disrespect.**

*Cultural relationships* are founded on principles of openness and collaboration developed collectively with groups of parents and others in the community as a whole. When they are engaged in change efforts, schools often decide upon their internal professional response first, then take a managerial approach to informing their community later through meetings or newsletters. Teachers and principals often fear washing their "dirty linen" in public for fear it will occasion criticism and disrespect. Yet, counterintuitively, when schools involve communities with them in the uncertainties of change before the internal professional response has been decided, assistance, support and understanding are much more likely to be forthcoming (Ainley, 1993). Instead of schools seeing the community's involvement in change as tantamount to displaying dirty linen, it is perhaps better to see successful change as entailing bringing the community into the school's "beautiful laundrette"—a communal place to work and conversation where the community does its washing together.

Connecting the school to the community through market relations or managerialism, marginalizes many social groups who are unable to exercise choices, or who, like many women, working class people and ethnic minorities, feel emotionally uncomfortable with councils, committees and the other rationalized procedures of formal bureaucracies. Although we have known this for a long time (e.g., Young & Willmont, 1957; Jackson, 1968), we somehow continue to repeat the errors of history. As a way of going deeper in linking school and community, Mary Henry suggests pursuing a number of feminist principles that address the emotional aspects of these important relationships. These are:

> **What is worth fighting for in our schools is ultimately the needs of learning among and caring for students.**

- "a feminist view of school and community centers on the project of community building"
- "all decision-making policy and practice start from a notion of caring"
- "leaders and workers including parents and community people, act as co-workers, forming lateral relationships and cross relationships centered around the core technology of teaching and learning"
- "professional educators are social workers as well as teachers: schools are responsive to social needs"

In this feminist view of working with parents and the community "authentic casual contact or informal relations between parents and educators may be more important than formalized events" (Henry, 1994:18).

## CONCLUSION

What is worth fighting for in our schools is ultimately the needs of learning among and caring for students. As our schools become more and more permeable, we must now consider how to take that struggle outside the walls of school into the wider community beyond and how to bring the community into the school to pursue this struggle with us. If our struggle is for the needs of all children and not just for the elite few, then markets and managerialism will help us little in our quest. They will merely strike a deeper emotional wedge between marginalized communities and the schools that claim to serve them. Openness, informality, care, attentiveness, lateral working relationships, reciprocal collaboration and candid vibrant dialogue are the basic ingredients of effective school-community collaboration, not merely emotional icing which adorns it. They are the basic, day-to-day foundation on which successful decision-making, committee work and general governance will depend. The struggle for positive educational change must now move beyond the school in order to enrich what goes on within it. It must fully engage our hearts as well as our minds. And it must extend emotionally beyond the internal management of schools themselves to the high powered politics of educational reform and restructuring above them. That, I believe, is how we need to redefine educational change—broadening it beyond the school, and deepening it emotionally and morally within ourselves, in order to benefit the children that we teach.

## REFERENCES

Acker, S. (1995). Gender and teachers' work. In M. Apple (Ed.), *Review and Research in Education,* 21. Washington, D.C.: AERA.

Ainley, J. (1993). Parents in the transition years. In A. Hargreaves, K. Leithwood, and D. Gerin-Lajoie. *Years of transition: Times for change.* Toronto: Ontario Ministry of Education and Training.

Ball, S. T. (1993). *Culture, cost and control: Self management and entrepreneurial schooling in England & Wales.* Philadelphia: Falmer Press.

Barlow, M. & Robertson, H-j. (1994). *Class warfare: The assault on Canada's schools.* Toronto: Key-Porter Books.

Bauman, Z. (1992). *Intimations of postmodernity.* London: Routledge.

Ben-Peretz, M. (1996). Women as teachers: Teachers as women. In Goodson, I. and A. Hargreaves. (Eds.), *Teachers' Professional Lives.* Philadelphia: Falmer Press.

Benlenky, M. F., Clinchy, B. M., Goldberger, N. R., and Tarule, J. M. (1986). *Women's ways of knowing.* New York: Basic Books.

Blackmore, J. (1995). *A taste for the feminine in educational leadership.* Unpublished paper, School of Education, Deakin University.

Bridges, W. (1994). *Jobshift.* Reading, Mass.: Addison-Wesley.

Caldwell, B. & Spinks, J. (1992). *Leading the self-managing school.* Philadelphia: Falmer Press.

Calvert, J. & Kuehn, L. (1994?). *Pandora's box: Corporate power, free trade and Canadian education.* Toronto: Our schools/Our Selves Education Foundation.

Campbell, R. J. & Neill, S. (1994). *Primary teachers at work.* London: Routledge.

Conference Board of Canada (1991). *Employability skills profile.* Ottawa: National Bureau and Education Centre.

Damasio, A. (1994). *Descartes' error: Emotion, reason and the human brain.* New York: Grosset/Putnam.

Day, C., Hall, C., Gammage, P., & Coles, M. (1993). *Leadership and curriculum in the primary school: The roles of senior and middle management.* London: Paul Chapman Publishing Ltd.

Deal, T. & Peterson, K. (1994). *The leadership paradox: Balancing logic and artistry in schools.* San Francisco: Jossey Bass.

Dehli, K. (1995). *Travelling tales: Thinking comparatively about education reform and parental "choice" in post-modern times.* Paper presented at the Annual Meeting of the American Educational Research Association, San Francisco, April.

Delpit, L. (1988). The silenced dialogue: Power and pedagogy in educating other people's children. *Harvard Educational Review, 58*(3), 280–98.

Elkind, D. (1993). School and family in the post-modern world. *Phi Delta Kappan,* 77(1), 8–14.

Emberley, P. and Newell, W. (1994). *Bankrupt education: the decline of liberal education in Canada.* Toronto: University of Toronto Press.

Etzioni, A. (1993). *The spirit of community.* London: Fontana Press.

Farber, R. (1996). *Management of the absurd: Paradoxes in leadership.* New York: Simon & Schuster.

Ferguson, K. (1984). *The feminist case against bureaucracy.* Philadelphia, PA: Temple University Press.

Fried, R. L. (1995). *The passionate teacher.* Boston: Beacon Press.

Fullan, M. (1991). *The new meaning of educational change.* with S. Stiegelbauer, New York: Teachers College Press.

Giddens, A. (1990). *Modernity and self-identity.* Cambridge: Polity Press.

————. (1995). *Beyond left and right.* Stanford: Stanford University Press.

Gilligan, C. (1982). *In a different voice: psychological theory and women's development.* Cambridge: Harvard University Press.

Goleman, D. (1996). *Emotional intelligence.* New York: Bantam Books.

Gordon, R. M. (1987). *The structure of emotions: Investigations in cognitive philosophy.* Cambridge: Cambridge University Press.

Grace, G. (1995). *The changing culture of educational leadership in England.* Paper presented to the Annual Meeting of the American Educational Research Association, San Francisco, April.

Handy, C. (1994). *The age of paradox.* Cambridge, MA: Harvard Business Press.

Hargreaves, A. (1989). *Curriculum and assessment reform.* Toronto: OISE Press.

————. (1994). *Changing teachers, changing times: Teachers' work and culture in the postmodern age.* Toronto: OISE Press.

————. (1995). Development and desire: A postmodern perspective. In Guskey, T. & Huberman, M. (Eds.), *Professional Development in Education: New Paradigms and Practices.* New York: Teachers' College Press.

Hargreaves, A. (1997). The emotions of educational change. In Hargreaves, A. (Ed.), *Rethinking educational change with heart and mind: The 1997 ASCD yearbook.* Alexandria, VA: 1997 Association for Supervision and Curriculum Development.

Hargreaves, A., Earl, L., & Ryan, J. (1996). *School for change.* Philadelphia: Falmer Press.

Hargreaves, A. & Fullan, M. (1996). *What's worth fighting for out there?* Toronto: Ontario Public School Teachers' Federation and New York: Teachers' College Press.

Hargreaves, A. & Goodson, I. (1992). *Schools for the future: Towards a Canadian vision.* Paper prepared for Employment & Immigration Council, Innovations and Programs Branch, August.

Hargreaves, A. and Goodson, I. (1996). Teachers' professional lives: aspirations and actualities In I. Goodson and A. Hargreaves (Eds.), *Teachers' Professional Lives.* New York: Falmer Press.

Hargreaves, D. (1995). School culture, school effectiveness and school improvement. *School Effectiveness and School Improvement,* 6(1). 23–46.

Harvey, D. (1989). *The condition of postmodernity.* Oxford: Blackwell.

Henry, M. E. (1994). *Parent-school partnerships: Public school reform from a feminist perspective.* Paper presented at the annual meeting of the American Educational Research Association, New Orleans.

Hochschild, A. R. (1983). *The managed heart: Commercialization of human feeling.* Berkeley: University of California Press.

Hoggart, R. (1995). *The way we live now.* London: Chatto and Windus.

Huberman, M. (1993). *The lives of teachers.* London: Cassell and New York: Teachers' College Press.

Ignatieff, M. (1993). *Blood and belonging.* London: Chatto & Windus.

Ingvarsson, L., Chadbourne, R. & Culton, W. (1994). *Implementing new career structures for teachers: a study of the advanced skills teacher in Australia.* Paper presented at the Annual Meeting of the American Educational Research Association, San Francisco, April 18–22.

Jackson, B. (1968). *Working class community.* London: Routledge.

James, W. (1917). *Selected papers on philosophy.* London: J. M. Dent & Sons.

Johnson, S. M. (1990). *Teachers at work.* New York: Basic Books.

Lash, S. & Urry, J. (1994). *Economies of signs and space.* London: Sage.

Leithwood, K. (1993). *Contributions of transformal leadership to school restructuring.* Address presented to the 1993 Convention of the University Council for Educational Administration, Houston, Texas, October.

Leithwood, K. Jantzi, D., & Fernandez, A. (1993). *Secondary school teachers' commitment to change: The contribution of transformal leadership.* Paper presented at the Annual Meeting of the American Educational Research Association, Atlanta, Georgia, April.

Livingstone, D. (1993). Lifelong education and chronic underemployment: Exploring the contradiction. In Arisef, P. & Axelrod, P. (Eds.), *Transitions: Schooling and Employment in Canada.* Toronto: Thomas Educational Publishing Co.

Logan, L., Sacks, J. & Dempster, N. (1994). Who said planning was good for us?: School development planning in Australian primary schools. *Report of the Primary School Planning Project.* Brisbane: Griffith University.

Menzies, H. (1989). *Fast forward and out of control: How technology is changing our life.* Toronto: MacMillan of Canada.

Morris, H. (1925). *The village college, being a memorandum on the provision of educational and social facilities for the countryside with special reference to Cambrigeshire.* Cambridge: Cambridge University Press.

Mortimore, P. & Mortimore, J. (1994). *Managing associate staff.* London: Paul Chapman Publishing.

Nias, J. (1989). *Primary teachers talking.* London: Routledge & Kegan Paul.

Noddings, N. (1992). *The challenge to care in schools.* New York: Teachers' College Press.

Oatley, K. (1992). *Best laid schemes: The psychology of emotions.* Cambridge: Cambridge University Press.

Postman, N. (1992). *Technopoly: The surrender of culture to technology.* New York: Alfred A. Knopf.

Rheingold, H. (1993). *The virtual community: Homesteading on the electronic frontier.* New York: Addison-Wesley.

Rosenholtz, S. (1989). *Teachers' workplace.* New York: Longman.

Sacks, O. (1995). *An anthropologist on Mars.* Toronto: Alfred A. Knopf.

Sarason, S. (1971). *The culture of the school and the problem of change.* Boston: Allyn & Bacon.

———. (1990). *The predictable failure of educational reform.* San Francisco: Jossey-Press.

Schlechty, P. (1990). *Schools for the twenty-first century: Leadership imperatives for educational reform.* San Francisco: Jossey-Bass.

Senge, P. (1990). *The fifth discipline: The art and practice of the learning organization.* New York: Doubleday.

Sergiovanni, T. J. (1994). *Building community schools.* San Francisco: Jossey-Bass.

Shields, R. (Ed.). (1992). *Lifestyle shopping.* London: Routledge.

Soja, E. W. (1989). *Postmodern geographies.* London: Verso.

Stoll, L. & Fink, D. (1996). *Changing our schools.* Milton Keynes: Open University Press.

Tabin, Y. & Coleman, P. (1991). *Joining the old boys club?: Women's careers as school principals in British Columbia, Canada 1980–1990.* Paper presented at the annual meeting of the American Educational Research Association, Chicago, Illinois, April 3–7, 1991.

Waller, W. (1932). *The sociology of teaching.* New York: Wiley.

Wells, A. (1993). Public funds for private schools: Politics and first amendment considerations. *American Journal of Education, 101*(3), 209–33.

Woods, P. (1979). *The divided school.* New York: Routledge.

———. (1993). *Critical events in teaching and learning.* London: Falmer Press.

Woods, P. & Jeffrey, B. (1996). *Teachable moments.* Buckingham: Open University Press.

Wynn, J. (1994). Continuing inequalities into new times. In *Schooling What Future?: Balancing the Education Agenda.* Deakin, Australia: Deakin Centre for Education and Change.

Young, M. & Willmott, P. (1957). *Family and kinship in East London.* London: Routledge & Kegan Paul.

# The Complexity of the Change Process

by Michael Fullan

P roductive educational change roams somewhere between overcontrol and chaos (Pascale, 1990). There are fundamental reasons why controlling strategies don't work. The underlying one is that the change process is uncontrollably complex, and in many circumstances "unknowable" (Stacey, 1992). The solution lies in better ways of thinking about, and dealing with, inherently unpredictable processes.

How is change complex? Take any educational policy or problem and start listing all the forces that could figure in the solution and that would need to be influenced to make for productive change. Then, take the idea that unplanned factors are inevitable—government policy changes or gets constantly redefined. Key leaders leave, important contact people are shifted to another role, new technology is invented, immigration increases, recession reduces available resources, a bitter conflict erupts, and so on. Finally, realize that every new variable that enters the equation—those unpredictable but inevitable noise factors—produce ten other ramifications, which in turn produces tens of other reactions and on and on.

As you think through the reality of the previous paragraph there is only one conclusion: "No one could possibly come to figure out all these interactions" (Senge, 1990, p. 281). As one of Senge's participants exclaimed after being engaged in an exercise to map out all the complexities of a particular problem:

> All my life, I assumed that somebody, somewhere knew the answer to this problem. I thought politicians knew what had to be done, but refused to do it out of politics and greed. But now I realize that nobody knows the answer. Not us, not them, not anybody. (p. 282)

From *Change Forces,* 1993, pp. 19–41. © 1993 by Taylor and Francis International Publishers. Reprinted with permission.

Senge makes the distinction between "detailed complexity" and "dynamic complexity." The former involves identifying all the variables that could influence a problem. Even this would be enormously difficult for one person or a group to orchestrate. But detailed complexity is not reality. Dynamic complexity is the real territory of change: "when 'cause and effect' are not close in time and space and obvious interventions do not produce expected outcomes" (*ibid,* p. 365) because other "unplanned" factors dynamically interfere. And we keep discovering, as Dorothy in Oz did, that "I have a feeling that we are not in Kansas anymore." Complexity, dynamism, and unpredictability, in other words, are not merely things that get in the way. They are normal!

Stacey (1992) goes even further. Since change in dynamically complex circumstances is non-linear, we cannot predict or guide the process with any precision:

> While Senge concludes that cause and effect are distant from each other in complex systems and therefore difficult to trace, this article concludes that the linkage between cause and effect disappears and is therefore impossible to trace. (p. 78)

Stacey concludes:

> The long-term future of such organizations is completely unknowable because the links between specific actions and specific outcomes become lost in detail of what happens. We can claim to have achieved something intentionally only when we can show that there was a connection between the specific action we took and the specific state we achieved; in other words, that what we achieved was not materially affected by chance. Since it is impossible to satisfy this condition when we operate in a chaotic system, it follows that successful human organizations cannot be the realization of some shared intention formed well ahead of action. Instead, success has to be the discovery of patterns that emerge through actions we take in response to the changing agendas of issues we identify. (p. 124)

What all this means is that productive change is the constant "search for understanding, knowing there is no ultimate answer" (*ibid,* p. 282). The real leverage for change, says Senge involves:

- Seeing interrelationships rather than linear cause—effect chains, and
- Seeing processes of change rather than snapshots. (*ibid,* p. 73)

The goal then is to get into the habit of experiencing and thinking about educational change processes as an overlapping series of dynamically complex phenomena. As we develop a non-linear system language, new thinking about change emerges:

> The sub-conscious is subtly retrained to structure data in circles instead of lines. We find that we "see" feedback processes and system archetypes everywhere. A new framework for thinking is embedded. A switch is thrown, much like what happens in mastering a foreign language. We begin to dream in the new language, or to think spontaneously in its terms and constraints. When this happens in systems thinking, we become . . . "looped for life." (*ibid*, p. 366)

Sounds complicated? Yes. Impractical? No. It is eminently more practical than our usual ways of introducing change, if for no other reason than that the latter does not work. Indeed, wrong solutions to complex problems nearly always make things worse (worse than if nothing had been done at all).

So, what is this new language for harnessing the forces of change? Chart 1 (see page 36) contains eight basic lessons arising from the new paradigm of dynamic change.[1] Each one is somewhat of a paradox and a surprise relative to our normal way of thinking about change. They go together as a set, as no one lesson by itself would be useful. Each lesson must benefit from the wisdom of the other seven.

## LESSON 1: YOU CAN'T MANDATE WHAT MATTERS
**(The more complex the change, the less you can force it.)**
Mandates are important. Policymakers have an obligation to set policy, establish standards, and monitor performance. But to accomplish certain kinds of purposes—in this case, important educational goals—you cannot mandate what matters, because what really matters for complex goals of change are skills, creative thinking, and committed action (McLaughlin, 1990). Mandates are not sufficient and the more you try to specify them the more narrow the goals and means become. Teachers are not technicians.

To elaborate, you can effectively mandate things that: (i) do not require thinking or skill in order to implement them; and (ii) can be monitored through close and constant surveillance. You can, for example, mandate the cessation of the use of the strap, or mandate a sales tax on liquor or petrol. These kinds of changes do not require skill on the part of implementers to comply; and provided that they are closely monitored they can be enforced effectively.

---

# CHART 1:
# The Eight Basic Lessons of the New Paradigm of Change

Lesson One:      You Can't Mandate What Matters
                 (The more complex the change the less you can force it)

Lesson Two:      Change is a Journey not a Blueprint
                 (Change is non-linear, loaded with uncertainty and excitement and sometimes perverse)

Lesson Three:    Problems are Our Friends
                 (Problems are inevitable and you can't learn without them)

Lesson Four:     Vision and Strategic Planning Come Later
                 (Premature visions and planning blind)

Lesson Five:     Individualism and Collectivism Must Have Equal Power
                 (There are no one-sided solutions to isolation and groupthink)

Lesson Six:      Neither Centralization Nor Decentralization Works
                 (Both top-down and bottom-up strategies are necessary)

Lesson Seven:    Connection with the Wider Environment is Critical for Success
                 (The best organizations learn externally as well as internally)

Lesson Eight:    Every person is a Change Agent
                 (Change is too important to leave to the experts, personal mind set and mastery is the ultimate protection)

---

Even in the relatively simple case—detailed, not dynamic complexity—almost all educational changes of value require new: (i) skills; (ii) behavior; and (iii) beliefs or understanding (Fullan, 1991). Think of: computers across the curriculum, teachers' thinking and problem solving skills, developing citizenship and teamwork, integration of special education in regular classrooms, dealing with multiculturalism and racism, working with social agencies to provide integrated services, responding to all students in the classroom, cooperative learning, monitoring the performance of students.

All of these changes, to be productive, require skills, capacity, commitment, motivation, beliefs and insights, and discretionary judgment on the spot. If there is one cardinal rule of change in human condition, it is that you cannot *make* people change. You cannot force them to think differently or compel them to develop new skills. Marris (1975) states the problem this way:

> When those who have the power to manipulate changes act as if they have only to explain, and when their explanations are not at once accepted, shrug off opposition as ignorance or prejudice, they express a profound contempt for the meaning of lives other than their own. For the reformers have already assimilated these changes to their purposes, and worked out a reformulation which makes sense to them, perhaps through months or years of analysis and debate. If they deny others the chance to do the same, they treat them as puppets dangling by the threads of their own conceptions. (p. 166)

In addition to the introduction of more and more mandated requirements, there is the general expectation in education that more and more innovation is needed. School people often respond to this expectation in a knee-jerk fashion adopting the latest "hot" items (site-based management, peer coaching and mentoring, restructuring, cooperative learning, whole language, etc.) It is no denial of the potential worth of particular innovations to observe that unless deeper change in thinking and skills occur there will be limited impact. It is probably closer to the truth to say that the main problem in public education is not resistance to change, but the presence of too many innovations mandated or adopted uncritically and superficially on an *ad hoc* fragmented basis.

The result, as Pascale (1990) observes: "not surprisingly, ideas acquired with ease are discarded with ease" (p. 20). New ideas of any worth to be effective require an in-depth understanding, and the development of skill and commitment to make them work. You cannot mandate these things. The only alternative that works is creating conditions that enable and press people to consider personal and shared visions, and skill development through practice over time. The more that mandates are used the more that fads prevail, the more that change is seen as superficial and marginal to the real purpose of teaching. The more that you "tighten" mandates, the more that educational goals and means get narrowed, and consequently the less impact there is.

Lesson 1 says that the acid test of productive change is whether individuals and groups develop skills and deep understandings in relation to new solutions. It finds mandates wanting because they have no chance of accomplishing these substantial changes even for single policies let alone for the bigger goals of moral purpose and the reality of dynamic complexity. Mandates alter some things, but they don't affect what matters. When complex change is involved, people do not and cannot change by being told to do so. Effective change agents neither embrace nor ignore mandates. They use them as catalysts to re-examine what they are doing.

**Change is a never-ending proposition under conditions of dynamic complexity.**

## LESSON 2: CHANGE IS A JOURNEY, NOT A BLUEPRINT

**(Change is non-linear, loaded with uncertainty, and sometimes perverse.)**

I have already made the case in this article that change is a never-ending proposition under conditions of dynamic complexity. Another reason that you can't mandate what matters is that you don't know what is going to matter until you are into the journey. If change involved implementing single, well-developed, proven innovations one at a time, perhaps it could be blueprinted. But school districts and schools are in the business of implementing a bewildering array of multiple innovations and policies simultaneously. Moreover, restructuring reforms are so multifaceted and complex that solutions for particular settings cannot be known in advance. If one tries to match the complexity of the situation with complex implementation plans, the process becomes unwieldy, cumbersome and usually wrong.

I think of the school in England described by McMahon and Wallace (1992) engaged in school development planning. Experienced in the planning process, working together, and committed to the plan they produced, they nonetheless encountered a series of unanticipated problems: staff training sessions had to be postponed because of delays in the production of national guidelines; a training project had to be deferred because the teacher appointed to run it had left after six weeks, leaving a vacancy which could not be filled for

several months; the headteacher became pregnant and the arrangements had to be made for a temporary replacement; the Government
introduced a series of new changes that had to be accommodated—
and on and on. I think of the group in the Maritimes in Canada with
whom we were working who defined change as "likened to a
planned journey into uncharted waters in a leaky boat with a muti-
nous crew."

Thus, a journey into the partially known or unknown is an apt
metaphor. As we will see, so many of the other lessons feed into and
corroborate this one. Even well developed innovations represent
journeys for those encountering them for the first time. With skills
and understanding at stake—never acquired easily—it could not be
otherwise. Other more complex reforms represent even greater
uncertainty because more is being attempted, but above all because
the solution is not known in advance. "Route and destination," says
Stacey (1992), "must be discovered through the journey itself if you
wish to travel to new lands" (p. 1). In the face of unpredictable
change, "the key to success lies in the creative activity of making
new maps" (p. 1).

Under conditions of uncertainty, learning, anxiety, difficulties,
and fear of the unknown are *intrinsic* to all change processes, especially at the early stages. One can see why a risk-taking mentality
and climate are so critical. People will not venture into uncertainty
unless they or others appreciate that difficulties are a natural part of
any change scenario. And if people do not venture into uncertainty,
no significant change will occur (see Lesson 3—problems are our
friends).

We know that early difficulties are guaranteed. The perverse
part is that later stages are unpredictable as well. It is true that in
cases of eventual success there are great highs, ecstatic feelings of
accomplishment, and moments of deep personal satisfaction and
well being. With greater moral purpose and change agent capacity,
the chances are greater that there will be more successes than failures. But sometimes things get worse rather than better even if we
are doing all the right things. And sometimes they get better even if
we are making mistakes. As dynamic complexity generates sur-
prises, for better or for worse, there is an element of luck. Non-luck
comes into play in how we relate to these unanticipated events, not
in whether we can prevent them in the first place. Sometimes they
will be overwhelmingly frustrating and bad, and we won't be able to

do a thing about it. People who learn to control their inner experiences, while contending with the positive and negative forces of change will be able to determine the quality of their lives (Csikszentmihalyi, 1990). Productive educational change, like productive life itself, really is a journey that doesn't end until we do.

## LESSON 3: PROBLEMS ARE OUR FRIENDS

**(Problems are inevitable, but the good news is that you can't learn or be successful without them.)**

It follows from almost everything I have said that *inquiry* is crucial. Problems are endemic in any serious change effort; both within the effort itself and via unplanned intrusions. Problems are necessary for learning, but not without a capacity for inquiry to learn the right lessons.

> **Problems are necessary for learning, but not without a capacity for inquiry to learn the right lessons.**

It seems perverse to say that problems are our friends, but we cannot develop effective responses to complex situations unless we actively seek and confront the real problems which are in fact difficult to solve. Problems are our friends because it is only through immersing ourselves in problems that we can come up with creative solutions. Problems are the route to deeper change and deeper satisfaction. In this sense effective organizations "embrace problems" rather than avoid them.

Too often change-related problems are ignored, denied, or treated as an occasion for blame and defense. Success in school change efforts is much more likely when problems are treated as natural, expected phenomena, and are looked for. Only by tracking problems can we understand what has to be done next in order to get what we want. Problems need to be taken seriously, not attributed to "resistance" or the ignorance or wrong-headedness of others. Successful change management requires problem-finding techniques like "worry lists," and regular review of problem-solving decisions at subsequent meetings to see what happened. Since circumstances and context are constantly changing, sometimes in surprising ways, an embedded spirit of constant inquiry is essential. Says Pascale (1990, p. 14) "inquiry is the engine of vitality and self-renewal."

Louis and Miles (1990) found that the least successful schools they studied engaged in "shallow coping"—doing nothing, procrastinating, doing it the usual way, easing off, increasing pressure—while the successful schools went deeper to probe underlying reasons and to make more substantial interventions like comprehensive restaffing, continuous training, redesigning programs, and the like. Successful schools did not have fewer problems than other schools—they just coped with them better. Moreover, the absence of problems is usually a sign that not much is being attempted. Smoothness in the early stages of a change effort is a sure sign that superficial or trivial change is being substituted for substantial change attempts. Later on, once mastered, changes can produce incredible highs through seemingly easy effort. There is nothing like accomplished performance for increasing self-esteem and confidence to go to even greater heights.

Avoidance of real problems is the enemy of productive change because it is these problems that must be confronted for breakthroughs to occur. Senge (1990, p. 24) paints the negative case:

> All too often, teams in business tend to spend their time fighting for turf, avoiding anything that will make them look bad personally, and pretending that everyone is behind the team's collective strategy—maintaining the *appearance* of a cohesive team. To keep up the image, they seek to squelch disagreement; people with serious reservations avoid stating them publicly, and joint decisions are watered-down compromises reflecting what everyone can live with, or else reflecting one person's view foisted on the group. If there is disagreement, it's usually expressed in a manner that lays blame, polarizes opinion, and fails to reveal the underlying differences in assumptions and experience in a way that the team as a whole could learn.

Problems are our friends is another way of saying that *conflict is essential* to any successful change effort:

> People do not provoke new insights when their discussions are characterized by orderly equilibrium, conformity, and dependence. Neither do they do so when their discussions enter the explosively unstable equilibrium if all-out conflict or complete avoidance of issues . . . People spark new ideas off each other when they argue and disagree—when they are conflicting, confused, and searching for new meaning—yet remain willing to discuss and listen to each other. (Stacey, 1992, p. 120)

The proper way to deal with confusion, observes Saul (1992, p. 535), "is to increase that confusion by asking uncomfortable questions until the source of the difficulties is exposed." Yet we do the opposite by affirming rhetorical truths and covering up conflict.

A pattern is beginning to emerge. Substantial change involves complex processes. The latter is inherently problem rich. A spirit of openness and inquiry is essential to solving problems. Change is learning. Pascale (1990, p. 263) summarizes why problems are our friends:

> Life doesn't follow straight-line logic; it conforms to a kind of curved logic that changes the nature of things and often turns them into their opposites. Problems then, are not just hassles to be dealt with and set aside. Lurking inside each problem is a workshop on the nature of organizations and a vehicle for personal growth. This entails a shift; we need to value the *process* of finding the solution—juggling the inconsistencies that meaningful solutions entail.

In short, problems are our friends; but only if you do something about them.

## LESSON 4: VISION AND STRATEGIC PLANNING COME LATER

### (Premature visions and planning can blind.)

Visions are necessary for success but few concepts are as misunderstood and misapplied in the change process. Vision come later for two reasons. First, under conditions of dynamic complexity one needs a good deal of reflective experience before one can form a plausible vision. Vision emerges from, more than it precedes, action. Even then it is always provisional. Second, *shared* vision, which is essential for success, must evolve through the dynamic interaction of organizational members and leaders. This takes time and will not succeed unless the vision-building process is somewhat open-ended. Visions coming later does not mean that they are not worked on. Just the opposite. They are pursued more authentically while avoiding premature formalization.

Visions come later because the process of merging personal and shared visions takes time. Senge (1990) provides an illuminating discussion of the tension between personal and collective ideals.

> Shared vision is vital for the learning organization because it provides the focus and energy for learning. While adaptive learning is possible

> without vision, generative learning occurs only when people are striving to accomplish something that matters deeply to them. In fact, the whole idea of generative learning—"expanding your ability to create"—will seem abstract and meaningless *until* people become excited about some vision they truly want to accomplish.
>
> Today, "vision" is a familiar concept in corporate leadership. But when you look carefully you find that most "visions" are one person's (or one group's) vision imposed on an organization. Such visions, at best, command compliance—not committment. A shared vision that many people are truly committed to, because it reflects their own personal vision. (p. 206)

And,

> Organizations intent on building shared visions continually encourage members to develop their personal visions. If people don't have their own vision, all they can do is "sign up" for someone else's. The result is compliance, never commitment. On the other hand, people with a strong sense of personal direction can join together to create a powerful synergy toward what I/we truly want. (Senge, 1990, p. 211)

By contrast, the old and dead wrong paradigm is still being promulgated, such as Beckhard and Pritchard's (1992) recommendations for vision-driven change. There are four key aspects, they say: creating and setting the vision; communicating the vision; building commitment to the vision; and organizing people and what they do so that they are aligned to the vision (p. 25). Not!

In their study of 26 plants over a five-year period, Beer, Eisenstat and Spector (1990) conclude just the opposite:

> Change efforts that begin by creating corporate programs to alter the culture of the management of people in the firm are inherently flawed even when supported by top management. (p. 6)
>
> The programmatic approach often falsely assumes that attempts to change how people think through mission statements or training programs will lead to useful changes in how people actually behave at work. In contrast our findings suggest that people learn new patterns through their interaction with others on the job. (p. 150)

Stacey (1992) extends these ideas starting with a critique of the vision-driven model which prescribes the following:

> . . . form a vision of the future state we desire to achieve, persuade others to believe in it as well, and then together, if we get our facts right, we will be able to realize it. In this view, top management

action will take the form of trying to find out in advance what is likely to happen. Managers will prepare forecasts, and they will go off for weekends to formulate visions and missions. They will mount comprehensive culture change programs of persuasion and propaganda to get people through-out the organization to commit to a new vision. But if the belief upon which these actions are based is unfounded, they will have wasted their time and probably missed doing what was really necessary for success. (p. 125)

Further:

Reliance on visions perpetuates cultures of dependence and conformity that obstruct the questioning and complex learning necessary for innovative leadership. (p. 139)

Recall Stacey's advice that "success has to be the discovery of patterns that emerge through actions we take in response to the changing agendas of issues we identify" (p. 124). Stacey concludes:

The dynamic systems perspective thus leads managers to think in terms, not of the prior intention represented by objectives and vision, but of continuously developing agendas of issues, aspirations, challenges, and individual intentions. The key to emerging strategy is the effectiveness with which managers in an organization build and deal with such agendas of issues.

This perspective produces a different definition of intention in an organization. Instead of intention to secure something relatively known and fixed, it becomes intention to discover what, why, and how to achieve. Such intention arises not from what managers foresee but from what they have experienced and now understand. It is intention to be creative and deal with what comes, not intention to achieve some particular future state. (p. 146)

In short, the critical question is not whether visions are important, but *how* they can be shaped and reshaped given the complexity of change. Visions die prematurely when they are mere paper products churned out by leadership teams, when they are static or even wrong, and when they attempt to impose a false consensus suppressing rather than enabling personal visions to flourish.

And yes, vision can die or fail to develop in the first place if too many people are involved at the beginning, when leaders fail to advocate their views, when superficial talk rather than grounded inquiry and action is the method used. Another paradox. Trying to get everyone on board in advance of action cannot work because it does not connect to the reality of dynamic complexity. Understanding this process puts the concept of ownership in perspective. Ownership cannot be achieved *in advance* of learning something new.

Deep ownership comes through the learning that arises from full engagement in solving problems. In this sense, ownership is stronger in the middle of a successful change process than at the beginning, and stronger still at the end than at the middle or beginning. Ownership is a process as well as a state. Saying that ownership is crucial begs the question, unless one knows how it is achieved.

Strategic planning is also called into question. Spending too much time and energy on advance planning, even if it builds in principles of flexibility, is a mistake. Participation, elaborate needs assessment, formal strategic plans are uncalled for at the outset of complex change processes. Louis and Miles (1990) call this the evolutionary perspective.

> The evolutionary perceptive rests on the assumption that the environment both inside and outside organizations is often chaotic. No specific plan can last for very long, because it will either become outmoded due to changing external pressures, or because disagreement over priorities arises within the organization. Yet, there is no reason to assume that the best response is to plan passively, relying on incremental decision. Instead, the organization can cycle back and forth between efforts to gain normative consensus about what it may become, to plan strategies for getting there, and to carry out decentralized incremental experimentation that harnesses the creativity of all members to the change effort . . . Strategy is viewed as a flexible tool, rather than a semi-permanent expansion of the mission. (p. 193)

The development of authentic shared vision builds on the skills of change agentry: personal vision building through moral purpose, inquiry, mastery, and collaboration. Collective vision-building is a deepening, "reinforcing process of increasing clarity, enthusiasm, communication and commitment" (Senge, 1990, p. 227). As people talk, try things out, inquire, re-try—all of this jointly—people become more skilled, ideas become clearer, shared commitment gets stronger. *Productive change is very much a process of mobilization and positive contagion.*

"Ready, fire, aim" is the more fruitful sequence if we want to take a linear snapshot of an organization undergoing major reform. Ready is important, there has to be some notion of direction, but it is killing to bog down the process with vision, mission, and strategic planning, before you know enough about dynamic reality. Fire is action and inquiry where skills, clarity, and learning are fostered. Aim is crystallizing new beliefs, formulating mission and vision statements and focusing strategic planning. Vision and strategic planning come later; if anything they come at *step 3,* not step 1.

> **Fire is action and inquiry where skills, clarity, and learning are fostered.**

In working on reform in teacher education in Toronto, we have experienced this sequence over the past five years. When we started in 1988, we deliberately rejected launching immediately into large-scale strategic planning, or establishing yet another task force. Instead we began with a few readiness principles: work on the teacher education continuum, link teacher development and school development, commit to some field-based programs, work in partnership with schools, infuse our efforts with continuous inquiry. The firing part took the form of establishing a number of field-based pilot projects with different teams of faculty and cohorts of student teachers, and entering into action-oriented agreements like the Learning Consortium. Near the end of year 3 we were ready to focus our aim, by establishing a Strategic Planning Committee and hiring an external consultant to facilitate the process with the committee and the faculty as a whole. In faculty-wide retreat with student representatives we generated images of what we should be striving for which were grounded in people's experiences through the pilot projects and other ideas. I believe, we were far more able to be clear (the aim) through this sequence than we would have had we started with the development of (what would have been) an abstract and/or partially-owned mission statement and strategic plan. There is still debate and unresolved issues, but we are now in a far better position to pursue reforms with greater clarity of purpose as we enter new phases, driven (this time) by shared vision.

Thorah Elementary School, northeast of Toronto in our Learning Consortium, is another case in point. Starting on a small scale (the Principal and two teachers out of a staff of 23), the school developed from an individualistic to a highly collaborative culture over a three-year period; not by starting with a vision, but by working toward a shared vision generated through their actions (Fullan, 1992).

Pascale (1990) also captures the ready-fire-aim sequence when he analyzes how the Ford Motor company developed a widely shared mission and values statement in the 1980s.

> In hindsight, a major factor in the wide acceptance of this statement [Ford's vision and values] is that its principles were *enacted* for several years before they were value statements the other way around, and the product is dismissed as PR hype. (p. 170)

Charismatic, high flying leaders and premature strategic planning are blinding because they "distract us from our *own* possibilities" (*ibid*, p. 265). In the new paradigm of change organizations will have to reverse traditionally held assumptions about vision and planning. By so doing they will "arrive at" deeper and more powerful shared visions which inspire committed action on a day-to-day basis throughout the organization. But "arrival" as we have seen is only temporary; the most powerful shared visions are those that contain the basis for further generative learning and recognize that individual and organizational development will always be in dynamic tension. Recognizing, indeed valuing this tension, and incorporating values and mechanisms for continually processing it is essential.

Contending with the forces of change is a never-ending process of finding creative ways to struggle with inherently contentious factors—and none more so than Lesson 5.

## LESSON 5: INDIVIDUALISM AND COLLECTIVISM MUST HAVE EQUAL POWER

**(There are no one-sided solutions to isolation and groupthink.)**
Productive educational change is also a process of overcoming isolation while not succumbing to groupthink. Paradoxes provide the seeds for learning under conditions of dynamic complexity:

> Paradox serves us by setting up polar opposites and affirming both sides. Two factors, mutual exclusivity and simultaneity are essential for a genuine paradox . . .
>
> It is useful to draw a distinction between two types of problems: *convergent* problems (such as balancing your checkbook) that deal with distinct, quantifiable problems amenable to logic, and *divergent* problems (how to reorganize the production department) that are not quantifiable or verifiable, and that do not lend themselves to a single solution. When one solves a convergent problem, one literally

estimates it. There is nothing wrong with that. Divergent problems, however, cannot be prematurely eliminated, and benefit from the lateral thinking that paradox evokes. (Pascale, 1990, p. 110)

There are a few more endemic paradoxes in humankind than the creative tension between individual and group development. As with all paradoxes there are no one-sided solutions. To illustrate let us trace through the problem of isolation in search of a solution.

Teaching has long been called a "lonely profession," always in pejorative terms. The professional isolation of teachers limits access to new ideas and better solutions, drives stress inward to fester and accumulate, fails to recognize and praise success, and permits incompetence to exist and persist to the detriment of students, colleagues, and the teachers themselves. Isolation allows, even if it does not always produce, conservatism and resistance to innovation in teaching (Lortie, 1975).

Isolation and privatism have many causes. Often they can seem a kind of personality weakness revealed in competitiveness, defensiveness about criticism, and a tendency to hog resources. But people are creatures of circumstance, and when isolation is widespread, we have to ask what it is about our schools that creates so much of it.

Isolation is a problem because it imposes a ceiling affect on inquiry and learning. Solutions are limited to the experiences of the individual. For complex change you need many people working insightfully on the solution and committing themselves to concentrated action together. In the words of Konosuke Matsushita, founder of Matsushita Electric Ltd.,

> Business, we know, is now so complex and difficult, the survival of firms hazardous in an environment increasingly unpredictable, competitive and fraught with danger, that their continued existence depends on the day-to-day mobilization of every ounce of intelligence. (quoted in Pascale, 1990, p. 27)

Educational problems are all the more complex, and collaborative, "learning enriched" schools do better than those lingering with the isolationist traditions of teaching (Rosenholtz, 1989; Fullan and Hargreaves, 1991). So what do we do? We drive a good idea to extremes. Collaboration is celebrated as automatically good. Participatory site-based management is the answer. Mentoring and peer coaching are a must. Well, yes and no. Pushed to extremes collaboration becomes "groupthink"—uncritical conformity to the group, unthinking acceptance of the latest solution, suppression of individual dissent (CRM Films, 1991). People can collaborate to do the wrong things, as well as the right things; and by collaborating too closely they can miss danger signals and learning opportunities.

In moving toward greater collaboration we should not lose sight of the "good side" of individualism. The capacity to think and work independently is essential to educational reform (Fullan and Hargreaves, 1991). The freshest ideas often come from diversity and those marginal to the group. Keeping in touch with our inner voice, personal reflection, and the capacity to be alone are essential under conditions of constant change forces. Solitude also has its place as a strategy for coping with change (Storr, 1988).

> When from our better selves, we have too long
> Been parted by the hurrying world, and droop,
> Sick of its business, its pleasures tired,
> How gracious, how benign, is Solitude
> (Wordsworth, *The Prelude,* cited in Storr, 1988)

Groups are more vulnerable to faddism than are individuals. The suppressing role of groups is clearly portrayed in Doris Lessing's (1986) *Prisons We Choose To Live Inside.*

> People who have experienced a lot of groups, who perhaps have observed their own behavior, may agree that the hardest thing in the world is to stand out against one's group, a group of one's peers. Many agree that among one's most shameful memories are of saying that black is white because other people are saying it. (p. 51)

Group-suppression or self-suppression of intuition and experimental knowledge is one of the major reasons why bandwagons and ill-conceived innovations flourish (and then inevitably fade, giving change a bad name). It is for this reason that I see the individual as an undervalued source of reform. Lessing puts it this way: "it is my belief that it is always the individual, in the long run, who will set the tone, provide the real development in society" (p. 71).

The dark side of groupthink is not just a matter of avoiding the dangers of overconformity. Under conditions of dynamic complexity different points of view often anticipate new problems earlier than do like-minded close-knit groups. Pascale elaborates:

> Internal differences can widen the spectrum of an organization's op-
> tions by generating new points of view, by promoting disequilibrium
> and adaptation. There is, in fact, a well-known law of cybernetics—
> the law of requisite variety—which states that for any system to adapt
> to its external environment, its internal controls must incorporate vari-
> ety. If one reduces variety inside, a system is unable to cope with va-
> riety outside. The innovative organization must incorporate variety
> into its internal processes. (p. 14)

Thus, a tight-knit shared culture is not a desirable end-point:

> The dynamic systems perspective leads to a view of culture as emer-
> gent. What a group comes to share in the way of culture and philoso-
> phy emerges from individual personal beliefs through a learning
> process that builds up over years. And if the learning process is to
> continue, if a business is to be continually innovative, the emphasis
> should be on questioning the culture, not sharing it. A dynamic sys-
> tems perspectives points to the importance of encouraging counter
> cultures in order to overcome powerful tendencies to conform and
> share cultures strongly. (Stacey, 1992, p. 145)

Strong sharing and non-sharing cultures are both defective
because they have the effect of creating boundaries that are respectively too tight or too loose (Stacey, 1992). Some degree of multiple
cultures is essential for questioning the *status quo* in the face of continually changing and contentious issues in the environment. Canon
and Honda, for example, hire some managers from other organizations "for the express purpose of establishing sizable pockets of new
cultures" (Stacey, 1992, p. 198).

It is for these reasons that having a healthy respect for individuals and personal visions is a source of renewal in inquiry-oriented
organizations. When the future is unknown and the environment
changing in unpredictable ways, sources of difference are as important as occasions of convergence. Because conflict (properly managed) is essential for productive change, i.e., because problems are
our friends, the group that perceives conflict as an opportunity to
learn something, instead of as something to be avoided or as an
occasion to entrench one's position, is the group that will prosper.
You can't have learning in groups without processing conflict.

However, we can overcompensate for groupthink by glorifying
the individual, stressing autonomy, and failing to work on shared
visions thereby dispersing energy. We come full circle—isolation
is bad, group dominance is worse. Honoring opposites simultaneously—
individualism and collegiality—is the critical message.

## LESSON 6: NEITHER CENTRALIZATION OR DECENTRALIZATION WORKS

**(Both top-down and bottom-up strategies are necessary.)**

Centralization errs on the side of overcontrol, decentralization errs towards chaos. We have known for decades that top-down change doesn't work (you can't mandate what matters.) Leaders keep trying because they don't see any alternative and they are impatient for results (either for political or moral reasons). Decentralized solutions like site-based management also fail because groups get preoccupied with governance and frequently flounder when left on their own (Fullan, 1991, pp. 200–9). Even when they are successful for short periods of time, they cannot stay successful unless they pay attention to the center and vice-versa. Pascale (1990) puts it this way, in examining the Ford case:

> Change flourishes in a "sandwich." When there is consensus above, and pressure below, things happen. While there was no operational consensus at the top as to precisely what should be done at Ford, the trips to Japan caused many senior managers to agree that the problems lay in the way the organization worked. This might not have led anywhere, however, were it not for pressures for change coming from rank and file. (pp. 126 and 128)

Control at the top as many reform-minded leaders have found, is an illusion. No one can control complex organizations from the top. The key question (or more accurately the constant contention) as Senge (1990, p. 287) says is "how to achieve control without controlling." He continues:

> While traditional organizations require management systems that control people's behavior, learning organizations invest in improving the quality of thinking, the capacity for reflection and team learning, and the ability to develop shared visions and shared understandings of complex business issues. It is these capabilities that will allow learning organizations to be both more locally controlled and more well coordinated than their hierarchical predecessors.

Similarly, it is a mistake for local units, even operating under decentralized schemes to ignore the center (see Lesson 7). For example, school and district development must be coordinated. It is possible for individual schools to become highly collaborative despite their districts, but it is not possible for them to stay collaborative under these conditions. Personnel moves, transfers, selection and promotion criteria, policy requirements, budget decisions including staff development resources all take their toll on schools if the relationship is not coordinated (see Fullan, in press).

Put differently, the center and local units *need each other.* You can't get anywhere by swinging from one dominance to another. What is required is a different two-way relationship of pressure, support and continuous negotiation. It amounts to simultaneous top-down bottom-up influence. Individuals and groups who cannot manage this paradox become whipsawed by the cross-cutting forces of change.

## LESSON 7: CONNECTION WITH THE WIDER ENVIRONMENT IS CRITICAL

**(The best organizations learn externally as well as internally.)**
Many organizations work hard on internal development but fail to keep a proactive learning stance toward the environment. This fatal flaw is an old as evolution. Smith (1984) makes this profound observation:

> For a social entity such as an organization to reflect on itself, it must have a system representing both itself and the context in which it is imbedded. That's where nonequilibrium comes in. A social system that promotes paradox and fosters disequilibrium (i.e., encourages variation and embraces contrary points of view), has a greater chance of knowing itself (as the by-product of continually reexamining its assumptions and juggling its internal tensions). This in turn generates a reasonable likelihood of being aware of the context in which it operates. (quoted in Pascale, 1990, p. 289)

Dynamic complexity means that there is constant action in the environment. For teachers and schools to be effective two things have to happen. First, individual moral purpose must be linked to a larger social good. Teachers still need to focus on making a difference with individual students, but they must also work on school-wide change to create the working conditions that will be most effective in helping all students to learn. Teachers must look for opportunities to join forces with others, and must realize that they are part of a larger movement to develop a learning society through their work with students and parents. It is possible, indeed necessary, for teachers to act locally, while conceptualizing their roles on a higher plane.

Second, to prosper, organizations must be actively plugged into their environments responding to and contributing to the issues of the day. They must engage state policies, not necessarily implement them literally, if they are to protect themselves from eventual imposition. But most fundamentally, learning organizations know that expectations and tensions in the environment contain the seeds of future development. There are far more ideas "out there" than "in here." Successful organizations have many antennae to tap into and to contribute to the demands of change which are constantly churning in the environment. They treat the internal and external milieu with equal respect. Seeing "our connectedness to the world" and helping others to see it is a moral purpose and teaching/learning opportunity of the highest order.

## LESSON 8: EVERY PERSON IS A CHANGE AGENT
**(Change is too important to leave to the experts.)**

There are two basic reasons why *every person* working in an enterprise committed to making continuous improvements must be change agents with moral purpose. First, as we have seen, since no one person can possibly understand the complexities of change in dynamically complex systems, it follows that we cannot leave the responsibility to others. Second, and more fundamental, the conditions for the new paradigm of change cannot be established by formal leaders working by themselves. Put differently, each and every teacher has the responsibility to help create an organization capable of individual and collective inquiry and continuous renewal, or it will not happen.

Formal leaders in today's society are generated by a system that is operating under the old paradigm. Therefore, they are unlikely to have the conceptions and instincts necessary to bring about radical changes consistent with the new mindset we have been describing in this article. Saul (1992) claims that the "age of reason" has become bastardized, while burying common sense and moral purpose:

> The rational advocacy of efficiency more often than not produces inefficiency. It concentrates on how things are done and loses track of why. It measures costs without understanding real costs. This obsession with linear efficiency is one of the causes of our unending economic crisis . . . Worst of all, it is capable of removing from

democracy its greatest strength, the ability to act in a non-conventional manner, just as it removes from individuals their strength as nonlinear beings . . . How could a civilization devoted to structure, expertise and answers evolve into each other than a coalition of professional groups? How, then, could the individual citizen not be seen as a serious impediment to getting on with business? (Saul, 1992, pp. 582–583)

It is only by individuals taking action to alter their own environment that there is any chance for deep change. The "system" will not, indeed cannot, do us any favors. If anything, the educational system is killing itself because it is more designed for the *status quo* while facing societal expectations of major reform. If teachers and other educators want to make a difference, and this is what drives the best of them, moral purpose by itself is not good enough. Moral purpose needs an engine, and that engine is individual, skilled change agents pushing for changes around them, intersecting with other like-minded individuals and groups to form the critical mass necessary to bring about continuous improvements.

## CONCLUSION

There are exciting, but no comfortable positions in contending with the forces of change because one must always fight against overcontrol on the one hand, and chaos on the other. There is a pattern underlying the eight lessons of dynamic change and it concerns one's ability to work with polar opposites: simultaneously pushing for change while allowing self-learning to unfold; being prepared for a journey of uncertainty; seeing problems as sources of creative resolution; having a vision, but not being blinded by it; valuing the individual and the group; incorporating centralizing and decentralizing forces; being internally cohesive, but externally oriented; and valuing personal change agentry as the route to system change.

What this analysis means is that the current struggle between state accountability and local autonomy, *both* are right. Success depends on the extent to which each force can willingly contend with if not embrace the other as necessary for productive educational change. In so doing, learning all eight lessons and recognizing their dynamic interdependency is essential.

The change process is exceedingly complex as one realizes that it is the *combination* of individuals and societal agencies that make a difference. Teachers are major players in creating learning societies, which by definition are complex. Development is "the continuing improvement in the capacity to grow and to build ever more connections in more varied environments" (Land and Jarman, 1992, p. 30). Internal connections (within oneself, within one's organization) and external connections (to others and to the environment) must co-exist in dynamic interplay.

As the scale of complexity accelerates in post-modern society our ability to synthesize polar opposites where possible, and work with their co-existence where necessary, is absolutely critical to success. One starts with oneself, but by working actively to create learning organizations, both the individual and the group benefit.

## NOTE

1. I am indebted to Matt Miles who has developed several of these lessons (see Fullan and Miles, 1992).

## REFERENCES

Beer, M., Ersenstat, R. and Spector, B. (1990). *The Critical Path to Corporate Renewal.* Boston, MA, Harvard Business School Press.

CRM Films. (1991). *Groupthink.* Carlsbad, CA, CRM.

Csikszentmihalyi, M. (1990). *Flow: The Psychology of Optimal Experience.* New York, NY, Harper Collins Publisher.

Fullan, M. (1991). "The best faculty of education in the country: A fable," submitted to the Strategic Planning Committee. Faculty of Education, University of Toronto.

Fullan, M. (1992). *Successful School Improvement.* Buckingham, UK. Open University Press.

Fullan, M. and Hargreaves, A. (1991). *What's Worth Fighting for in Your School?* Toronto, Ontario, Ontario Public School Teachers' Federation; Andover, MA, The Network; Buckingham, UK, Open University Press; Melbourne, Australia, Australian Council of Educational Administration.

Land, G. and Jarman, B. (1992). *Break-point and Beyond.* New York, Harper Business.

Lessing, D. (1986). *Prisons We Choose to Live Inside.* Toronto, CBC Enterprises.

Lortie, D. (1975). *School Teacher: A Sociological Study.* Chicago, IL, University of Chicago Press.

Louis, K. and Miles, M. B. (1990). *Improving the Urban High School: What Works and Why*. New York, Teachers College Press.

McLaughlin, M. (1990). "The rand change agent study revisited." *Educational Researcher, 5*, pp. 11–15.

McMahon, A. and Wallace, M. (1992). "Planning for development in multi-racial primary schools." paper presented at the annual meeting of the American Educational Research Association, San Francisco.

Marris, P. (1975). *Loss and Change*. New York, Anchor Press/Doubleday.

Pascale, P. (1990). *Managing on the Edge*. New York, Touchstone.

Rosenholtz, S. (1989). *Teachers' Workplace: The Social Organization of Schools*. New York, Longman.

Saul, J. R. (1992). *Voltaire's Bastards: The Dictatorship of Reason in the West*. New York, The Free Press.

Senge, P. (1990). *The Fifth Discipline*. New York, Doubleday.

Smith, K. (1984). "Rabbits, Jynxes, and organizational transitions," in Kimberley, J. and Quinn, R. (Eds). *Managing Organizational Transitions,* Homewood, IL, Irwin.

Stacey, R. (1992). *Managing the Unknowable*. San Francisco, CA, Jossey-Bass.

Storr, A. (1988). *Solitude*. London, Flamingo Press.

# Cultures of Teaching and Educational Change

by Andy Hargreaves

O ver the previous quarter century, research on educational change has come to attain stature and significance as an important and legitimate field of study in its own right. This evolving field of educational change is grounded in and has also influenced a complex collection of approaches to bringing about educational change in practice. Thus, studies of educational change have been variously concerned with the implementation of organizational innovations (Gross et al., 1971; House, 1974; Havelock, 1973; Huberman & Miles, 1984); with managed or planned educational change (Hall & Loucks, 1977; Leithwood, 1986); and with mandated educational reform (Berman & McLaughlin, 1978; McLaughlin, 1990; Sikes, 1992). Studies have also been conducted of how educational change is experienced or initiated by educators themselves in relation to the contingencies of their own practice (Richardson, 1991), their stage of career development (Huberman, 1993), the context of their school or subject department (Louis & Miles, 1990; Lieberman, Saxl & Miles, 1988; Hargreaves et al., 1992; McLaughlin & Talbert, 1993) and a host of other subjectively relevant phenomena as described in Fullan's (1991) definitive review of the field.

In the past few years, school restructuring has presented the most visible face of educational change at the highest levels of policy (Murphy, 1991) and in many individual efforts to bring about school-level change (Lieberman, 1995). Changing the structures of time and space in schooling along with the roles teachers play and the positions they occupy with those structures, has been at the center of worldwide efforts to transform the most basic features of

From *International Handbook of Teachers and Teaching.* © pending by Kluwer Academic Publishers, Reprinted with permission.

schooling in terms of classes, subjects, grades and departments. Historians have demonstrated that these structures of schooling have proved especially resilient to change over the years and have repeatedly undermined successive efforts to bring about improvements in teaching and learning (Cuban, 1984; Tyack & Tobin, 1994). This is why structural reform now occupies much of the educational change agenda.

Yet, because of the way they have been implemented, many of the good intentions of school restructuring have placed literal and metaphorical impositions upon the lives and work of teachers. Structural reforms have too often been built on teachers' backs, mandated

**No educational changes are foolproof or flawless.**

without their involvement or consent. Many initiatives in school restructuring and reform have not even had good intentions to commend them. In some places, newly created national curricula have placed burdens of detailed content on teachers, content that has often been inappropriate for the diverse backgrounds and learning styles of the students who make up these teachers' classes (Hargreaves, 1989). Elsewhere, movements towards self-managing schools have not so much devolved real responsibility to teachers, as loaded them up with the busy work that used to be handled by central office (Smyth, 1993). Not surprisingly, principals and headteachers, whose managerial hand is often strengthened by self-management, seem to be much more enamored of this educational change than classroom teachers whose time is eaten up by its consequences (Bishop & Mulford, 1996).

Given these limits of school restructuring as a sole strategy of educational change, other writers on and advocates of change in education have focused on developing the motivations and capacities of teachers, and on building productive working relationships among them as an alternative approach to change. They have recommended *reculturing* schools as well as *restructuring* them (Hargreaves, 1995; Fullan, 1993).

It is this shift towards *cultural* alongside *structural* strategies of educational change that I want to address in this article. Elsewhere, I have emphasized the importance of culture in the life and renewal of organizations, and as a vital area of investigation for understanding how the fundamental fabric of schooling persists or changes over time (Hargreaves, 1986; 1994). However, no educational changes are foolproof or flawless. All changes have drawbacks as well as advantages. Specific changes can benefit students and teachers but also do them great harm. It all depends on how they are interpreted and how they are used. All change efforts, even and especially those to which we are most passionately committed, therefore need to be subjected to periodic questioning, criticism and review. We need to be vigilant about how changes can be misused and watchful of unintended negative consequences that our eagerness for improvement may initially prevent us from seeing.

It is time, I believe, for the concept of school *culture* and the strategy of *reculturing* schools to be opened to just this kind of questioning. In the very midst of growing interest in and advocacy for school *reculturing,* some stock-taking and soul-searching is now due—not so as to dismiss or demolish the concept of culture in educational change, but so as to review it and rebuild it in a more morally grounded and politically hard-headed way.

My task in this article, then, is to explore some rather more disquieting aspects of school cultures, and their rise to prominence in the contemporary agenda of educational change. How are cultures of schooling and especially of teaching being promoted and represented? Which aspects of teacher cultures are being highlighted and which ones played down? What is it about the current context of educational change that seems to call forth cultural solutions? How can we explain this cultural turn in the theory and practice of educational change, and what stance should we take towards it? In order to address these questions, it is first necessary to examine the particular context of educational change in which the concept of culture is currently being used and understood.

## CHAOS, COMPLEXITY AND CONTRADICTION IN TEACHING

Teaching in much of the Western world today is bedevilled by a number of fundamental paradoxes or contradictions. Among the more striking ones are that:

- Many vital areas of decision-making about curriculum content and responsibility for judging the performance of students are being taken out of teachers' hands and centralized. Conversely, moves towards decentralization are making teachers collectively responsible for the results they secure from their students, and for making their schools places where such results are achievable.

- Individual school improvement (including collaborative teacher commitment to norms of continuous learning) is being promoted and celebrated with increasing urgency and enthusiasm. Meanwhile, many systems of state schooling and the resources and supports they can offer teachers in their workplaces, are being actively dismantled and undergoing widespread deterioration.

- There is increasing support for teacher professionalism among governments who used to resist it, in terms of establishing professional standards, and creating self-regulating bodies which will monitor and enforce these standards. At the same time, teacher redundancies, salary caps and a multitude of reforms imposed on teachers without their involvement and consent, have significantly undermined the professional status and judgment that teachers value (Hargreaves & Goodson, 1996; Robertson, 1996).

- In many parts of the world, more and more women teachers are moving into positions of school leadership and are bringing more feminine and feminist orientations to the role with them. However, the "leadership" of wider school systems and the policies that emanate from them are as non-negotiable masculine and managerial as ever, if not more so (Blackmore, 1995).

Centralization is being accompanied by decentralization; professionalization by deprofessionalization. Commitments to individual school improvement are occurring alongside collapses of wider system support. More women are moving into school leadership while what they have to lead and manage seems less and less viable and defensible. What do these contradictions amount to? What do they mean? How should the teaching profession and the educational research community respond to them?

Some of the more avant-garde theorists of educational leadership and change do more than merely describe contradictions such as these. They virtually revel in them. Reinvented as paradoxes, chaos and complexity, these deeply painful contradictions for practitioners have become symbolic tokens of hope and exhortation in what is often an academic ecstasy of change theory and change advocacy. In their book, *The Leadership Paradox,* Deal and Peterson (1995) urge their readers to accept "the seemingly contradictory approaches" to school leadership which emphasize its technical and expressive aspects respectively, "as a paradox to be embraced and creatively addressed" (p. 9). Similarly, Handy (1994:18) argues that:

> Paradoxes are like the weather, something to be lived with, not solved, the worst aspects mitigated, the best enjoyed and used as clues to the way forward. Paradox has to be accepted, coped with and made sense of, in life, in work, in community and among the nations.

Senge (1990) points to dynamic complexity being a normal state of affairs in contemporary organizations. This complexity amounts to difficulties of tracing cause and effect when the consequences of our actions may not become evident until they are far removed in space and time. The existence of this dynamic complexity, argues Senge, is one of the fundamental reasons why we need to develop our organizations so that they have improved capacity to learn from and to solve ongoing problems. Taking up Senge's argument, one of Fullan's influential texts on educational change contends that "as the scale of complexity accelerates in post-modern society, our ability to synthesize polar opposites where possible, and work with their co-existence where necessary, is absolutely critical to success" (Fullan, 1993:41). While trying to take a more critical approach to educational paradoxes, some of my own writing has also overly emphasized their positive aspects and spoken more of paradoxes as exciting opportunities than crushing constraints (Hargreaves, 1995). It is not difficult to write books that celebrate the value of "Thriving on Chaos," (Peters, 1988) when you are flying first-class to your next five-figure speech! Looking down at the chaos from the edge of the stratosphere can make it seem pretty interesting. Those who are surrounded by all the chaos aren't usually so convinced. The confusions and contradictions that infuriate teachers are the paradoxes and complexities admired by academics and their acolytes. As a source of authority on educational change, the scholarly pen, it seems, is considerably stronger than the teacher's word!

There are at least three reasons why it is not sufficient to explain the contradictions in teachers' work simply in terms of chaos theory, complex systems or paradoxical demands.

First, the paradoxes, complexities and uncertainties of present times are not just random, accidental, or mysterious. Take, for example, the growing social and moral uncertainty that we currently experience in education and elsewhere. This uncertainty propels educators into inventing missions and visions for their schools, leads parents to subscribe to charter schools and other schools of choice that accord with their own religious or social values and pushes policy-makers into imposing centralized curricula that bear the reassuring stamp of certainty upon them. This uncertainty is not just a product of systemic complexity, of organizational forces we cannot control that have no will or agency. It has very specific causes. Elsewhere, I have argued that the pervasive social and moral uncertainty which afflicts contemporary culture is part of a postmodern condition driven by changes in the circulation of information, ideas and entertainment; by multicultural migration and international travel; and by international economic restructuring (Hargreaves, 1994; Kenway, 1995). These forces create increased moral uncertainty as ideas, information and belief systems come into greater content, they produce greater scientific uncertainty as information-flow is accelerated and knowledge is disconfirmed at an ever-increasing rate; and they help create contrary impulses to reinvent ideas of community and national identity (not least through education) in order to counter these trends toward globalization (Hargreaves, 1994; also Harvey, 1989).

> **Perhaps the most disturbing aspect of the advent of social and moral uncertainty is what Giddens (1995) calls *manufactured uncertainty*.**

Perhaps the most disturbing aspect of the advent of social and moral uncertainty is what Giddens (1995) calls *manufactured uncertainty*.[1] This is a condition where postmodern chaos and complexity to some extent result from willful attempts by governmental, corporate and financial powers to maximize their interests of profitability and control by keeping labor forces flexible, interest groups fragmented, and everyone off-balance (also Jameson, 1990; Barlow & Robertson, 1994).

When companies out-source their contracts, opt to use more temporary labor and fire their employees only to rehire them again as consultants (but without pensions or other benefits), it is not coping with complexity or becoming a learning organization that is uppermost in their priorities, but making the labor force more exploitable and manipulable to protect company profits and achieve other management ends. The loss or reassignment of teachers' jobs similarly creates individual career uncertainties that are the product of states with shrinking budgets seeking higher control over their expensive professional labor costs. Lastly, the chaos of multiple innovation and of intensified reform efforts is often a sign of governments in panic; trying with increasing desperation to secure reforms through education when they know that in the context of worldwide economic restructuring, successful reform in employment and the economy may well continue to elude them. In a postmodern age of rapid information flow and associated economic and cultural change, much of our present uncertainty may be inevitable and some of it may even be desirable (Slattery, 1995). But the origins of some of that uncertainty are also manufactured and malevolent. Many aspects of the contemporary paradoxes, chaos and complexity in our social and educational condition should therefore not be causes for celebration but for fundamental critique. The literature of educational change has largely avoided this challenge.

The second problem of explaining the changes confronting teachers in terms of chaos and complexity is that some of these paradoxes and complexities are rooted in struggles for power and in conflicting visions of what educational change is for and who will benefit from it. For example, telling teachers that their classrooms should cultivate and recognize multiple intelligences marks an attempt to create more elusive and equitable kinds of education where all students' chances for achievement are increased. Meanwhile, judging schools and teachers by standardized test scores privileges one or two kinds of intelligence above all others and divides schools, teachers, and students in terms of their ability to succeed at them. Many teachers have to deal with this paradox of intelligence and expectation every day: a paradox that is not a consequence of accident or muddle, but of conflicting social and political values being played out in the classrooms of our nations. In much of the educational and organizational change literature, such paradoxes and complexities are presented as inevitable: the only challenge is how to work with them. Yet restructurings of labor, uncertainties of employment, erosions of equity and intensified and expanded work expectations are parts of many contemporary paradoxes that are politically undesirable and morally indefensible. These are paradoxes that should be attacked, not accommodated.

Third, and most importantly for this article, some of the paradoxes and complexities that teachers experience amount to people taking or advocating interior psychic responses of an individual and interpersonal nature to external problems whose origins are more political and structural. This interior turn towards the self, personal relationships and lifestyle choices as a focus for empowerment and change is a common characteristic of postmodern times. Many have been critical of this interior turn. Taylor (1991:15) has argued that "the culture of self-fulfillment has led many people to lose sight of concerns that transcend them. And it seems obvious that it has taken trivialized and self-indulgent forms." Lasch (1979) has complained about the growth of a culture of narcissism where therapies and ideologies of personal growth and human potential are grounded in delusions of individual omnipotence where people cannot see the boundaries between themselves and the world around them, where they confuse personal change with social change, or where they see the second as resulting from the first. And elsewhere I have explained the impact of what I call *the boundless self* on much of the theory and practice of teacher development, where teacher development has been described in terms of personal development, or of "storying" and "restorying" one's life and career, in ways that can easily become pious, narcissistic and self-indulgent (Hargreaves, 1994; 1996). It is odd and also ominous that when the work of teaching is being externally restructured like never before, vast areas of the literature and practice of teacher development are turning teachers inwards to individual reflection, personal wellness and the telling of individual stories as the place where solutions can be found (Hargreaves & Goodson, 1996). It was the conservative Margaret Thatcher who said there is no such thing as society; there are only individuals—and there are few better moral warnings against the dangers of abandoning collective projects for individual ones than that!

> **"The culture of self-fulfillment has led many people to lose sight of concerns that transcend them."**

Despite these problems, other writers have seen sources of strength in this interior turn towards lifestyle, the self and personal relationships. Giddens (1991) persuasively argues that the collapse of scientific certainty and unquestioned expertise throws people back on their own reflexive resources for making their own choices and directing their own lives. Personal reflexiveness and self-help sought through others, he argues, can be sources of personal empowerment and positive social change compared to people's previous dependence on expert science or state control. This reflexiveness, Giddens claims, can bring about transformations in gender politics and the relationships of intimacy, as men become more able to turn inward to their emotional lives so that they have more insight into and awareness of their close relationships with others (Giddens, 1992). Elsewhere, Giddens (1995) extends his argument to claim that the interior turn towards self-development and personal reflexivity can even help dissolve the old distinctions between "left" and "right" as lifestyle politics brings together traditional conservatives and environmental radicals around "green" issues that impact upon people's quality of life.

When self-reflexivity is connected to moral action and political consciousness, this can help us find a new moral ground and authority for our actions (Taylor, 1989; Grimmett & Neufeld, 1994). This kind of self-reflexivity is preferable to the narcissism and self-indulgence of personal self-development undertaken purely as a psychological quest. But it is hard not to wonder whether Giddens' celebrations of self-reflexivity and lifestyle politics reflect on abandonment of European class politics for California cults of personal growth as a source of theoretical inspiration. More than this, however, whether the interior turn towards the self is celebrated or critiqued, I want to argue that it is not just its *form* that may be problematic (as personally self-indulgent rather than morally and politically authentic), but the very *prominence* which this interior turn has come to occupy within the theory and practice of educational and social change.

**School-level improvement is a popular response to the collapse of system-level support.**

We live in the world of widespread educational reform, where politically and structurally imposed problems are commonly seen as calling for personal and interpersonal solutions. School-level improvement is a popular response to the collapse of system-level support. More and more macho approaches to imposed educational reform are being implemented and accommodated through the relationship-centered and commitment-building qualities possessed by increasing numbers of women moving into school leadership. A fundamental irony of educational change in the postmodern world, therefore, is that externally imposed problems are being accompanied by discourses and practices of interior solutions, such as stress management, individual wellness, reflective practice, personal narrative and school-level change.

The social-psychological, interior landscapes of schooling are places where much of the attention of policy and leadership is being focused to accommodate the pressures of global economic restructuring and sweeping educational reform. It is not wider systemic change which educators are increasingly asked to initiate, or indeed to resist, but the small local areas, the 15% or so of their immediate work environment which, it is claimed, they will reasonably be able to control (Morgan, 1996). This is a dangerous seduction. It encourages teachers and principals to tend to their own gardens while leaving large-scale restructuring to others. It accepts that policy should be imposed on teachers, and not be a process in which teachers should participate themselves (Darling-Hammond, 1995). It extols the virtues of gradualism, but has no place for the courageous resistance of a Gandhi. The focus upon the interior landscapes of schooling along with attempts to redesign those interior landscapes are therefore important and troubling educational phenomena. Central to this inward shift of focus and energy is the concept of school culture. It is one aspect of this culture, the culture of teaching, that I want to address in the rest of this article.

## THE SIGNIFICANCE OF TEACHER CULTURES

Culture is central to the life of schools, as it is to the life of any organization. For Williams (1961: 63), the study of culture involves "the study of relationships between elements in a whole way of life" and "the attempt to discover the nature of the organization which is the complex of these relationships." For Page (1987: 82), the culture of a school comprises "a set of beliefs, values and assumptions that participants share . . . while the beliefs are often tacit and regarded as self-evident by members of the culture, they nevertheless provide a powerful foundation for members' understanding of the way they and the organization operate." Among many writers, especially those whose concern is with analyzing corporate culture, it is what is shared subjectively among people that best defines the life of the organization. In a much repeated phrase of Deal and Kennedy's (1983:5), culture can be defined as "the way we do things around here." For Schein (1985:6), the essence of culture is "the deeper level of basic assumptions and beliefs that are shared by members of an organization, that operate unconsciously, and that define in a basic, 'taken-for-granted' fashion, an organization's view of itself and its environment."

Other writers are more inclined to suspend the notion of shared-ness being central to the definition of culture. Goodenough (1957:167), for example, has written that

> culture is not a material phenomenon; it does not consist of things, people, behavior or emotions. It is rather an organization of these things. It is the forms of things that people have in mind, their models for perceiving, relating and otherwise interpreting them.

Elsewhere, I have gone further than this and distinguished the *content* from the *form* of teacher cultures (Hargreaves, 1992, 1994). The *content* of culture refers to the substantive attitudes, beliefs, values and ways of life that members of an organization, or a sub-group within it, hold in common. The content of a teacher culture may be found in allegiances to subject knowledge, commitments to child-centeredness, acceptance of low standards, placing a strong focus on care and community, concentrating upon the academic elite, giving pride of place to sports and to its "jocks," and so forth.

The *form* of teacher cultures, by contrast, describes the patterns of relationship and forms of association among members of that culture. The form of teacher cultures may, for example, be *individualized* with teachers working independently and in isolation from each other (Lortie, 1975; Flinders, 1988; McTaggart, 1989), *collaborative* where teachers work together and share ideas and materials as a single professional community (Nias et al., 1989; Johnson, 1990); *balkanized* where teachers are separated into and work together in different sub-groups such as grade-levels or subject departments which are at best indifferent and at worst actively hostile to one another (Hargreaves & Macmillan, 1995); or characterized by *contrived collegiality* where collaboration is mandated, imposed and regulated by managerial decree in terms of measures like compulsory team-teaching or required collaborative planning (Hargreaves, 1994). These four forms almost certainly do not exhaust all possible forms of teacher culture schools. Sociometric and social network analyses may, in the future, establish complex maps of patterns of association among teachers, where other forms become apparent. One hypothetical possibility, for example, is *satellite cultures* where a core, dominant culture in the school is surrounded by several, peripheral satellite subgroups.[2]

It is through cultures of teaching, that teachers learn what it means to teach, and what kind of teacher they want to be, within their school, subject department or other professional community. Cultures of teaching, in this respect, form frameworks for occupational learning. Concluding her study of two high schools, Page (1987:96) remarked that "understanding the cultures of schools is crucial to understanding the work of teachers." As Walker (1932:375) said, "teaching makes the teacher." It is a "boomerang that never fails to come back to the hand that threw it." And while there are characteristics of the occupation as a whole that shape the life, work and culture of teaching (Waller, 1932; D. Hargreaves, 1980) *where* you are a teacher, and *how* the work of teaching is organized in that place, will significantly influence the kind of teacher you will become.

> **Cultures of collaboration among teachers seem to produce greater willingness to take risks.**

In his classic study of the *Culture of the School and the Problem of Change,* Sarason (1971:59) argues that efforts to understand educational change must take account of three types of social relationship: "those among the professionals within the school setting, those among the professionals and the pupils, and those among the professionals and the different parts of the larger society." These relationships are what make up much of the culture of the school. In addition to teacher cultures being important for framing teachers' work, and for filtering educational change, they also appear to have important consequences for student learning. In particular, cultures of collaboration among teachers seem to produce greater willingness to take risks, to learn from mistakes, and to share successful strategies with colleagues that lead to teachers having positive senses of their own efficacy, beliefs that their children can learn, and improved outcomes in that learning as a result (Rosenholtz, 1989; Ashton & Webb, 1986). How strong the professional cultures or communities of teaching are in particular departments, schools or even whole systems, seems to be really crucial for how satisfied teachers feel and how well students achieve in those places (McLaughlin, 1996; McLaughlin & Talbert, 1993).

To sum up: cultures of teaching affect the actions of teachers in significant ways. They affect how teachers approach and define their work, how they respond to change, and how much agency they feel they have in making a difference in the lives and futures of their students. The importance for educational research and practice of understanding teacher cultures should therefore not be underestimated. Unfortunately, however, this understanding is often placed in the service of educational purposes that are distinctly suspect. These purposes even shape how the understanding of teacher cultures is pursued; how the research on cultures of teaching is constructed. Both the theory and the practical formation of teacher cultures are highly vulnerable to colonization by interests outside of teaching which seek to control it. One of the biggest problems facing the field of teacher cultures is its colonization by the purposes of educational management, by the kinds of change that educational managers and leaders want to bring about, and by the ways in which such change is typically implemented.

## THE COLONIZATION OF TEACHER CULTURES

A criticism of early and classical anthropology and its study of different cultures has been its covert or unintended colonialism (Waite, 1996).[3] Classical anthropology and ethnography, it is suggested, charted other cultures so they might be tamed and controlled more easily (Clifford & Marcus, 1986). It even arranged "primitive" cultures along hierarchies which permitted them to be classified and evaluated accordingly (Vidich & Lyman, 1994). In this way, primitive cultures were colonized not only economically and religiously, but also intellectually, through anthropological methods and forms of inquiry.

Contemporary studies of corporate cultures and school cultures often show the same tendencies to guide how we understand people's meanings in order to assist the interests of management. School cultures in general and teacher cultures in particular are frequently investigated and understood from the leader's point of view. Sergiovanni (1984), for instance, creates an understanding of school culture from the standpoint of the needs and priorities of the school leader. Much of the organizational culture literature takes a similar line; directing itself to the question of how leaders can build strong cultures to fulfill the organization's purposes. Bates (1987) has articulated a fundamental critique of this orientation: "Company managers," he says, "have been attempting to construct and impose company cultures for a very long time" (p. 80). The literature on corporate management, he continues, emphasizes culture-building as a way for management to increase its control over members of the organization. Successful management depends on "getting the culture right" (p. 81). Bates (1987:82) concludes that:

> advocates of corporate culture are conducting cultural analysis on behalf of managers. They are not, for example, incorporating a consideration of the interests of workers into their analysis, except for the assumption that what is good for the corporation, is good for workers too.

Conversely, Bates then wonders "what an analysis of corporate culture might look like if it were conducted on behalf of the managed." Just as cultural and economic imperialism colonized the cultures of primitive societies so, in many respects, is corporate management colonizing and controlling the cultures of its workforces. This process of managerial colonization is happening in education too, with respect to teacher cultures, where much of the theoretical inspiration is drawn from the corporate domain. This colonization can be seen in four domains:

- in the literature of school leadership, which places high value on the culture-building behaviors of school principals or headteachers
- in the creation and regulation of cultures of collaboration among teachers that are bureaucratic and managerialist in form
- in value-laden representations of teacher cultures and of cultural change in teaching that highlight their positive, optimistic elements and neglect or suppress their more troubling or disturbing dimensions
- in treating the cultural lives of teachers as a kind of "bounded irrationality" that should be open to management and manipulation by school leadership.

## LEADERSHIP AS CULTURE BUILDING

Many contemporary models of educational leadership in the form of instructional, servant or transformational leadership, identify culture-building (usually alongside problem-solving) as one of the main priorities of principalship (Deal & Peterson, 1995; Leithwood, 1992; Sergiovanni, 1984). Following the literature on corporate culture, where the chief executive's task is seen as establishing a vision, being the founder of the culture, rewarding those who commit to it and "letting go" those who don't (Deal & Kennedy, 1983), writing on educational leadership similarly see culture-building among the staff as the prime responsibility of the principal (rather than anyone else). As Gronn (1995) noted, where they are seen to be effective at mobilizing team efforts, theoretically and conceptually, these leaders are accorded all the individual credit. Such leaders, he says, are poor models for democratic change. Although they are inclusive and involving and often place a sincere emphasis on caring, relationships and building collaborative cultures of trust and support, many of these principals, especially at the elementary school level, adopt paternalistic or maternalistic stances towards their staffs

**Culture-building is other people's responsibility as well as the principal's.**

(e.g., Nias et al., 1989). In this respect, as I have argued elsewhere, it is more than a little ironic that many principals refer to their schools and their staffs as "families" (Hargreaves, 1994). There is little ambiguity about who is the parent and who are the children here!

I do not wish to imply through this critique that principals should play no part in culture-building; that they should refrain from encouraging collaboration or shared professional learning, for example. But culture-building is other people's responsibility as well as the principal's. Teacher leadership and team leadership need to be given more practical and theoretical emphasis in the creation of school cultures, in addition to the leadership offered by principals (e.g., Fullan, 1995). And it should be recognized that the cultures which *teachers* create and recreate are often divergent from and sometimes disruptive of those which their principals are trying to create. Nor do these cultures always amount to resistance which principals should overcome. They also offer possibilities for insight and learning that might help principals develop themselves. Interestingly, Macmillan (1995) has found that where it is the policy to rotate principals through different schools, enduring staff cultures often successfully resist the change efforts of leaders who are merely passing through. The robust cultures that teachers are often able to create frequently enable them to survive their principals and successfully "wait them out." These properties of teacher cultures receive less than their proper due in a leadership literature that is geared to managing and manipulating teacher cultures rather than learning from and strengthening them as independent sources of educational improvement and change.

Feminist scholarship has raised further questions about the cultural aspects of educational leadership. In an especially insightful paper, Blackmore (1995) has described how increasing numbers of women in the principalship are becoming "the emotional middle-managers" of educational change; using women's ways of organizing, knowing and caring (Gilligan, 1982; Belenky et al., 1986) to smooth the path of organizational development and change. Blackmore argues that these women principals are taking "soft," human relations decisions as malleable middle-managers, while the top (largely male) executive and financial managers take the "hard decisions" which circumscribe the scope of self-determination for individual schools in which the middle-managers work. This top-level culture is a predominantly masculine one that mandates system-wide changes, cuts jobs, shrinks budgets, imposes testing requirements and demands detailed paperwork for administrative accountability. Under the aegis of empowerment, meanwhile, women principals use emotional management to build commitment and collaboration, offsetting resistance to the changes and stimulating the desire to make them work. The growth of such emotional middle-management in a broader policy context where teachers have less representation and little voice, is one of the more disturbing features of the interior turn towards culture, emotions and personal growth in school-level change; for all this is occurring at a time when schools are being privatized, public education is being dismantled, supports are being withdrawn and the conditions of teachers' work are being restructured all around them. One of the more worrying effects of this pattern of change is on women principals themselves. Emotional labor takes its toll on their health and their personal lives as they try desperately to build caring cultures and positive change in policy contexts that are deeply inimical to them (see also Hochschild, 1983).

## CONTRIVED COLLEGIALITY

The attempted managerable colonization of teacher cultures by management is perhaps most evident in a phenomenon that I have called *contrived collegiality* (Hargreaves, 1992; 1994). Collaboration can be a burden as well as a blessing, especially once administrators take it over and convert it into models, mandates, and measurable profiles of growth and implementation. For the spontaneous, unpredictable and dangerous processes of teacher-led collaboration, administrators sometimes prefer to substitute the safe simulation of contrived collegiality: more perfect, more harmonious (and more controlled) than the reality of collaboration itself.

Such *safe simulations* (Baudrillard, 1983; Eco, 1990) of collaboration among teachers occur when spontaneous, voluntary and difficulty-to-control forms of teacher collaboration are discouraged or usurped by administrators who capture it, contain it and contrive it through compulsory cooperation, required collaborative planning, stage-managed mission statements, labyrinthine procedures of school development planning, and processes of collaboration to implement non-negotiable programs and curricula whose viability and practicality are not open to discussion.

The characteristic features of contrived collegiality are that it is:

- *administratively regulated.* It does not evolve from teachers' own initiative but is an administrative imposition that requires teachers to meet and work together.
- *compulsory.* It makes working together a matter of compulsion as in mandatory team teaching, peer coaching or collaborative planning. Contrived collegiality affords little discretion to eccentricity, individuality or solitude.
- *implementation-oriented.* It requires or "persuades" teachers to work together so as to implement other people's mandates—be these the principal's, the district's, or those of the wider system. Collaboration here is secured in the service of goals defined by others.
- *fixed in time and space.* It occurs in particular places at particular times. Contrived collegiality requires teachers to work together in times and places that are administratively determined by others.
- *predictable.* It is designed to bring about relatively predictable outcomes. Control over its purposes and regulation of its time and placement are all designed to increase this predictability.

It is not so much that contrived collegiality is a manipulative, underhand way of tricking passive teachers into complying with administrative agendas. Teachers are very quick to see through such contrivances. Rather, the administratively simulated image of collaboration becomes a self-enclosed world of its own. In this sense, the major problem raised by safely simulated contrived collegiality is not one of control and manipulation but one of superficiality and wastefulness. Contrived collegiality does not so much deceive teachers, as delay, distract and demean them.

The inflexibility of mandating collegiality makes it difficult for programs to be adjusted to the purposes and practicalities of particular school and classroom settings. It overrides the discretionary judgments of teacher professionalism. And it diverts teachers' efforts and energies into simulated compliance with administrative demands that are inflexible and inappropriate for the settings in which they work. Worst of all, by making collaboration into an administrative device, contrived collegiality can paradoxically suppress the desires that teachers have to collaborate and improve among themselves.

## VALUE-LADEN REPRESENTATIONS

A third way in which school and teacher cultures can and have become colonized by the purposes of management can be seen in how such cultures are commonly portrayed and represented in the relevant literature. While no representations or images of the world around us are free from value, some kinds of social scientific representation that portray patterns in human thinking and behavior, are especially normative in nature. These kinds of conceptual patterning do not merely portray differences or variations in human conduct. The very way in which these variations are arranged strongly implies distinctions of good and bad, better and worse.

Bipolar, dichotomous representations draw such distinctions particularly sharply. Thus, Susan Moore Johnson (1990) eloquently represents cultures of teaching as follows:

> In the ideal world of schooling, teachers would be true colleagues working together, debating about goals and purposes, coordinating lessons, observing and critiquing each other's work, sharing successes and offering solace, with the triumphs of their collective efforts far exceeding the summed accomplishments of their solitary struggles. The real world of schools is usually depicted very differently with teachers sequestered in classrooms, encountering peers only on entering or leaving the building. Engaged in parallel piecework, they devise curricula on their own, ignoring the plans and practices of their counterparts in other classrooms or grades. . . . Although such portrayals are often exaggerated, they contain more truth than most of us would like to believe. (Johnson, 1990:148)

Such portrayals present collaboration and collegiality as things to be aspired to, while individualism and isolation are processes to be eradicated or avoided. Solitude, eccentricity, and creative individuality also have their place in teaching; yet these bipolar portrayals of teacher culture present individualism and collaboration as mutually exclusive. They leave no room for individual and solitary pursuits to be recognized and appreciated in the broader panoply of teachers' work (Hargreaves, 1993; Fullan & Hargreaves, 1996).

Some analyses of teacher cultures present them not in dichotomous terms, but as an arrangement of points on a continuum. Little (1990) for example, has identified four kinds of collegiality relations among teachers and has arranged them along a continuum. She describes scanning and storytelling, help and assistance and sharing as relatively weak forms of collegiality. She argues that if collaboration is limited to anecdotes and help-giving only when asked, or to pooling existing ideas without examining and extending them, it can confirm the status quo. A fourth kind of collegial relation appears much further along Little's continuum. This is joint

**Joint work embraces activities like team teaching, shared planning, mutual observation, action research, and mentoring.**

work, and for Little it represents the strongest form of collaboration. Joint work embraces activities like team teaching, shared planning, mutual observation, action research, and mentoring. She argues that it implies and creates stronger interdependence, shared responsibility, collective commitment and greater readiness to participate in the difficult business of review and critique.

The continuum is a popular device for representing variations in educational practice. It allows finer discriminations to be made than straight polar opposites allow. This is certainly true for cultures of teaching. There is much more to cultures of teaching than their being collaborative or individualized, good or bad. A continuum of teacher collaboration holds out the promise of being able to chart and push progress towards ever more sophisticated interpretations and implementations of collaboration. But sometimes, the urge to measure and manage can obstruct the search for meaning. This can happen with educational continuums in two ways. First, quite complex and disparate behaviors may be clustered amorphously together into a single stage, level or point on the continuum for the sake of simple and convenient measurement, when in practice the specific behaviors often do not belong together at all. One may, for instance, perform brilliantly in some areas of collaborative work but poorly in others. Great team problem-solvers may be poor emotional supporters. Teachers who may be excellent in nurturing junior colleagues, may flinch when having to face conflicts with equals or superiors. It is impossible to capture these complexities and distinctions on a single scale of collaborativeness.

A second point is that educational continuums often embody implicit values where movement along the continuum is construed as growth or progress towards a better state. However, progress along a continuum does not guarantee continuation towards progress. For example, Little's continuum tends to value forms of collaboration that are more intellectual, inquiry-based and task-centered over ones which are organized more informally around principles and purposes of care, connection and storytelling. In a critique of Little's work, Tafaaki (1993:102) however, shows that in their exchange of narratives and stories, teachers are not merely "gossiping" for amusement or moral support. Indirectly, through these stories, they are also learning about the moral principles which guide each other's work and that, if sufficiently shared, might provide a basis for further associations among them. These "communal caring" cultures are most likely to be found in the feminine, feminized, though not necessarily feminist world of elementary teaching (Acker, 1992). Such cultures may not operate like rational seminars of rigorous intellectual inquiry, but alongside and within the practices of care and connection, they do incorporate inquiry and reflection in more implicit, informal and incidental ways. Representing teacher cultures along normative continuums of development and progress does not allow these sophisticated distinctions to be captured and portrayed.

> **Progress along a continuum does not guarantee continuation towards progress.**

Thus, we need to take care in how we portray teacher cultures; not just in crude polarities or normative continuums that guide us towards the researcher's or leader's visions of improvement and progress, but in terms of more complex typologies or other kinds of representation which place the purposes of curiosity and understanding before the rush to betterment and action.

## BOUNDED IRRATIONALITY

A fourth way in which teacher cultures have been managerially colonized really pervades the other three. The prior sections have revealed a growing normative tradition in writing on educational change, leadership and schools as workplaces. In this tradition, teacher cultures are treated as embodying a kind of "bounded irrationality" where the inefficient, irrational, dangerous and resistant components of teachers' lives and work can be captured, contrived and controlled for purposes of managerial manipulation. In a trenchant critique of the more general literature of organizational culture, Jeffcutt (1993:32) observes that this literature "is distinguished by heroic quests for closure." It is a literature, he argues, that is dominated by two broad representational styles. *Epic* forms portray great cultural leaders who come into an organization and in the face of failure and catastrophe, manage to turn its culture around. In education, case studies of great transformational leaders (Leithwood, 1992) or of principals who have worked with their staffs to turn failing schools around exemplify this *epic* mode. *Romantic* forms, meanwhile, stress placid or pulsating qualities of collaboration and teamwork that help create cultures of organizational harmony. Case studies of exemplary principals building positive cultures of care and support (e.g., Nias et al., 1989) illustrate the presence of this *romantic* mode in educational writing.

Such representational strategies, Jeffcutt argues, "expose an overriding search for unity and harmony that suppresses division and disharmony." Much less common in the literature of leadership and change are representations of organizational culture that take *tragic* or *ironic* forms. Here, obstacles triumph, opponents gain their revenge, heroic quests are unsuccessful and organizations collapse. In the educational research literature, such tragic and ironic accounts of marginalized, resistant or subversive teacher cultures are less likely to be found in the expansive and improvement-oriented landscape of educational change than in the scholarly crevices of educational sociology and anthropology (e.g., Riseborough, 1980). In the general literature of school culture and educational change, however, what predominates are epic and romantic representational styles which embody "*bounded irrationality,* functioning to harmonize, integrate, and unify organization" (Jeffcutt, 1993:32).

## CONCLUSION

For me, this has been an unusual but important paper to write. I have devoted considerable time in recent years, both in my writing and in my practical work with teachers and administrators in the field to build an understanding and appreciation of the *cultural* dimensions of teaching and of educational change. I have seen this as an especially important task, given a context of structural reforms that pay no heed to the humanity of teaching; to the motivations, dispositions and capacities that teachers bring to their work, or to the collegial relationships and sheer emotional labor through which teaching is done. It remains a passionate mission of mine to have educational policy-makers and administrators recognize how important the quality and character of human relationships among teachers are for the quality of their classroom work, and to help them see the damage that can be done to these vital relationships when mandated reforms are oblivious to them. For these reasons, I believe that recognizing and embracing the cultural dimensions of teaching and educational change remain essential to understanding what teachers do, why they do it, and how they might do it better.

**The interior turn that cultural strategies of educational change represent is not an innocent one.**

Yet it seems equally clear to me that the cultural turn in the literature and practice of educational change should not be celebrated prematurely or advocated naively. The interior turn that cultural strategies of educational change represent is not an innocent one. It occurs alongside and not instead of massive exterior strategies of school reform and restructuring in which many teachers appear to have little interest and even less involvement. While school-level cultural change may deserve praise and merit support in principle, in the context of parallel policy moves to dismantle public education and diminish the professional independence of teachers, its growing popularity should be seen as more suspect.

This article has been written to address this disturbing coalescence of seemingly contradictory forces. One of these forces turns leaders inwards to the cultural development of their staffs when the sources of their schools' problems should also be fought and contested "out there." It advocates cultural solutions to what are often structural and political problems. And it tries to harness the emotional energies of teachers and secure their commitment to imposed change, while placing managerial boundaries around this "irrationality," and around the unpredictable outcomes that unfettered collaborative cultures among teachers might otherwise unleash.

I am not recommending that we abandon teacher cultures as part of a proper focus for understanding or initiating educational change. But I *am* advising that we temper our enthusiasm about cultural approaches to change and take time to reflect on the ways in which teacher cultures are being widely colonized by the interests and purposes of management at this time of worldwide structural reform. In light of this analysis, while keeping teacher cultures within our investigative sights, I believe we would do well to pursue three courses of action in educational practice and research. First, we should recognize and support teachers as active agents in developing and maintaining their own cultures, not just as cultural construction materials which administrators can assemble in their own image. Second, we should cultivate and learn from studies of teacher cultures that are tragic and ironic as well as ones that are more epic or romantic. Third, our change theories and practices should address how teachers and principals can turn outwards in their change strategies to fight the assault on public education and the attrition of their professionalism, as well as turning inwards to develop the cultures and capacities of their own immediate staffs.

Cultures of teaching can be a vital key to positive educational change, or they can unlock a Pandora's box of emotional adaptation to imposed reforms that hold out few benefits for students or their teachers. The keys of school culture have been cut. It is now up to teachers, administrators and educational researchers to open the right doors with them.

## NOTES

1. My use of the term here is somewhat different from Giddens. His usage is more general—manufactured uncertainty resulting from what humankind has created, rather than from plagues, famines, earthquakes or other natural events.

2. Jorges de Lima of the University of Azores in Portugal is currently undertaking such a social network analysis of teacher cultures in two secondary schools.

3. I am very grateful to Duncan Waite for the communication we have had around his work on school culture and anthropology for the way it has contributed to my understanding of colonization of culture.

## REFERENCES

Acker, S. (1992). Creating careers: Women teachers at work. *Curriculum Inquiry,* 22(2), 141–163.

Ashton, P. & Webb, R. (1986). *Making a difference: Teachers' sense of efficacy and student achievement.* New York: Longman.

Barlow, M. and Robertson, H.–j. (1994). *Class warfare: The assault on Canada's schools.* Toronto: Key Porter Books.

Bates, R. (1987). Corporate culture, schooling and educational administration. *Educational Administration Quarterly,* November, 23(4), 79–115.

Baudrillard, J. (1983). *Simulations.* Columbia University, NY: Semiotext.

Belenky, M. F., Clinchy, B. M., Goldberger, N. R. & Tarule, J. M. (1986). *Women's ways of knowing.* New York: Basic Books.

Berman, P. & McLaughlin, M. (1978). *Federal programs supporting educational change: V8 implementing and sustaining innovations.* Santa Monica, CA: Rand Corporation.

Bishop, P. W. & Mulford, R. (1996). Empowerment in four Australian primary schools: They don't really care. *International Journal of Educational Reform,* 5(2), 193–204.

Blackmore, J. (1995). *A state for the feminine in educational leadership.* Unpublished paper, Faculty of Education, Deakin University, Australia.

Clifford, J. & Marcus, G. E. (Eds.). (1986). *Writing culture: The politics and poetics of ethnography.* Berkeley: University of California Press.

Cuban, L. J. (1984). *How teachers taught: Constancy and change in American classrooms 1890–1980.* New York: Longman.

Darling-Hammond, L. (1995). Policy for Restructuring. In A. Lieberman (Ed.), *The work of restructuring schools.* New York: Teachers College Press.

Deal, T. & Kennedy, A. (1983). Culture and school performance. *Educational Leadership,* 40(5), 14–15.

Deal, T. & Peterson, K. (1995). *The leadership paradox.* San Francisco: Jossey- Bass.

Eco, U. (1990). *Travels in hyperreality.* San Diego, CA: Harcourt Brace Jovanovich.

Flinders, D. J. (1988). Teachers' isolation and the new reform. *Journal of Curriculum and Supervision,* 4(1), 17–29.

Fullan, M. (1995). Broadening the concept of teacher leadership. *New Directions.* Detroit: National Staff Development Council.

———. (1991). *The new meaning of educational change.* With S. Stiegelbauer. New York: Teachers College Press.

Fullan, M. & Hargreaves, A. (1996). *What's worth fighting for in your school?* (Second edition). New York: Teachers' College Press.

Giddens, A. (1995). *Beyond left and right.* Stanford: Stanford University Press.

———. (1992). *The transformation of intimacy.* Stanford: Stanford University Press.

———. (1991). *Modernity and self-identity.* Cambridge: Polity Press.

Gilligan, C. (1982). *In a different voice.* Cambridge, MA: Harvard University Press.

Goodenough, W. H. (1957). Cultural anthropology and linguistics. In Garvin, P. L. (Ed.), *Report of the Seventh Annual Round Table Meeting on Linguistics and Language Study.* Washington, D.C.: Georgetown University Press, 167–173.

Grimmett, P. & Neufeld, J. (Eds.). (1994). *Teacher development and the struggle for authenticity.* New York: Teachers College Press.

Gronn, P. (1995). Greatness revisited: The current obsession with transformational leadership. *Leading and Managing,* 1(1), 14–27.

Gross, N., Giacquinta, J. & Bernstein, M. (1971). *Implementing organizational innovations: A sociological analysis of planned educational change.* New York: Basic Books.

Hall, G. E. & Loucks, S. (1977). A developmental model for determining whether the treatment is actually implemented. *American Educational Research Journal,* 14(3), 263–276.

Handy, C. (1994). *The age of paradox.* Cambridge, MA: Harvard Business Press.

Hargreaves, A. (1996). Revisiting voice. *Educational Researcher,* January/February, 1–8.

———. (1995). Renewal in the age of paradox. *Educational Leadership,* 52(7), 14–19.

———. (1994). *Changing Teachers, Changing Times.* London: Cassell, New York: Teachers College Press, Toronto: OISE Press.

———. (1993). Individualism and individuality: Reinterpreting the teacher culture. *International Journal of Educational Research,* 19(3).

———. (1992). Cultures of teaching: A focus for change. In Hargreaves, A. & Fullan, M. (Eds.), *Understanding Teacher Development.* London: Cassell and New York: Teachers College Press.

———. (1989). *Curriculum and Assessment Reform.* Toronto: OISE Press.

———. (1986). *Two Cultures of Schooling: The Case of Middle Schools.* Lewes: Falmer Press.

Hargreaves, A. & Goodson, I. (1996). Teachers' professional lives: Aspirations and actualities. In Goodson, I. & Hargreaves, A. (Eds.), *Teachers' professional lives.* New York: Falmer Press.

Hargreaves, A. & Macmillan, R. (1995). The balkanization of teaching. In Little, J. W. & Siskin, L. S. (Eds.), *Subjects in question.* New York: Teachers College Press.

Hargreaves, D. (1980). The occupational culture of teaching. In P. Woods (Ed.), *Teacher Strategies.* London: Croom Helm.

Harvey, D. (1989). *The condition of postmodernity.* Oxford: Basil Blackwell.

Havelock, R. (1973). *The change agent's guide to innovation in education.* Englewood cliffs, N.J.: Educational Technology Publications.

Hochschild, A. R. (1983). *The managed heart: Commercialization of human feeling.* Berkeley: University of California Press.

House, E. (1974). *The politics of educational innovation.* Berkeley, CA: McCutchan.

Huberman, M. (1993). *The lives of teachers.* London: Cassell and New York: Teachers College Press.

Huberman, M. & Miles, M. (1984). *Innovation up close.* New York: Plenum Press.

Jameson, F. (1991). *Postmodernism: Or the cultural logic of late capitalism.* London & New York: Verso.

Jeffcutt, R. (1993). From interpretation to representation. In Hassard, J. & Pracker, M. (Eds.), *Postmodernism and organizations.* London: Sage, 25–48.

Johnson, S. M. (1990). *Teachers at work.* New York: Basic Books.

Kenway, J. (1995). *Reality bytes.* Unpublished paper, Faculty of Education, Deakin University, Australia.

Lasch, C. (1979). *The culture of narcissism.* New York: W. W. Norton.

Leithwood, K. (1992). The move toward transformational leadership. *Educational Leadership,* 49(5), 8–12.

———. (Ed.). (1986). *Planned change through the process of review, development and implementation.* Toronto: OISE Press.

Lieberman, A. (Ed.). (1995). *The work of restructuring schools.* New York: Teachers College Press.

Lieberman, A., Saxl, E. R. & Miles, M. B. (1988). Teachers' leadership: Ideology and practice. In Lieberman, A. (Ed.), *Building a professional culture in schools,* 148–66. New York: Teachers College Press.

Little, J. W. (1990). The persistence of privacy: Autonomy and initiative in teachers' professional relations. *Teachers College Record,* 91(4), 509–36.

Lortie, D. (1975). *Schoolteacher.* Chicago: University of Chicago Press.

Louis, K. S. & Miles, M. (1990). *Improving the urban high school: The what and the how.* New York: Teachers College Press.

McLaughlin, M. (1996). Rebuilding teacher professionalism in the United States. In Hargreaves, A. & Evans, R. (Eds.), *Bringing teachers back in.* Buckingham: Open University Press.

————. (1990). The rand change agent study revisited: macro perspectives and micro realities. *Educational Researcher,* December, 11–16.

McLaughlin, M. & Talbert, J. (1993). *Contexts that matter for teaching and learning.* Stanford University, CA: Center for Research on the Context of Secondary School Teachers.

McTaggart, R. (1989). Bureaucratic rationality and the self-educating profession: The problem of teacher privatism. *Journal of Curriculum Studies,* 21(4), 345–361.

Morgan, G. (1996). Finding your 15%: The art of mobilizing small changes to create large effects. *Focus on educational change,* Vol. 1.

Murphy, J. (1991). *Restructuring schools: capturing and assessing the phenomena.* New York: Teachers College Press.

Nias, J., Southworth, G. & Yeomans, R. (1989). *Staff relationships in the primary school.* London: Cassell.

Page, R. (1987). Teachers' perceptions of students: A link between classroom, school cultures and the social order. *Anthropology and Education Quarterly,* 18, 77–97.

Peters, T. (1988). *Thriving on chaos. Handbook for management revolution.* London: Macmillan.

Richardson, V. (1991). How and why teachers change? In S. C. Conley & B. S. Cooper (Eds.), *The school as a work environment.* Needham, MA: Allyn & Bacon.

Riseborough, G. (1980). Teacher careers and comprehensive school. *Sociology,* 15(3).

Robertson, S. (1996). Teachers' work, restructuring and postfordism: Constructing the new "professionalism." In Goodson, I. & Hargreaves, A. (Eds.), *Teachers' professional lives.* New York: Falmer Press.

Rosenholtz, S. (1989). *Teachers' workplace.* New York: Longman.

Sarason, S. (1971). *The culture of the school and the problem of change.* Boston: Allyn & Bacon.

Schein, E. (1985). *Organizational culture and leadership.* San Francisco: Jossey-Bass.

Senge, P. (1990). *The fifth discipline: The art and practice of the learning organization.* New York: Doubleday.

Sergiovanni, T. J. (1984). Leadership and excellence in schooling. *Educational Leadership,* 41(5), 4–13.

Sikes, P. (1992). Teacher development and imposed change. In Fullan, M. & Hargreaves, A. (Eds.), *Teacher development and educational change.* New York: Falmer Press.

Slattery, P. (1995). A postmodern vision of time and learning: A response to the National Education Commission Report Prisoners of time. *Harvard Educational Review,* 65(4), Winter, 612–633.

Smyth, J. (Ed.). (1993). *The socially critical self-managing school.* London & Philadelphia: Falmer Press.

Tafaaki, I. (1992). *Collegiality and women teachers in elementary and middle school settings: The caring relationship and nurturing interdependence.* Doctor of Education Thesis, University of Massachusetts.

Taylor, C. (1989). *Sources of self.* Cambridge, MA: Harvard University Press.

———. (1991). *The malaise of modernity.* Concord, Ontario: Anasi Press.

Tyack, D. & Tobin, W. (1994). The grammar of schooling: Why has it been so hard to change? *American Educational Research Journal,* 31(3), Fall, 453–480.

Vidich, A. J. & Lyman, S. M. (1994). Qualitative methods: Their history in sociology and anthropology. In Denzin, N. K. & Lincoln, Y. S. (Eds.), *Handbook of qualitative research.* Thousand Oaks, CA: Sage, 23–59.

Waite, D. (1996). Anthropology, sociology and supervision. In Firth, G. R. & Pajak, E. F. (Eds.), *Handbook of research in school supervision.* New York: Scholastic, Inc.

Waller, W. (1932). *The sociology of teaching.* New York: John Wiley.

Williams, R. (1961). *The long revolution.* Harmondsworth: Penguin Books.

# Section 2

# Leadership and Change

Nothing is more important and more elusive than the role of leadership in educational reform. Neither passive nor aggressive, leadership seems to work. There is also a problem with the volume and nature of the countless books on leadership. This literature is often misleading as it offers the latest model, which at last, promises to supply the right answer. Or it is less than helpful when it contains inspiring images (like the learning organization) with little practical guidance to what it means in practice.

Helen Gunter provides a very important critique of management theory and its misuses. She argues that there is no silver bullet, but rather a series of fads; and that there is no substitute for the hard work of action, reflection-in-action, and development of learning organizations. Similarly, in my article on leadership for change, I critique the limitations of existing leadership theories on the one hand, and develop case examples of the application of new theories on the other. In this way, we see how these new ideas lead to very different analysis and actions in dealing with "resistance and conflict" and "the development of collaborative cultures."

Leadership includes teacher development and new roles for teachers. Judith Warren Little shows how the dominant professional development model (training and coaching) is inadequate to the conceptions and requirements of teaching. Put another way, we need different assumptions about professional development and teacher leadership. These assumptions must align with the new model of change embedded in the articles in this book. The principles of professional development outlined by Little are organic and more in tune with the changes in the workplace advocated in Section 3.

# Chaotic Reflexivity

by Helen Gunter

C onsider the following extract from a book on leadership and management:

> This is not an article of conclusions, cases, or exemplary practices of excellent companies. It is deliberately *not* that kind of article, for two reasons. First, I no longer believe that organizations can be changed by imposing a model developed elsewhere. So little transfers to, or even inspires, those trying to work at change in their own organizations. Second, and much more important, the new physics cogently explains that there is no objective reality out there waiting to reveal its secrets. There are no recipes or formulae, no checklists or advice that describe "reality." There is only what we create through our engagement with others and with events. Nothing really transfers; everything is always new and different and unique to each of us.
>
> (Wheatley, 1994, p. 7)

How long will it be before an education management product on leadership and management in educational institutions will have such a reflective process both at the beginning and throughout? What Wheatley (1994) records in her book is not just an explanation of the "new physics" but the impact it has had on her thinking and her practice as a management consultant. Such a process can be stimulated by life event(s), interaction article(s). The preface of this article shows that for me it was all three, for Wheatley (1994) it was the reading of Capra's *The Turning Point,* and for Lewin (1992), *Life at the Edge of Chaos* is more meaningful as a result of visiting Chaco Canyon and the rainforest.

---

From *Rethinking Education: The Consequences of Jurassic Management,* 1997, pp. 83–103. © 1997 by Helen Gunter. Reprinted with permission.

The process of reflection and reflexivity is essential to learning. We could ask: what effect does your subject specialism have on your view of the world, your value systems and, ultimately, what and how you engage in a consultantancy or an INSET activity? Wheatley (1994) notes the dominance of engineers as actual or role models for strategic management theorists, and yet we very rarely see acknowledgment of these ontological and epistemological foundations of their work. Does being a physicist mean that you generate a different type of education management product to a social scientist? The book from which this article is adapted from is about sharing with you the various critiques of education management as a part of encouraging a debate about the Education Management Industry. This article in particular is about asking you to engage in the reflective process and to dig deeper than we have gone so far. By getting in touch with the scientific roots of education management we may even touch some raw nerves within the social sciences in general.

Participants within the Education Management Industry could engage in a process of reflection and reflexivity through the use of Chaos Theory. What is interesting here is the adoption and use of the term Chaos Theory, which in scientific and research circles is known as non-linear dynamics. If the book was in a "management-by-ringbinder" publication then the title would be there, and as long as I made my value system clear by a statement on the first loose-leaf page, then you the reader would be quite happy to accept or reject on this basis. It is more complex than this, as my adoption of Chaos Theory rather than non-linear dynamics is central to the core themes of the book, i.e., the link between theory and practice and research and practice. This point has been illustrated by Hayles (1990):

> "chaos theory" and the "science of chaos" are not phrases usually employed by researchers who work in these fields. They prefer to designate their area as nonlinear dynamics, dynamical systems theory, or, more modestly yet, dynamical systems methods. To them, using "chaos theory" or the "science of chaos" signals that one is dilettante rather than an expert. (p. 8)

Hayles (1990) goes on to argue that she will use Chaos Theory, as it encapsulates her research process and interests as "part of my project to explore what happens when a word such as 'chaos,' invested with a rich tradition of mythic and literacy significance, is appropriated by the sciences and given a more specialized meaning." For me, this debate illustrates how the use of words and labels can be significant in understanding the struggles over status, knowledge and what is defined as intellectual rigor. A key critique of this book could be that I am operating in the very "management-by-ringbinder" mode that I am worried about. Dipping into science theory in order to provide a strategy for education management to get itself out of the hole it has dug itself into is hardly legitimate when my critique is based on the consumerist approach behind the content of many education management products. The simplest defense might be to say that I had to use education management approaches in order to be bought, read and understood. This would be patronizing, unproductive and incorrect. The answer lies within an aspect of education management history and writings. Education management is generally regarded in the UK as a field of application rather than a discipline (Glatter, 1972, p. 51). As Harries-Jenkins (1984) has stated:

> we are looking at a field of management studies characterized by a considerable flexibility of discipline boundaries. A major feature of this has always been the exceptional permeability of these boundaries, so that the development of research and theory in this context has long relied on the work of scholars in such established disciplines as economics, political studies, psychology, and sociology. (p. 215)

This echoes the writings of Baron and Taylor (1969), Glatter (1972, 1979), Bone (1982) and Hughes (1978) and gives perspective to the tensions in the development of education management as a field of application. Hughes (1978) argues that a field of application is concerned with "showing awareness and sensitivity in relation to the problems and concerns of the practitioners who provide the justification of the whole enterprise" (p. 10). In this way the writings of the scientific movement (e.g., Taylor, 1911; Fayol, 1916) were close to the practitioner, but too restricted in scope; the phenomenologists put emphasis on the individual in the field in their interpretation of the management context; and the Theory Movement turned away from the practical application to develop a general theory of administration. Hughes (1978) goes on to argue that currently the best way to understand a field of application is by the use of an analogy with medicine:

> Medical Science is a body of knowledge, the elements of which are
> drawn selectively from a number of sources on the basis of their
> relevance to clinical practice. These elements are derived from sub-
> disciplines of the natural sciences, Physics, Chemistry and Biology an
> also from clinical experience; the knowledge is organized about prob-
> lems of practice. From such a viewpoint, understanding, co-operative
> relationship between a clinician and the analysis, i.e. between the
> practitioner and the academic, is seen as all-important. (p. 10)

Within this framework, the practitioner or clinician communicates
with the analyst or academic on what is needed; and the analyst/
academic can provide an overview and direction to the clinician/
practitioner's work. Therefore practitioner demand and the articulation of problems with education led to a response from academics
in the form of courses and research. Academics then turned to theoretical concepts and models in the social sciences in order to meet
the need:

> It was the field of practice which presented the problem and provided
> the initial stimulus, the research itself required an analysis of concepts
> drawn from the social sciences, the final outcome was to make some
> contribution, it is hoped, to improve practice (any small contribution
> to further theory development being an additional bonus).
>
> (Hughes, 1978, p. 10)

What the theory-practice and academic-practitioner divide is
about status: is a field of application as distinct from a pure discipline or a body knowledge of a lower status? Hughes (1978) argues
that:

> the precise boundary between the pure and the applied may be hard to
> determine, and the traffic in inspiration, ideas and techniques moves
> in both directions. I therefore have little sympathy with the view
> sometimes expressed that an applied science is a somewhat inferior
> form of knowledge to which the high academic standards of the pure
> disciplines do not apply. When I hear such remarks I almost wish that
> the phase "applied science" had never been invented. (p. 13)

Agreed! But since Hughes (1978) wrote those wise words it is clear
that they have not been listened to, as evidence of a two-way traffic
is absent in the business of education management products. We are
all concerned in education with the same issues, and while the focus
may be different for some, the key issue is whether such specificity
becomes blinkered. The theory-practice divide is a false dichotomy

and, as I have said earlier, the justification of this statement has to be more than a debate about the amount and type of practitioner experience which dominates much education management writing.

An interesting way of moving this issue forward is to consider how and why we label social processes. Empowerment, discourse, vision and other popular words would benefit from an understanding of what they really are about and how they could/should be utilized. There are no agendas within this book; if I call Chaos Theory by that title it is not because I am appealing to the common populist mode but because the title furthers our understanding. I agree that I could be labeled a 'dilettante' as I am not a professional scientist ("O" level biology, grade 5, 1974), but I don't have to be an expert in science in order to gain an understanding of the science foundations to my subject expertise. Subject boundaries are an artificial creation that has more to do with power and exclusivity than it has to do with knowledge creation. I am not consuming scientific concepts in order to promote a management solution, but rather looking at how science can illustrate the failure of such solutions. We learn by analogy, and the use of metaphor triggers recognition and imagination. I will therefore talk about Chaos Theory not as part of an amateur-expert struggle, but because it best describes the scientific processes in which all our work is rooted. How ideas are presented is essential to our work as it enables it to be inclusive or exclusive, and nowhere is this better illustrated than in how science and scientists are presented in the media, and how stereotypes act as barriers to what science is really about and its importance to everyday life. Technical terms like the Latin names for plants are something that the so-called "amateur gardener" finds of interest as well as the expert. They are part of a shared language in which words, labels and descriptions, when challenged by all participants, facilitate communication, understanding and an appreciation of the plurality of work context and outcomes. Do you know why your use words and phrases like cost effectiveness, efficiency, accountability and delegation? Do you challenge your use of them and consider whether and why you have been co-opted into the language and therefore the ideology of management? The education profession is an educated profession, but why do we persist in

> **The theory-practice divide is a false dichotomy.**

educating professionals to do, rather than to think? As Inglis (1985) has powerfully argued:

> The deadly banalities of the management consultant and the techno-cratic expert are universally deployed to justify arbitrary closure, redundancy, the dereliction of building (plant, as they say), as well as the gross, philistine and self-seeing foreshortening of a humane edu-cation. All of us have innumerable such stories to tell. But through it all, with unshakable self-satisfaction, the managerialists pursue their unimpeded way, entitling new courses "the management of contrac-tion," "the organization of decline," or most risible of all, "falling rolls." The inanity of the disciplinary diction should have been enough to kill it off. Stuck with a latter-day and pretentious account of the policy sciences as being capable of bringing about rational progress and the accurate predictions which would permit this con-summation, no senior manager ever has recourse to such traditional concepts as wisdom, sagacity, utter accident, sainthood, passion, trag-edy, historical understanding. No curriculum advises middle manag-ers to pick at random from Hegel, Turgenev, Dickens, Kierkegaard, Einstein, the Buddha, Aristotle, Prince Kropotkin, Hannah Arendt, Rosa Luxemburg, Chinua Achebe. (pp. 105–6)

No education management product asks practitioners to look at the history of science and how it enables us to understand and explain current thinking and practice in a range of fields including management. Chaos Theory can explain why we cannot predict outcomes for some complicated systems like the weather or earth-quakes or gambling. Chaos Theory is a fundamental paradigm shift and challenges the foundations on which our lives and work are based. Our view of the world is rooted in the natural sciences and further study illustrates that this is based on the seventeenth-century Newtonian legacy. Let us consider that Kogan (1979) argues:

> that it is the task of social scientists to take things apart. I assume that it is the task of politicians and administrators to make sure that things are brought back together again . . . (p.8)

Such an approach is based on the world as a well-ordered and pre-dictable machine: things can be taken apart, analyzed and put back together again without damage. By separating out knowledge into subjects in places of learning, or organizations into departments and roles, we assume that we can understand the whole by investigating the part. Turbulence and disturbance to the system is therefore nega-tive and a problem. In this world, the emphasis is on either rising above the practical and being characterized as thinkers, or for the practitioner keeping the machine running smoothly, and solving problems. You either do or do not get your hands dirty. Chaos is literally "chaotic:" the imperative is to control change in order to prevent entropy. As Wheatley (1994) has said:

> Machines wear down; they eventually stop. . . . This is a universe, we feel, that cannot be trusted with growth, rejuvenation, process. If we want progress, then we must provide the energy, the momentum, to reverse decay. By sheer force of will, because we are the planet's consciousness, we will make the world hang together. We will resist death. (p. 17)

Education management products are designed on seventeenth century assumptions with an emphasis on managerialist techniques and systems, and creating a fear of understanding human relationships. Human resource management, in spite of the rhetoric of empowerment, ownership and collegiality, is still based on control, stability, order and the equilibrium of organizational fit with the environment. This is not a denial that Newtonian physics does not have validity (Toffler, 1984), and as Lewin (1992) has argued, getting a human to the moon and back is based on the laws of motion and predictability which can be simulated and tested. However, it is time to acknowledge non-literacy in the natural and social world. As Sungaila (1990b) has argued, we cannot allow scientific revolutions to pass us by unnoticed, rather we are alive and we should conceptualize the universe accordingly:

> Machines are not natural. They are not alive. Our world is both. Our students, our schools, our school systems, are alive. So are our language, our culture, our society. Our systems of thought, including our discipline of educational administration, are living systems too. And science has at last begun to grasp the basic principles on which living systems operate. They are self-renewing and self-organizing. (p. 6)

This has implications for research and we may compare the act of taking things apart with the implications of Schroedinger's cat for the social scientist. A cat is placed in a box and no one can see inside it. Poison or food can be released at any time; the probability of food or poison is 50:50. When the release mechanism goes, what is the cat's fate? We do not know until we look, and therefore the act of observation creates the cat's situation, ". . . it is impossible to say that the cat is living or dead until we observe it. . . . Before we peer

in, the cat exists as probabilities. Our nosiness determines its fate"
(Wheatley, 1994, pp. 59–60).

What this illustrates is that there is a different type of knowledge if we stop investigating on the basis of objective reality. The
world of the observer and observed, researcher and researched has
been shattered. Furthermore, the Newtonian machine view of the
universe elevated humans as a part of a rational process separate
from nature. We have lost touch with a respect for the earth and in
the late twentieth century we now have the opportunity to revisit that
culture, not just through ecology, but through a different understanding of control. As Prigogine and Stengers (1984) have argued,
science is more than "manipulating nature, but it also an attempt to
understand it, to dig deeper into questions that have been asked
generation after generation" (p. 291). We have spent the last three
hundred years trying to prove that natural and social are different,
but as Sungaila (1990b) has shown, "it is now discovered, that the
same dynamics underpin *both* natural *and* social life" (p. 7; italics in
original). Quantum mechanics is a world of discovery rather than
scientific method. Particles are not objects, things, items, or units
which are independent of each other. Relationships are what matter.
A particle exists and only be seen in connection with something else.

Therefore, the closed system of the Newtonian machine has
been challenged by the open system in which continued existence is
through the constant exchange of energy with the environment. Within
closed systems things can be determined and events reversed, but
within open systems:

> The irreversibility of such systems implies that they have histories
> and that they evolve. Discussing an open system then must involve
> some description of the historical development of the system.
>                                         (Sawada & Caley, 1985, p. 14)

The message for education management is loud and clear. We have
seen real history does not figure much in education management
products as they assume that open systems can be subjected to the
predictive control mechanisms, reversibility processes and determination of the clock and machine.

Hayles (1990) has identified two different emphases in Chaos
Theory which is tied up in the complexity of: there is order within
chaos, and there is order out of chaos. Firstly, there is the work of
Prigogine who, with Stengers, wrote *Order out of Chaos* (1984), and

argued that chaos and order are not opposites. Prigogine's Nobel Prize (1977) work on dissipative structures shows how certain chemical processes can lead to self-organization. As energy dissipates the system does not die, but rather there is a regenerative and self-renewing process taking place:

> open systems have the possibility of continuously importing free energy from the environment and of exporting entropy. They don't sit quietly by as their energy dissipates. They don't seek equilibrium. Quite the opposite. To stay viable, open systems maintain a state of non-equilibrium, keeping the system off balance so that it can change and grow. They participate in an active exchange with their world, using what is there for their own renewal. Every organism in nature, including us, behaves in this way. (Wheatley, 1994, p. 78)

The system is autopoetic, in which there is a drive for renewal. The system has a boundary that both identifies distinction an integration with the environment, and so I am not a single entity isolated in space but part of a turbulent living network in which I am both individual and social. Therefore, as Toffler (1984, p. xv) argues, ". . . surely biological and social systems are open, which means that the attempt to understand them in mechanistic terms is doomed to failure."

A second emphasis in Chaos Theory is about order within chaos or what has been known as "bounded instability." This is based on the work of Lorenz, and what are known as "strange attractors" (see Gleick, 1987, p. 90). Hayles (1990) describes this as:

> Whereas truly random systems shown no discernible pattern when they are mapped into phase space, chaotic systems contract to a confined region and trace complex patterns within it. The discovery that chaos possesses deep structures of order is all the more remarkable because of the wide range of systems that demonstrate this behavior. They range from lynx for returns to outbreaks of measles epidemics, from the rise and fall of the Nile River to eye movements in schizophrenics. (pp. 9–10)

Therefore, order within chaos enables us to consider the "strange attractors" within organizations, and not just computer modeling. For Wheatley (1994), a potent, strange attractor is *meaning,* in which individuals in hostile environments are able to ask and find answers to "why?":

> If we search to create meaning, we can survive and even flourish. In chaotic organizations, I observed just such phenomenon. Employees

were wise enough to sense that personal meaning-making was their
only route out of chaos. In some ways, the future of the organization
became irrelevant. They held onto personal coherence because of the
meaning attractor they created. Maybe the organization didn't make
sense, but their lives did. (pp. 134–5)

While there is debate among chaos theorists, it is possible to
identify some features (Hayles, 1990; Griffiths et al., 1991) of
chaotic systems that enable us to gain a different understanding of
social processes. Firstly, systems are *non-linear,* in that cause and
effect are distant. A small cause can have a large effect, and *sensitivity to local conditions* (butterfly effect) can *amplify* the input through
*feedback* loops. Therefore the flap of a butterfly's wings could cause
a thunderstorm in another part of the world:

> For small pieces of weather . . . any prediction deteriorates rapidly.
> Errors and uncertainties multiply, cascading upward through a chain
> of turbulent features, from dust devils and squalls up to continent-
> sized eddies that only satellites can see. (Gleick, 1987, p. 20)

Secondly, systems are *complex,* and different approaches to scale
and measurement are needed. A coastline cannot be measured in the
same way as a triangle in which there is an instrument and a precise
process based on the truth and accuracy of objective scales and numbers. Mandlebrot's fractals are patterns which are *self-similar* in that
they look the same or similar on every scale or dimension in which
they are examined.

Chaos Theory has been applied in science to astronomy, physi-
ology, demography, mathematics and meteorology, and within the
field of economics some interesting work has been done by Curtis
(1990) and Radzicki (1990). The applicability to the social sciences
is a matter of dispute. Percival (1991) has argued that:

> Science takes words and shapes their meanings to its own ends, and
> "chaos" is no exception. The state of Lebanese politics and British
> education may look chaotic, but you cannot study them using chaos
> theory. (p. 16)

We may well ask: why not? Recently, writers have begun to recognize the validity of Chaos Theory to social processes within organizations and are moving away from the usual way of seeing "chaos"
and "the crucial turn comes when chaos is envisioned not as an
absence or void but as a positive force in its own right" (Hayles,
1990). Therefore, Gleick (1987) has argued:

> Now that science is looking, chaos seems to be everywhere. . . .
> Chaos appears in the behavior of the weather, the behavior of an air-
> plane in flight. . . . No matter what the medium, the behavior obeys
> the same newly discovered laws. That realization has begun to change
> the way business executives make decisions about insurance, the way
> astronomers look at the solar system, the way political theorists talk
> about the stresses leading to armed conflict. . . . Chaos breaks across
> the lines that separate scientific disciplines. (p. 5)

Books and articles are appearing in which Chaos Theory has influenced the thinking of the writer (Ferchat, 1990; Nilson, 1995), and
some interesting analysis has been done by Nonaka (1988), who
uses self-organization as a means of understanding and creating self-
renewal in Japanese business. Most work has been located within
the business sector by Stacey (1991, 1992, 1993), in challenging the
orthodoxy of strategic management and using Chaos Theory to illustrate how successful companies achieve by using instability to innovate. Also recommended is the excellent reflexive study by Wheatley
(1994) on how Chaos Theory can enable our understanding of leadership to develop through conceptualizing organizations differently:

> If organizations are machines, control makes sense. If organizations
> are process structures, then seeking to impose control through perma-
> nent structure is suicide. If we believe that acting responsibly means
> exerting control by having our hands into everything, then we cannot
> hope for anything except what we already have—a treadmill of effort
> and life-destroying stress. (p. 23)

For Wheatley, the lessons of quantum mechanics are clear for organizations, and as a consultant her focus has shifted, "now I look
carefully at how a workplace organizes its relationships; not its
tasks, functions, and hierarchies, but the patterns of relationship and
the capacities available to form them" (p. 39).

In education there is no equivalent to Stacey and Wheatley, but
as we have seen, there is a growing disquiet about managerialism in
the critique of site-based management. Within the broader field of
education management text books we do find the work of Weick
(1988) and Cohen and March (1989), in which the reality of the
world of rational and costed plans, job descriptions and evaluation
schedules is questioned. Weick argues that organizations are
"loosely coupled," while Cohen and March identify the American
college and university as "organized anarchies" in which decision-
making can be best understood as a "garbage can":

> A key to understanding the processes within organizations is to
> view a choice opportunity (an occasion on which an organization is
> expected to produce a decision) as a garbage can into which various
> problems and solutions are dumped by participants. The mix of
> garbage in a single can depends partly on the labels attached to the
> alternative cans; but it also depends on what garbage is being produced
> at the moment, on the mix of cans available, and on the speed with
> which garbage is collected and removed from the scene. (p. 111)

What is interesting is that this world is not reflected in education
management products, otherwise the "recipes" and "maps" would
not produce the solutions. Even within mainstream education
management writings there is some difficult. Weick (1988, pp. 61–2)
admits to a "neutral, if not mildly affectionate stance towards the
concept" of loose coupling but does acknowledge that it could be
met with hostility. We may wonder why in spite of Bell's (1989)
argument that hierarchy with vertical and horizontal divisions should
be abandoned there is still an emphasis on management control
through, for example, teams to deal with issues of "problematic
goals," "unclear technology," and "fluid participation" within organized anarchies (Weick, 1988). The drive for stability and consensus
is strong for those who present ambiguity models within the mainstream literature. Weick (1976) is quoted by Bush (1995) as follows:

> If there is a breakdown in one portion of a loosely coupled system
> then this breakdown is sealed off and does not affect other portions of
> the organization . . . when any element misfires or decays or deterio-
> rates, the spread of this deterioration is checked in a loosely coupled
> system . . . A loosely coupled system can isolate its trouble spots and
> prevent the trouble from spreading. (pp. 116–17)

Disorder is conceptualized as negative and has to be managed. Bush
(1995) is concerned that management accountability means that this
disorder cannot be tolerated: "action must be taken to remedy the
weakness if the institution is to thrive in a period of heightened market and public accountability" (p. 117).

These issues are reflected in other debates over organizational
structure and behavior. Turner (1977) is prepared to argue in favor
of educational institutions as "unpredictable, anarchic organizations
with no clear boundaries and a turbulent environment" (in Westoby,
1988, p. 83) but his co-writer is concerned with accountability. As
Packwood (1977) states:

The hierarchy, through its properties of accountability and authority, is a rational attempt to combine the activities of many in securing desired ends. Without accountability the organization runs as "catch as catch can" and any outcome depends upon the power of the individuals concerned. Education is too important for that and it cannot solely depend upon short-term decisions. The result would be unhappy, uneducated children and unhappy, frustrated staff.

(Westoby, 1988, p. 84)

In replying, Turner (1977) begins to touch on chaotic issues of how a context is conceptualized. If we want line-managed accountability then we must structure accordingly, but if we see the importance of relationships and information flows then the accountability becomes one of professional dialogue and partnership. While this type of discussion is clearly evident within the broader education management literature, what is missing is that ambiguity and organized anarchy are not taken a stage further by considering how disorder can lead to a positive process of creative self-renewal.

Clearly we have to come to terms with whether the pure excitement and enthusiasm for Chaos Theory makes it just a novelty, and it is open to abuse. In the battle for recognition and consecration within the field of education management, language and specialist terminology could be used to exclude people. All the work currently being done on Chaos Theory illustrates that it is not a bandwagon that is rolling through like Total Quality Management and Competences, but is fundamental to understanding social and educational processes. In Australia, Sungaila (1990a) has argued that there is an "emerging synthesis in the natural and social sciences" (p. 6), and therefore educational observers and practitioners cannot ignore the transformation in science and its applicability to understanding educational systems. Furthermore, work by Snyder et al. (1995) based at the University of Florida challenges the "utility of a linear construct of planned change..." and contends that, "Chaos Theory provides a useful mental model of guiding change as leaders garner the energy from unpredictable events for realizing transformation goals" (p. 2). In spite of all the books and training on how to plan, structure and identify objectives for a quality teaching and learning strategy, we are all aware of the creative process within the classroom and that it is definitely not linear; cause and effect are often not closely related. This is nowhere better illustrated than in concerns being raised about the OFSTED inspection process in England and Wales, where Russell (1994) has argued that the inspection framework is a systems approach which "is not only conceptually opposed to randomness and maverick creativity. If applied really well it leaves no room for the serendipity that may inspire excellence" (p. 311). Hence, even though very able and knowledgeable people may be involved in the inspection process, the report may fail to bring about school improvement because, "to inspire the effort needed in schools to bring about change there has to be that 'ah ha' of recognition when the report is read" (p. 313). Cziko (1989) has raised questions about educational research based on the rational and predictive certainties of Newtonian physics. He uses the butterfly effect to question the linearity of learning and progression rooted in current educational structures:

> The butterfly effect of chaotic phenomena constitutes a particularly vexing curse for psychometricians because no matter how reliable and valid a test may be, identical scores on a pretest will inevitably lead to unpredictable differences on posttest of later achievement. (p. 19)

This clearly has messages for much value-added and school improvement research. For Cziko (1989), in social science research:

> We must, however, always guard against the temptation to make hard and fast predictions of human behavior and devise "cookbook" solutions to problems based on our understanding because, as argued here, it is a serious error to believe that one can predict the future based on what has happened in the past.
>
> Though such research might (indeed, *should*) lead the implementation and dissemination of innovative educational practices, it must be realized that regardless of the extent of prior research, accurate prediction of outcomes is not possible, and so continuous monitoring and fine-tuning is essential to any educational undertaking. (p. 23)

Cziko's paper has provoked debate in the form of a reply by Lehrer et al. (1990), in which they question whether behavior is always indeterminate, and therefore it "does not mean that behavior is not predictable *within certain tolerances*. The challenge for a theory is to specify these tolerances" (p. 17). What would be interesting for the Education Management Industry is to examine how the "tolerances" have been very narrowly defined to the techniques and language of management, and how a reflective and reflexive process from within the sciences may facilitate challenge and review.

Griffiths et al. (1991) recognize that their "foray into chaotic modeling is a bit 'quick and dirty' because of the limitations on data and case construction and the post hoc character of the analysis," but they are positive about the appeal of Chaos Theory and its "explanatory value" (p. 447). However, they are skeptical about it in relation to data collection and research design: if we search for "strange attractors" then we will find them. Furthermore, the predictive abilities of Chaos Theory are just as limited as what is already available within the social sciences. If we are in search of truth in the tradition of Newtonian physics then so be it, but, as Cziko (1989) argues, the kind of educational research which should take place is one which

> would involve a change from the orthodox "scientific" research perspective that attempts to predict and control to one that attempts "only" to describe, appreciate, interpret, and explain the social and individual behaviors as well as the cognitive processes relevant to understanding educational phenomena. Educational research from such a perspective would be essentially descriptive, with useful units of study varying from the macro level of community, school, and classroom to the more micro level of individual behaviors, feelings, and cognitive processes. (p. 23)

However, even though valuable work has started in the application of Chaos Theory to the educational context, the relevance may not be immediately clear. For the manager-practitioner schooled in the entrepreneurial mind-set, the science of fractals, strange attractors and the butterfly effect seem far removed from organizational behavior. Chaos Theory presents the view that to be successful a school or college needs to recognize that educational institutions are not linear but complex networks with equally complex feedback loops. Current orthodoxy is that schools and colleges operate a rational cycle of review, forecast, implementation and evaluation in relation to resource management. Therefore, curriculum and resource needs are identified and prioritized, and forecasts are made of pupil/student numbers and income linked to targets. This is informed by the development plan and the long-term vision of where the school/college wants to be at a given point in the future. During the annual cycle, negative feedback (e.g., changes to the funding formula) is prevented from causing a downward spiral or vicious cycle by monitoring, and adjustments are made in order to ensure stability. Similarly, positive feedback (e.g., increased demand for places in the sixth form) can form a virtuous cycle of success and must be prevented from leading to disintegration or "explosively unstable equilibrium" (Stacey, 1992, p. 62).

The drive for stability is a product of a retrospective view of education and of the perceived need to return to the golden age when the long-term was predictable and all you had to do was to teach. At the core of much man-

**The future cannot be visioned as it is unpredictable and depends on chance.**

agement training is the view that managers' concerns must be met by giving them the handbook containing the strategies and tools which will enable stability to return once again to schools and colleges. We see courses about controlling change by adopting the management tools of strategic manage-

ment, quality management and business planning, combined with stress and self-esteem courses to help managers deal with the guilt and angst when they don't work (Stacey, 1992).

Chaos Theory presents education managers with a third choice to either stability or disintegration, and that is to operate within "bounded instability" (Stacey, 1992, p. 21). A successful school or college would operate away from equilibrium between stability and disintegration. Management behavior is therefore operating in an environment of constant order and disorder. The future cannot be visioned as it is unpredictable and depends on chance. Feedback can produce behavior that is complex, in which a direct link between cause and effect cannot be seen. For Bowe et al. (1992), the complexity, speed and contradictory aspects of the change process "make a mockery of the neat and trite prescriptions offered in many of the 'how-to-do-it' management texts written to cash in on the ERA reforms" (p. 166). Therefore the future is created by the sensitive response to fluctuations in the environment rather than proactive and systematic installations of new structures and tasks. Perhaps education management products require new prescriptions: managers should not be following the John Major call to go "back to basics," in which history determines the future, nor should the manager yield to the idealism of visioning and let some picture of a desired future determine what you do today. What Chaos Theory enables the manager to do is to explore the issues in relation to what his happening now and recognize the choices from which the future will unfold. Sullivan's (1994) work has shown the importance of human relationships, and how systems co-evolve by a creative process of policy and organizational modification.

Teachers need not panic. The day-to-day issues are within control, it is the long-term issues that have the potential to use a creative or an extraordinary management approach using a chaotic perspective (Stacey, 1992). Furthermore, the future is not random in the ordinary sense of chaos in that it is "bounded instability." The weather patterns are not predictable, but they are within a boundary of, for example, the seasons. We might not be able to predict if there will be sun during the Wimbledon tennis championships, but we can recognize patterns and therefore predict that there will not be snow! If it were to snow, we would be able to see that each snowflake is unique as a result of fluctuations in the environment in which it was created, but we would also see "self-similarity" in that the flakes of frozen water can be categorized as snowflakes (Stacey, 1991).

What does the challenge of Chaos Theory mean for the Education Management Industry? The fundamental issue that the Education Management Industry has to grapple with is a confusion between order and control (Wheatley, 1994), and Hargreaves (1995) critique of Chaos Theory illustrates this, Hargreaves (1995) is rooted in a Newtonian view of the world and so the drive for observable control mechanisms is strong in order to maintain stability and meet the needs and wants of parents and children. "Corrective control" (p. 220) in relation to "targets, success criteria, action plans, and progress checks" is both possible and desirable through the working of open and closed feedback loops. For Hargreaves, monitoring and evaluation are as essential for whole institutional development as they are for effective teaching and learning. Buried within the article (p. 225) is an analysis of the importance of complex relationships, but they are marginalized to the tasks of information providers for monitoring and adjustment. If Hargreaves had begun with human relationships rather than with the management structures and tasks designed to keep management tidy, then he would have access to the creative energy among professionals. Closed loops may operate in thermostats where corrective control is about bringing "things" back on track, but not in human interactions. Chaos Theory enables us to understand that you are not necessarily out of control if you are not in control.

Furthermore, there is an obsession with problem-solving within education management products. The effective manager is provided with a series of stages, tasks and systems in order to be able to work through people to get the job done. Problem-solving is aided by controlling problem development by having a consensus value system, collective goals and a sense of purpose combined with collegiate team structures. This is an illusion, but it is being packaged (and repackaged) and sold to educational professionals under the guise of a right to manage. We cannot solve problems, rather it is the issues from which the problems are created that require investigation. Redefining a problem as an opportunity does not help, and in fact is mischievous. If I'm cold then I can switch on the heating, and if I am too warm then I can turn it off. Problem solved? The problem (feeling hot or cold) is seen as being linear, with cause and effect close together, and I am in control of the barrier that I have created. However, the technical action of flicking a switch and obtaining instant relief from cold or heat does not really solve the problem. I have been cold/hot in the past, and no doubt I will be cold/hot again in the future. The barrier that I have created has been there and will continue as along as I am a sentient being (though being cold/hot in my grave still means that the issue is thereof, but not a live one!). Furthermore, I may make choices independent of feeling hot or cold. I may decide to tolerate the cold in order not to have a large heating bill, or go for a walk to keep warm, and so on. In other words we create, we inherit, we define and we redefine problems. We can put in place short-term measures to deal with manifestations of the problem but we cannot "clear it up" or "settle it" or "close the book." We can never truly zero base. When the legal system completes a murder case the victim may be buried and the perpetrator in jail but the problem of that and other murders has not been resolved. Problems within social processes are non-linear, cause and effect are distant, and history helps to shape the present. Therefore for educational professionals the key concern is how tasks, processes and events are or are not conceptualized as a problem, and a problem which they as educationalists have to solve. Saul (1992, p. 7) has argued that "a civilization unable to differentiate between illusion and reality is usually believed to be at the tail end of its existence," and this has messages for the Education Management Industry in its construction of problem-solving imperatives and knowledge. In order to apply in this context, I will take the liberty of paraphrasing Saul (1992) and say that within the Education Management Industry reality is dominated by elites who have spent much of the last decade organizing teachers "around answers and around structures designed to produce answers" (p. 8). In this sense, elites are those who have power positions based on what is promoted as "expertise" in the form of books, videos, software, and inset courses. Management knowledge is controlled through these products; it is targeted, audience specific and exclusive to the management elite within a school. The language of accountability, performance indicators, consensus and quality gives legitimacy. This is an illusion and a dangerous one at that. As Saul (1992) states:

> Thus, among the illusions which have invested our civilization is an absolute belief that the solution to our problems must be a more determined application of rationally organized expertise. The reality is that our problems are largely the product of that application. The illusion is that we have created the most sophisticated society in the history of man. The reality is that the division of knowledge into feudal fiefdoms of expertise has made general understanding and coordinated action not simply impossible but despised and distrusted. (p. 8)

What is particularly "despised and distrusted" within education management products is the concept of professionalism. Traditionally, teachers have focused on professional issues to do with learning, assessment, standards, teaching style, subject context and concepts. Teachers recognized the importance of "general understanding" of these issues and how structural factors such as the economy had an impact, and also promoted "coordinated action" in the form of working with parents, and ultimately taking action if the issue was conceptualized as a problem that could undermine learning. Education professionals are told that they now have management problems to do with outcomes, accountability, improvement and change. The issues are not new to educational professionals, and if we strip away the managerialist jargon then we may be able to gain access to understanding that teaches have always been interested in outcomes, but not the ones which are measured in league tables. Teachers have always had a sense of accountability, but they question the current emphasis on leaving a paper trail of proformas and policy documents to prove that they are. Teachers have always been in favor of continuous improvement, but this has been invisible as much creative flair happens outside normal pupil-contact hours, and is not recognized by externally imposed criteria. Teachers have always driven change in teaching and learning styles, examination courses, new materials and technology. However, it has not always been welcomed by the tabloid media and the New Right, who have a different agenda.

Therefore, if educational professionals have failed at all, it has been in how educational and non-educational issues have been conceptualized as problems which they have to solve. Decentralization of the responsibility for educational issues to schools as a result of legislation such as the 1988 Education Reform Act has meant that the management model has been attractive. If schools not only *can* make a difference, (teachers have never denied this) but also *have to* make a difference, then schools will take on the structural economic and social problems around them. Equal opportunity policies are important for educational institutions, but they will not manage away the structural injustices in society. Furthermore, "management by ringbinder" will not provide the real authority to discharge those responsibilities when power over priorities and resources lies with government agencies. Perhaps what we need are management development courses and books which enable professionals to say: we understand that this is an important issue, and we would like to contribute to debate but it is not only our problem. I can expel a child for drug-pushing in the school playground but the school is not the cause of the drug problem; I can make a member of staff redundant but it does not resolve the under-resourcing of education and the structural weaknesses of the economy.

Educational professionals have not been quiet over many of these issues, and OFSTED report after report shows, for example, that schools have refused to solve the legislated problems surrounding collective worship and daily assemblies because it goes against professional judgment and equity. Nevertheless, it does not prevent education management products from continuing to peddle their quick fixes and patent medicines as cure-alls. It seems that professionals are able to live with the sentence in their OFSTED report which says they are not obeying the law. How long can such resistance last when new teachers are entering the profession trained in accordance with minimalist competences?

This needs to be put within a "bigger picture" and we could trace the development of the Education Management Industry to the worldwide dissatisfaction with education that has led to restructuring in the form of the self-managing school and college (Lawton, 1992; Gordon and Pearce, 1993) and the growth of technical and measurable management competencies. In proactively responding to the perceived need to do something, education management has been deluded into thinking it could problem-solve for practitioners. As Sungaila (1990b) has shown:

> Irrespective of how educational administrators are trained, and educational systems are structured and managed, public dissatisfaction will continue to manifest itself in one form or another. Such is the nature of educational reality. (p. 4)

Sungaila goes on to argue that those involved in professional development need not keep rushing to develop new courses, books and other product development as a means of demonstrating that they are worthy of existing either structurally or economically. In other words, education management cannot deal with parent, pupil and politician dissatisfaction with schools by collaborating with managerial agendas and making systemic reforms work. Schools will always be a complex issue as their existence and form are a matter for values, ethics, politics and interests. Conceptualizing a school as a small business based on entrepreneurial techniques will not manage these issues away. If educational professionals are unable to resist then we will have educational practitioners who are pragmatic problem-solvers rather than professionals who have a moral and ethical involvement in social issues, and are capable of being pragmatic but are also theorists and thinkers. Education management can only have a role to play for the practitioner if it looks at its role within, and contribution to, knowledge creation, and how it facilitates the practitioner's access to it. As Wheatley (1994) has stated:

> In our past explorations, the tradition was to discover something and then formulate it into answers and solutions that could be widely transferred. But now we are on a journey of mutual and simultaneous exploration. In my view, all we can expect from one another is new and interesting information. We can *not* expect answers. Solutions, as quantum reality teaches, are a temporary event, specific to a context, developed through the relationship of persons and circumstances. There will be no more patrons, waiting expectantly for our return, just more and more explorers venturing out on their own. (pp. 150–1)

Chaos Theory enables us to conceptualize education as a complex *human* system in which a full interplay of regenerative forces can take place. The implications of Chaos Theory lie in a debate about what the successful professional behaviors for teachers are. This is not an easy process and as we have seen it requires an engagement with fundamental issues to do with knowledge. For Wheatley (1994), the personal story of developing a new understanding of the universe unfolds throughout her book, and she states:

> the time I formerly spent on detailed planning and analysis I now use to look at the structures that might facilitate relationships. I have come to expect that something useful occurs if I link up people, units, or tasks, even though I cannot determine the precise outcomes. And last, I realize more and more that the universe will not cooperate with my desires for determinism. (pp. 43–4)

Action-thinking-action is real empowerment because it is based on "decentralizing the location of (and the authority for) knowledge creation" (Winter, 1991, p. 474). People do not just respond to the environment, they create it, and therefore what schools and colleges offer to current and potential customers is not about meeting customer needs but about shaping them. This is a new role for managers in being interventionist within the environment by seeing how small changes can have a considerable impact over time as "creative strategies emerge from instability in a seemingly unintended, uncoordinated manner" (Stacey, 1992, p. 20). The investment of time and energy in such dissipative structures is high, but turbulence does not interrupt or interfere—as Sawada and Caley argue, it "embodies information" (1985, p. 16). Hence the use of information and decision-making is by the use of analogy and intuition rather than analyzing cause and effect through modeling and statistical forecasting. Wheatley (1994, p. 117) acknowledges that "new knowledge" is from relationships and networks, and goes on to argue that thinking skills or "intellectual capital" is an essential resource for all workers. Visioning is not about knowledge creation, understanding or dissemination. Visioning is a delusion; its only function is to provide comfort for those uneasy about living with turbulent change. When people find themselves in new situations they learn while doing it and using previous activities to develop meaning and new strategies for creating the future (Stacey, 1992). Therefore, effectiveness is not just about measuring up to external and imposed criteria, but about professional judgment and professional standards.

The challenge for the Education Management Industry is to learn that contradiction and conflict are very creative, and that people within an organization will not learn if they are subject to the control of a strong value system, but they will learn if they know how to recognize disorder. It will be difficult to break out of the evangelical myth of the consensus and stability models, but effective management is about being a "bureaucracy buster" (Dumaine, 1991; Semler, 1989) and "equilibrium buster" (Jantsch in Wheatley, 1994). Organizations have traditionally recruited and rewarded on the basis of the formal skills which the organization defines as being valid and worthy of the title "skill." The butterfly effect allows us to recognize that one person can have an impact and therefore the lesson for teachers is to tap into and encourage the whole skills base of colleagues. When instability disrupts existing patterns of behavior, organizations can be left bereft of what to do as the old skills are redundant and the training courses for the new ones have not been designed. This is directly linked to equality of opportunity and access, as Gaskell (1992) has shown:

> Women have not had the power to insist that their skills be recognized and valued in the work-place. Their lack of ability to define the work as skilled is not simply a matter of cognition, but is the result of a social process that has had institutional consequences in relation to educational qualifications and opportunities for vocational training, as well as in relation to wages. (p. 113)

Therefore real equality of opportunity within educational organizations is about giving recognition to the skills and capacities which staff have as a result of the plurality of their lives.

When events or crises hit individuals and groups there is a spontaneous capacity to organize and respond. Groups form which are fluid and can network with each other while the issue is salient. Many pressure groups have been formed in this way: women at Greenham Common; various groups against the poll tax; miners' wives during the miners' strike of 1984–85. A recent example is the Friends of John McCarthy, for which Jill Morrell describes how:

> Nick [Toksvig] and I felt that we had to act; to go out to the Middle East and see what as happening for ourselves, to talk to people. . . . All our friends, and especially our colleagues at WTN, were enthusiastic and eager to help. When the management told Nick and me that we couldn't, as planned, go over Christmas and New Year because of staffing problems, colleagues switched their holidays around to make the trip possible. When we realized we would need to organize a small fund-raising evening to pay our way we found ourselves bombarded with help from all sides. It was as if John's friends had been waiting a long, long time to be able to help in some way. . . .
>
> (McCarthy and Morrell, 1993, pp. 113–15)

These people showed the capacity for self-organization in which
current behavior patterns are shattered by "the spontaneous formation of interest groups and coalitions around specific issues, communication about those issues, cooperation and the formation of
consensus on and commitment to a response to those issues"
(Stacey, 1993, p. 242).

Self-organization can be in many forms. It can happen within a
bureaucracy like the Friends of John McCarthy and the anti-live
animal export protest groups; or it can overthrow a bureaucracy, like
Solidarity in Poland. Such social interactions are based on collaboration rather than collusion: there is emphasis on open communication, active listening, a recognition of the learning opportunities.
There is the capacity for the individual to be self-motivated, self-
regulated and to value the self in order to facilitate action rather than
be steered from a distance by policy structures and agencies. This is
what Stacey (1993) calls "communities of practice" where:

> People performing closely similar tasks always form informal social
> groups in which they discuss what they are doing and the environ-
> ment they are doing it in. They gossip, repeat anecdotes, and tell war
> stories. They recount the difficulties they have experienced in carry-
> ing out particular tasks and others compare these with similar experi-
> ences they have had. What is going on when this happens is, however,
> far more important than pleasant social exchange. What is going on is
> in fact a vitally important form of learning. (pp. 348–9)

Therefore individuals are motivated by intrinsic rewards such as
a scene of achievement and feelings of self-worth rather than by
extrinsic rewards such as pay and promotion.

Organizations can utilize this energy and commitment in a creative way, enabling political activity to take place, rather than trying
to overlay it or eradicate it by formal structures. Political action in
the forming of coalitions around key issues and building power
blocs is the source of innovation and creativity. Micro-politics in
educational institutions has been documented (Ball, 1987), and more
recently Ganderton (1991) has identified the important role of the
"subversive" within the organization. The subversive is in contrast
to the "conformist" and "isolate" and is defined as someone who
through their attitude and viewpoints is seen to be "at variance with
the prevailing organizational view." (p. 32). However, as Ganderton
argues, both theory and management training identify the role of the
subversive as that of a saboteur and therefore:

> Management strategies have sought to marginalize/neutralize such
> people because they are assumed to be of only negative value. (p. 36)

However, Chaos Theory allows us to see the subversive or the maverick in a positive way as an enabler and emancipator. Hence the capacity for individual and group learning is great; Morrell (McCarthy
and Morrell, 1993) has shown the impact of the Friends of John
McCarthy at critical points in creating rather than visioning the future:

> The Friends' campaign achieved its objective, to make the hostages
> an issue in Britain; a political problem that would have to be resolved
> before the resumption of any meaningful relationship with Iran. (p. 495)

Spontaneous self-organizing groups cannot be controlled by managers, as membership is self-participating, self-empowering, self-
regulating and self-destructing (Stacey, 1993). Behavior is not
random but based on "self reference" (Jantsch, 1980, p. 26), i.e.,
disorder and turbulence generate information for change, but change
is within an environmental context. As Wheatley (1994) states,

> As it changes, it does so by referring to itself; whatever future form it
> takes will be consistent with its already established identity. . . .
> [Changes] always are consistent with what has gone on before, with
> the history and identity of the system. (p. 94)

Nowhere is this better illustrated than by contrasting self-organization with self-managing teams, as illustrated in Table 1. The main
message from the comparison outlined in the table is that managers
cannot install effective management systems but can intervene in the
energetic and creative human interactions already happening around
them. Therefore management training and development based on
strategies, tools, and rational cycles for proactively empowering
people is an expensive illusion. Leadership is a product of human
networks within a context rather than a product of role hierarchy and
contrived cultural norms. Furthermore, we cannot have a meaningful
debate about the quality of teaching and learning, and how to raise
levels of achievement for all children unless teachers take control
rather than wait to be given it. This is where the potential for real
school improvement is located. The growth of the expert manager in
education not only denies teacher professionalism by elevating
managerial knowledge and skills, but is also cutting off the professional from information analysis and interpretation. As Wheatley
(1994) has stated:

We often limit their potential because we circumscribe them with rules and chains of command or give them narrow mandates or restrict their access to information. But if we liberate them from those confines and allow them greater autonomy, constrained more by purpose than by rules or present expectations, then their potential for generating information is great. (p. 115)

---

### Table 1
### Comparing Self-Managing Teams
### and Self-Organization Networks

| Self-managing teams | Self-organization networks |
| --- | --- |
| A formally installed with clear terms of reference and a reporting imperative. Therefore legitimacy is organizationally defined. Can be temporary or permanent. | Informal temporary groups form spontaneously around issues. Legitimacy derived from the issue and can be in line with the formal organization or in conflict with it. |
| Are controlled through rules on how to operate by managers who have installed the team(s). Teams are proactively created often using team roles; e.g., Belbin to facilitate the process. | Cannot be controlled directly. Managers like anyone else can intervene to influence the boundaries. Group participants decide on who takes part and what the boundaries are. There are no predetermined roles and no leaders until they develop through social and political interaction. |
| Are intended to increase participation by flattening the traditional hierarchical structure. | Networks operate in conflict with and are constrained by the hierarchical structure. |
| Delegation of power to proactively created teams is supposed to lead to consensus. Norms are predetermined and ensure equilibrium: first, strategy and decision making are controlled by the vision and mission of the school/college; and second, the team process is controlled by INSET based on the linear model of forming, storming, norming, and performing. | Power is unequal and energizes the networks through conflict and also operates as a constraint. Control is through the political and social interactions, and norms emerge from this. This is destabilizing in that the networks are sometimes in line with the formal structure and sometimes in competition with it. |
| The hierarchy empowers the teams. | People empower themselves. |

Source: Derived from Stacey, 1993, p. 243.

The challenge for continuous professional development is in enabling teachers to understand the context in which they exercise their professional skills and knowledge. Perhaps it is time that teachers engaged in professing what is central to being a professional. Chaos Theory provides opportunities to explore how learning is about sharing and changing perceptions through group interaction which discovers, questions, makes critical choices and takes action. Effective organizations are more about resiliency than stability.

## REFERENCES

Ball, S. J. (1987) *The Micropolitics of the School.* London: Routledge.

Baron, G. and Taylor, W. (1969) *Educational Administration and the Social Sciences.* London: Athlone Press.

Bell, L. (1989) Ambiguity models and secondary schools: a case study. In Bush, T. (ed.) *Managing Education: Theory and Practice.* Buckingham: Open University Press.

Bone, T. R. (1982) Educational Administration. *British Journal of Educational Studies* 30(1), February, pp. 32–42.

Bowe, R. and Ball, S. with Gold, A. (1992) *Reforming Education and Changing Schools.* London: Routledge.

Bush, T. (1995) *Theories of Educational Management* (second edition). London: Paul Chapman Publishing.

Cohen, M. D. and March, J. G. (1969) Leadership and ambiguity. In Bush, T. *Managing Education: Theory and Practice.* Buckingham: Open University Press.

Curtis, R. K. (1990) Complexity and predictability: the application of chaos theory to economic forecasting. *Future Research Quarterly* Winter, 57–70.

Cziko, G. A. (1989) Unpredicability and indeterminism in human behavior: arguments and implications for educational research. *Educational Researcher* April, 17–25.

Dumaine, B. (1991) The bureaucracy busters. *Fortune,* June 17, 26–36.

Fayol, H. (1916) *Administration industrielle el generale.* Translated by Storrs, C. (1949) as *General and Industrial Management.* London: Pitman.

Ferchat, R. A. (1990) The chaos factor. *The Corporate Board* May/June, 8–12.

Ganderron, P. S. (1991) Subversion and the organization: Some theoretical considerations. *Educational Management and Administration* 19(1), 30–6.

Gaskell, J. (1992) *Gender Matters from School to Work.* Buckingham: Open University Press.

Glatter, R. (1972) *Management Development for the Education Profession.* London: Harrap.

Glatter, R. (1979) Education 'policy' and 'management': one field or two? In Bush T., Glatter, R., Goodey, J. and Riches, C. (eds) *Approaches to School Management.* London: Harper Educational Series.

Gleick, J. (1987) *Chaos.* London: Cardinal.

Gordon, L. and Pearce, D. (1993) Why compare? A response to Stephen Lawton. *Journal of Education Policy* 8(2), 175–81.

Griffiths, D. E., Weaver Hart, A. and Goode Blair, B. (1991) Still another approach to administration: chaos theory. *Educational Administration Quarterly* 27(3), 430–51.

Hargreaves, D. H. (1995) Self-managing schools and development planning—chaos or control? *School Organization* 15(3), 215–27.

Harries-Jenkins, C. (1984) Education Management: part 1. *School Organisation and Management Abstracts* 3(4), 213–33.

Hayles, N. K. (1990) *Chaos Bound: Orderly Disorder in Contemporary Literature and Science.* New York: Cornell University Press.

Hughes, M. G. (1978) *Education Administration: Pure or Applied?* Birmingham: University of Birmingham.

Inglis, F. (1985) *The Management of Ignorance.* Oxford: Basil Blackwell.

Jantsch, E. (1980) *The Self-organizing Universe.* Oxford: Pergamon.

Kogan, M. (1979) Different frameworks for education policy-making and analysis. *Educational Analysis* 1(2), 5–14.

Lawton, S. B. (1992) Why restructure?: an international survey of the roots of reform. *Journal of Education Policy* 7(2), 139–54.

Lehrer, R., Serin, R. C. and Amundson, R. (1990) Knowledge or certainty? A reply to Cziko. *Educational Researcher,* August-September, 16–19.

Lewin, R. (1992) *Complexity: Life at the Edge of Chaos.* New York: Macmillan.

McCarthy, J. and Morrell, J. (1993) *Some Other Rainbow.* London: Bantam.

Nilson, T. H. (1995) *Chaos Marketing.* Maidenhead: McGraw-Hill.

Nonaka, I. (1988) Creating organizational order out of chaos: self-renewal in Japanese firms. *California Management Review,* Spring, 57–73.

Packwood, T. (1977) The school as a hierarchy. *Educational Administrations* 5(2), 1–6. Reprinted in Westoby, A. (ed.). (1988) *Culture and Power in Educational Organizations.* Milton Keynes: Open University Press.

Percival, I. (1991) Chaos: A science for the real world. In Hall, N. (ed.). *The New Scientist Guide to Chaos.* Harmondsworth: Penguin.

Prigogine, I. and Stengers, I. (1984) *Order out of Chaos.* New York: Bantam.

Radzicki, M. J. (1990) Institutional dynamics, deterministic chaos, and self-organizing systems. *Journal of Economic Issues* 24(1), 57–102.

Russell, S. (1994) The "ah ha" factor. *Education,* October 21.

Saul, J. R. (1992) *Voltaire's Bastards.* New York: Free Press.

Sawada, D. and Caley, M. (1985) Dissipative structures: New metaphors for becoming in education. *Educational Researcher* 14(3), 13–19.

Semler, R. (1989) Managing without managers. *Harvard Business Review,* September-October, 76–84.

Snyder, K. J., Acker-Hocevar, M. and Wolf, K. M. (1995) Chaos Theory as a Lens for Advancing Quality Schooling. A paper presented to the Annual Conference of the British Educational Management and Administration Society, September 1995.

Stacey, R. D. (1991) *The Chaos Frontier.* Oxford: Butterworth-Heinemann.

———. (1992) *Managing Chaos.* London: Kogan Page.

———. (1993) *Strategic Management and Organisational Dynamics.* London: Plenum.

Sullivan, T. J. (1994) *System Metamorphosis: An Examination of Chaos Theory Applied to a System of School Organization Undergoing Policy Implementation.* Unpublished Doctoral Thesis, University of New England, Armidale, Australia.

Sungaila, H. (1990a) The new science of chaos: making a new science of leadership? *Journal of Educational Administration* 28(2), 4–23.

———. (1990b) Organizations alive: have we at last found the key to a science of educational administration? *Studies in Educational Administration,* No. 52, May, Commonwealth Council for Educational Administration.

Taylor, F. W. (1911) *Principles of Scientific Management.* New York: Harper.

Toffler, A. (1984) Science and change. Foreword to Prigogine, I. and Stengers, I. (1984). *Order out of Chaos.* New York: Bantam.

Turner, C. (1977) Organising educational institutions as anarchies. *Educational Administration* 5(2), 6–12. Reprinted in Westoby, A. (Ed.) (1988) *Culture and Power in Educational Organizations.* Milton Keynes: Open University Press.

Weick, K. E. (1976) Educational organizations as loosely coupled education. *Administrative Science Quarterly* 21, 1–19.

———. (1988) Educational organizations as loosely coupled systems. In Westoby, A. (ed.) (1988) *Culture and Power in Educational Organizations.* Milton Keynes: Open University Press.

Westoby, A. (ed.) (1988) *Culture and Power in Educational Organizations.* Milton Keynes: Open University Press.

Wheatley, M. J. (1994) *Leadership and the New Science.* San Francisco: Berrett-Koehler Publications.

Winter, R. (1991). Post-modern sociology as a democratic educational practice? Some suggestions. *British Journal of Sociology of Education* 12(4), 467–81.

# Leadership for Change

by Michael Fullan

> Wanted: A miracle worker who can do more with less, pacify rival groups, endure chronic second-guessing, tolerate low levels of support, process large volumes of paper and work double shifts (75 nights a year out). He or she will have carte blanche to innovate, but cannot spend much money, replace any personnel, or upset any constituency. (R. Evans, Education Week, April 12, 1995)

We have come a long way since the days of valuing leaders who "run a tight ship." We have gone through the phases of the principal "as administrator" and the principal "as instructional leader" to a broader and more fundamental notion of principal as change agent. In this article I take a critical approach to understanding the nature of the evolving role of school leadership, why it has changed, and what we need to know and to be able to do to make the leadership role more doable. While the focus is on "school" leadership (principal and teacher leadership), much of the analysis applies to "system" leadership involving superintendents and other central office staff.

The premise of the article is that we are obtaining a general appreciation of the new work of leaders, but that two problems remain: (1) the noise function in which misleading conceptions of leadership persist, and (2) to the extent that new conceptions are on the right track, they remain at a general level of understanding with little practical meaning about how to carry out the role at the operational level.

The article is organized in the following sections. First, the new context is analyzed to identify key underlying reasons why and how the role of school leadership has changed. Second, I discuss the broad conceptions of leadership with a view of sorting out less productive from more productive lines of thinking. The intent is to

From *International Handbook of Educational Leadership and Administration,* 1996, pp. 701–722. © 1996 by Kluwer Academic Publishers. Reprinted with permission.

capture how "leadership for change" might be conceptualized. Although this is still at a general level, the mindset of effective leadership is clearly articulated. Third (and this is the essence of the article), I present a number of "middle level" examples of how key problems of change would be specifically handled. This section on how "leadership for change in action" focuses on what leaders would actually do in real situations of complex change. This, I believe is missing from much of the literature and is obviously crucial for informing both understanding and action.

## THE NEW CONTEXT

I will not address here the broad issues of the age of paradox and chaos in postmodern society (although these issues do get introduced in the following two sections). Rather, we are interested in the more specific manifestations of these trends as they directly change the very context within which leadership must work. Eight trends in particular affect school leadership directly (see Fullan and Hargreaves, 1996; Hargreaves and Fullan, 1996).

> **School boundaries are becoming more transparent.**

First, there is a world-wide trend toward *self-managing* schools. This was meant a sea-change in the role of the school leader transforming responsibility towards whole school development, school development planning and the like. Developing collaborative work cultures with a focus on teaching and learning for all students has become a major mandate for school principals. The term self-managing, however, is misleading because the other trends, paradoxically mean that with greater autonomy comes greater permeability of boundaries and more visible accountability and involvement with other constituencies.

Second, part and parcel of the new devolution of authority— from Chicago to New Zealand and points in between—is new forms of *school-community governance*. Most directly this takes the form of legislated "local school councils" with new responsibilities and powers. The formal governance component as we shall see later, is only the most obvious structural aspect of a much more comprehensive realignment of parental/community-school relationships. In effect, school boundaries are becoming more transparent, and the work of the school not only much more visible but ultimately more intertwined with the family and the community (Epstein, 1995). School leadership, in turn, is radically affected. We are no longer talking about attempting to have cordial relationships with parents but rather developing more comprehensive learning systems in new public arenas, requiring new conceptions and skills that school leaders have hitherto never experienced.

Third, there is a trend to *reduce dependence on outside bureaucracy and regulation.* Because of the ambivalence of the state to "let go," this trend is difficult to interpret. It is the case, driven partly by the need to reduce expenditures and partly by the new conceptions described here, that there is a widespread reduction in the number of bureaucrats at both the regional and state levels. In these jurisdictions that have district school boards, it is not clear that this level of bureaucracy will survive as some of the powers devolve to local school councils while other powers are usurped upward to the state.

**Massive expansion of information technology brings with it greater global access to ideas and people.**

Fourth, while middle level bureaucracies are becoming simplified or eliminated, *the state is taking on new centralist roles.* Depending on the degree of centralizing tendencies this takes the form of developing state-wide curriculum frameworks, standards of practice, and accountability of performance and outcomes. School leaders, of course, must constantly negotiate this simultaneous centralization-decentralization terrain.

Fifth, there is more talk and action about *reinventing teacher professionalism* with increased standards of practice that in effect widen and deepen the role of the teacher, transcending the classroom door to new forms of collaboration and partnership within and outside the school. This reduction in the isolation of teachers is accompanied by new opportunities and expectations for teacher leadership. School leadership, then, becomes more complex. Every teacher is expected to exercise such leadership, and particular new teacher leadership roles become established. The principal finds himself or herself participating in the change of the teaching profession itself where the role of the traditional school leader is disappearing.

Sixth, massive expansion of *information technology* brings with it greater global access to ideas and people, and untold opportunities and headaches about how to manage the information explosion in relation to its positive potential and harmful downside.

Seventh, a focus on the *new learning outcomes* continues apace, defined less in terms of traditional content and more in terms of teaching for understanding and performance in a changing world. School leaders become embroiled in debates that are no less funda- mental than revisiting the question of the purpose of schools in a social and work world very different from the past.

Eighth, *multi-racial, gender and sexual politics* bring new styles of leadership and more visibility to issues of equity. The socio-political complexity of the role of the school leader comes with the new territory.

In short, to begin to understand "leadership for change," one must first understand basic changes in the social context.

## BROAD CONCEPTIONS OF LEADERSHIP

I wish the reader for the time being to accept the following premise: neither the passive facilitator leader who tries to be responsive to others, or the forceful charismatic leader is effective under the con- textual conditions just outlined. The former leader fails to stand for anything and the latter dominates the agenda.

Since vision-driven leadership tends to be a major component of leadership theory over the last decade, it is necessary to clarify the limitations of this view. Beckhard and Pritchard (1992) provide a succinct version of this conception. There are four key aspects, they say: creating and setting the vision; communicating the vision; building commitment to the vision; and alignment to the vision (p. 25). Similarly, Bennis and Nanus (1985) advocate four leader- ship strategies: I. Attention through Vision; II. Meaning through Communications; III. Trust through Positioning; IV. The Deploy- ment of Self through Positive Self-Regard.

Senge (1990), I believe, provides the definitive critique of the above image of leader as savior:

> Our traditional views of leaders—as special people who set the direc- tion, make key decisions, and energize the troops—are deeply rooted in an individualistic and nonsystemic world view. Especially in the West, leaders are *heroes*—great mean (and occasionally women) who "rise to the fore" in times of crises. Our prevailing leadership myths

are still captured by the captain of the cavalry leading the charge to rescue the settlers from the attacking Indians. So long as much myths prevail, they reinforce a focus on short-term events and charismatic heroes rather than on systemic forces and collective learning. At its heart, the traditional view of leadership is based on assumptions of people's powerlessness, their lack of personal vision and inability to master the forces of change, deficits which can be remedied only by a few great leaders. (p. 340)

Yet, we know that strong leadership is required to manage the barrage of problems and potential opportunities to make major reforms. In the remainder of this section I will develop a more balanced view of strong leadership which leads to the following two conclusions: (1) the conception of the leader of the future is becoming more articulated *at the broad level,* and (2) a corollary, it is very difficult to obtain from this literature what leaders would do at the operational level if they attempted to follow this conception in their own work.

A good place to start is Champy's (1995) recent excellent book on "re-engineering management." He claims, I think correctly, that there are four broad issues for managers of the future:

*Issues of purpose.* Insistently, persistently, relentlessly, the new manager must ask, "What for?" What is it that we're in business for? What is the process for? This product? This task? This team? This job? What are we doing here, anyway?

*Issues of culture.* If successful reengineering requires a change in a company's whole culture, as seems to be the case in many instances, how is it to be accomplished by the same management that did so well in the old culture? If it is true (and it is) that reengineering is unlikely to succeed where the corporate atmosphere is charged with fear (and its twin, mistrust), how do we generate another, better environment—one, say, of willingness and mutual confidence.

*Issues of process and performance.* How do we get the kind of processes we want? How do we get the performances we need from our people? How do we set the norms and standard, or measure results—for worker performance, management performance, and the performance of the whole enterprise? Reengineering usually demands radical objectives, leadership, and political skills to realize. But how do we know whether we have the stuff? What does it take to be a good manager today?

> *Issues of people.* Who do we want to work with? How can we find
> them both inside and outside the company? How do we get them to
> want to work with us? How do we know whether they're the kind of
> people we want? (p. 7)

Champy advocates that we should "lead experimentally," and that
"linear thinking, general strategy thinking, familiar thinking, conventional thinking, produce only comforting illusions, bland rigidi-
ties, complacent passivity, all the slow working recipes for disaster"
(pp. 32–33). What follows in Champy's book are many illustrations,
ideas and insights (and we shall draw upon some of them later), but
at the end of the book, one would be hard pressed to answer the
question: "what do I do now, where do I start?"

Senge (1990) also put us on the right track in his description of
the new work of the leader: as designer, as steward, as teacher. As
designers:

> The leaders who fare best are those who continually see themselves
> as designers and not crusaders. Many of the best intentioned efforts
> to foster new learning disciplines founder because those leading the
> charge forget the first rule of learning: people learn what they need to
> learn, not what someone else thinks they need to learn.
>     In essence, the *leader's task is designing the learning processes*
> whereby people throughout the organization can deal productively
> with the critical issues they face, and develop their mastery in the
> learning disciplines. This is new work for most experienced manag-
> ers, many of whom rose to the top because of their decision-making
> and problem-solving skills, not their skills in mentoring, coaching,
> and helping others learn. (p. 345, italics in original)

As stewards, leaders continually seek and oversee the broader purpose and direction of the organization:

> In a learning organization, leaders may start by pursuing their own
> vision, but as they learn to listen carefully to others' visions they
> begin to see that their own personal vision is part of something larger.
> This does not diminish any leader's sense of responsibility for the
> vision—if anything it deepens it. (p. 352)

Leader as teacher is not about teaching other people one's own vision:

> Leaders in learning organization have the ability to conceptualize their
> strategic insights so that they become public knowledge, open to chal-
> lenge and further improvement. . . . [Leader as teacher] is about fos-
> tering learning for everyone. Such leaders help people throughout the

organization develop systemic understandings. Accepting this responsibility is the antidote to one of the most common downfalls of otherwise gifted learners—losing their commitment to the truth. (p. 356)

As we move directly to the role of the principal we see similar conceptions of the leadership role. Deal and Peterson (1994) argue that principals must possess both technical and symbolic traits (logic and artistry):

Technical problems require the analytical, rational problem-solving capabilities of a well-organized manager. Symbolic dilemmas require the sensitive, expressive touch of an artistic and passionate leader. (p. 113)

Eight technical roles are identified: planner, resource allocator, coordinator, supervisor, disseminator, jurist, gatekeeper, analyst; as well as eight symbolic roles: historian, anthropological detective, visionary, symbol, potter, poet, actor, leader.

Goldring and Rallis (1993) recommend that principals must in combination be:

- The Facilitator: Enabling Internal Leadership
- The Balancer: Communicating Within the System Hierarchy
- The Flag Bearer and Bridger: Managing the Environment
- The Inquirer: Assessing Effectiveness and Developing School-Based Accountability

Similarly, Peterson (1993) states five values needed for leadership in tomorrow's school as compared to the present:

### Value 1: Openness to Participation

*Today's Value:* Our organization values employees listening to the organization's leaders and doing what the leaders tell them to do.

*Tomorrow's Value:* Our organization values employees actively participating in any discussion or decision affecting them. (p. 5)

### Value 2: Openness to Diversity

*Today's Value:* Our organization values employees falling in line with the overall organizational direction.

*Tomorrow's Value:* Our organization values diversity in perspectives leading to a deeper understanding of organizational reality and an enriched knowledge base for decision making. (p. 7)

**Value 3: Openness to Conflict**

*Today's Value:*          Our organization values employees communi-
                          cating a climate of group harmony and happiness.

*Tomorrow's Value:*   Our organization values employees resolving
                          conflict in a healthy way that leads to stronger
                          solutions for complex issues. (p. 8)

**Value 4: Openness to Reflection**

*Today's Value:*          Our organization values employees conveying
                          a climate of decisiveness. Firm decisions are
                          made and implemented without looking back.

*Tomorrow's Value:*   Our organization values employees reflecting
                          on their own and others' thinking in order to
                          achieve better organizational decisions. (p. 10)

**Value 5: Openness to Mistakes**

*Today's Value:*          Our organization values employees concentrating
                          on making no mistakes and working as effi-
                          ciently as possible.

*Tomorrow's Value:*   Our organization values employees acknowledg-
                          ing mistakes and learning from them. (p. 12)

Patterson concludes with the now familiar refrain of the need to
"lead within paradox" (p. 80).

Finally, in my own *Change Forces* eight lessons are identified
derived from the conclusion that change processes these days are
inevitably non-linear and chaotic, and that effective leaders are those
who are able to foster and/or capitalize on periodic patterns that
occur over time. The eight lessons themselves are laced with dilemmas
that require leaders to work with opposing tendencies by bringing them
into dynamic tension:

Lesson One:      **You Can't Mandate What Matters**
                 (The more complex the change the less you can
                 force it)

Lesson Two:      **Change is a Journey not a Blueprint**
                 (Change is non-linear, loaded with uncertainty and
                 excitement and sometimes perverse)

Lesson Three:   **Problems are Our Friends**
                 (Problems are inevitable and you can't learn
                 without them)

Lesson Four:   **Vision and Strategic Planning Come Later**
(Premature visions and planning blind)

Lesson Five:   **Individualism and Collectivism Must Have Equal Power**
(There are no one-sided solutions to isolation and groupthink)

Lesson Six:   **Neither Centralization Nor Decentralization Works**
(Both top-down and bottom-up strategies are necessary)

Lesson Seven:   **Connection with the Wider Environment is Critical for Success**
(The best organizations learn externally as well as internally)

Lesson Eight:   **Every Person is a Change Agent**
(Change is too important to leave to the experts, personal mind set and mastery is the ultimate protection)

(Fullan, 1993: 21–22)

As inspiring as this literature on the new role of leaders is, and as many specific descriptions of leaders that the same literature contains, I maintain that, at the end of the day, it is very difficult for even the committed reader to know what to do. For the latter we need a more middle-level theory of leadership that not only beckons, but also provides insightful examples of how leaders would manage typical paradoxical situations that they increasingly face. In fact, in the absence of more grounded analysis, the literature is misleading at worse and unhelpful at best. In reviewing over 200 studies of the role of the principal as change agent, Christensen (1994) found the literature dominated by prescriptions and sometimes descriptions with a very weak research and analytical base. As we shall see in the next section, in her own carefully documented study of the role of the principal, Christensen's findings provided insights that go beyond and in some cases contradict the characterization of leadership for change found in the literature.

## LEADERSHIP FOR CHANGE IN ACTION

Leadership for change requires an internalized mindset that is constantly refined through thinking, and action, thinking, action, etc. This cumulative learning produces an orientation and ability to exercise greater executive control over the forces of change, and a capacity to generate the most effective actions and reactions in accomplishing change. The result is both more specific and to a certain extent different than what the general literature would have us believe about the role of the principal.

Mintzberg (1994) in his definitive critique of strategic planning says "companies plan when they *have* intended strategies, not in order to get them" (p. 111, his italics). In a related interview, he offers this wise advice:

> Never adopt a technique by its usual name. If you want to do reengineering, or whatever, call it something different so that you have to think it through for yourself and work it out on your own terms. If you just adopt it and implement it, it is bound to fail. (1995: 27)

Put differently, there are no shortcuts. Leaders for change must immerse themselves in real situations of reform and begin to craft their own theories of change constantly testing them against new situations and against grounded accounts of others' experiences. In this section, I will illustrate what this new mindset for change looks like in action by taking four typical dilemmas faced by principals:

1. The case of Advocacy and Resistance with respect to given innovations or reforms
2. The Case of Whole School Reform
3. The Case of School Councils
4. The Case of Contending with State Policy

### Advocacy and Resistance

Leaders are urged to foster experimentation, but what if staff appears uninterested in trying new things? Principals are expected to promote some of the latest innovations but what if staff are not committed to doing so? If we look deeply enough the new conceptions of leadership gives guidance about how to handle these kinds of situations. Gitlin and Margonis (1995) state it this way:

> We believe teachers' initial expressions of cynicism about reform should not automatically be viewed as obstructionist acts to

> overcome. Instead, time should be spent looking carefully at those resistant acts to see if they might embody a form of good sense—potential insights into the root causes of why the more things change the more they stay the same. (pp. 386–387)

Their case study of site-based reform shows how a well-intentioned administrator went about promoting the innovation, working with career ladder teachers, attempting to overcome resistance on the part of teachers. On the surface the principal did most things that the literature on transformational leadership would endorse. For Gitlin and Margonis there was a failure to get at two root causes: new authority relations where teachers would indeed have more power; and need for examining the structures and availability of time to manage the new demands.

Let's build the case, however, in a more simple manner. Assume that you are a principal who is strongly committed to the increased use of technology. You are sincerely convinced that it is in the best interest of students to become technologically proficient. To keep the example uncomplicated we must leave aside a number of contextual questions we would have to have answered. We can contrast then, the old and the new way of approaching the situation. By the old, I mean the superficial reading of the literature. By the new, I mean a deeper understanding of leadership for change.

Your old way of thinking would be like the following: I am sure that technology is one of the keys to the future for my students; parents support it; I know that some teachers favor it, but others are going to be Luddites; How can I get some teacher leaders to support it? What kind of external resources and expertise can I generate to provide support and pressure to move forward? Maybe I can secure a few transfers and new appointments. My whole approach is advocacy and co-optation into an agenda that I am sure is right.

With the new mindset, I am equally convinced that technology is critical, but I approach it differently. Cutting the story short, let's say that I am having a staff session in which I am about to show a video segment that portrays a highly successful technology-based school in action. Instead of showing it to make my case, I present it differently. I randomly ask one half of the staff to view the video with a "positive lens" noting what might be in it for us; I ask the other half of the staff to view it "negatively or critically" by identifying what might be problematic or potentially negative for us. If I am sincere, I have legitimized dissent. I have made it easy for staff to speak up about concerns (which would come out later anyway in more subtle and/or inaccessible ways). I listen carefully, suspending my own advocacy, because I know that some fundamental problems will be identified and that people's fears, real or imagined, will need to be examined carefully. This information may lead me to go back to the drawing board or to work with staff on some preconditions that would have to be addressed; or to proceed into action on a "start small, thing big" basis, or to abandon high-profile technology in favor of a different approach.

There is no right answer in this case, but consider the underlying theory. This is what is meant in the new literature by "disagreement is not bad."

> A culture that squashes disagreement is a culture doomed to stagnate, because change always begins with disagreement. Besides disagreement can never be squashed entirely. It gets repressed, to emerge later as a pervasive sense of injustice, followed by apathy, resentment, and even sabotage. (Champy, 1995: 82)

The new leader then does not assume that it should go her or his way, values diversity and early disagreement as fundamental to breakthroughs, listens (really listens) to pick up cues and new ways of thinking. Once this becomes internalized it generates myriads of more productive actions and reactions to situations of change. Without this internalization and more sophisticated understanding it is easy to get mislead by the literature.

### The Case of Whole School Reform

Christensen (1994) conducted a thorough review of the literature on the role of the principal before launching her own investigation into the role of the principal in transforming an "Accelerated School" (Levin, 1995). As noted earlier, she analyzed over 200 studies. She portrayed the difference in the literature between the role of the principal in the traditional school vs the restructured school. Our interest here is how the conception in the restructured school stacks up against Christensen's findings in her own study—findings carefully documented through the analysis of over 1000 "critical incidents" of behavior, cross-validated in open-ended questions she asked in the five accelerated schools she studied.

The top behaviors cited in the literature were different in priority compared to those found by Christensen. The literature places "communicates goals," "shares decision-making," "creates/articulates school vision" and "supports staff" (the one overlap) at the top of the list. Christensen found that "fostering the process," "supporting staff," "promoting learning" and "promoting parent involvement" were the major behavior categories with "promote the vision of the school" as an important, but more distant priority (it ranked 10th in frequency out of 13 categories) (Christensen, 1994: 113).

We must be careful not to misinterpret these findings. They do not say, for example that creating a vision is unimportant. But they do put it in perspective, showing that it is subordinate in some ways to a more sophisticated process. Second, although we do not have the specifics here, it is crucial that leaders understand the discrete behaviors that made up the categories. For example, "use the governance process correctly" was one of 18 subcategories of "fostering the process" and itself had a dozen types of critical incidents of behavior such as:

- don't make administrative mandates that affect the whole school without going through the process
- make sure decisions are not made in a hurry
- don't take over meetings; be a co-participant
- get input from all stakeholders
- encourage consensus rather than voting (ibid., p. 120)

Similarly in interviews, the top "things a principal must do to be a good accelerated school principal" according to principals and teachers were:

- be willing to let go of control
- be supportive of staff
- be present
- stand up to the district
- be a real expert on the accelerated school process
- be positive
- believe every child is a success
- be open-minded; listen to everybody's opinions
- be sensitive to staff morale (ibid., p. 132)

It is obviously not helpful to try and memorize the list of behaviors, but a pattern is emerging. Effective principals extend as well as express what they value. They nurture a subtle process of enabling teachers to work together to generate solutions. It is easy for principals with good ideas to let themselves get seduced into "taking over." Prestine's (1994) study of a "Coalition of Essential Schools" reform that got bogged down, but eventually regrouped illustrates this problem clearly.

When progress was faltering, the principal became more and more concerned:

> Taking charge of the meetings, the principal assigned a series of discrete tasks, built around authentic assessment ideas, to be completed by faculty groups. In essence, nothing happened. As the principal noted, 'I gave an assignment. I can't believe I tried this. No one read the book. No one understood what I was talking about. It was like I was talking Swahili. The whole thing sort of fell flat.' (Prestine, 1994: 134)

Reflecting on this the principal observed:

> I allowed the faculty to push responsibility for their learning onto me. Even worse, I went out and provided the venue in which it would happen. I did something I swore I would never do—take responsibility for a school's behavior, for the learning of individual teachers. I took direct managerial responsibilities. Worse yet, the model I set up was exactly the kind of instruction I had never done as a teacher—that is, I give you an assignment and you do exactly as I told you to do. It was terrible as I came to understand what I had been doing. (ibid., p. 135)

As one of the teacher coordinators observed:

> We suddenly realized what was wrong. We realized that we did not have ownership anymore. . . He [the principal] seemed to know everything there was to know about it, so it was necessary to push it onto him. Once we did that, it was doomed to failure. (ibid., p. 135)

The point here is not that these mistakes can be eliminated. Rather the message is that you need enough of a working theory of leadership for change combined with mechanisms for personal and collective reflection, so that you inevitably self-correct, thereby deepening the internalization of theory and your capacity to act effectively the next time, and the time after that, and so on.

These developments are part and parcel of a more fundamental change in the culture of schools and in the evolution of the teaching profession itself, which go beyond the terms of reference of this chapter. Schools are not now learning organizations and for them to become so they must engage in a radical process of "restructuring, retiming and reculturing the school" (Fullan, 1995). The end result of this process is not yet known but the implications for the role of leadership are compatible with the formulations in this article. Leaders in learning organizations for example know that *both* individualism and collaboration must co-exist. They know that isolation is bad, but that collaboration has downsides too—not the least of which are balkanization and groupthink (Fullan, 1993). They know that differences, diversity and conflict not only are inevitable, but that they often contain the seeds of breakthroughs. Homogenous cultures are more peaceful, but are also more stagnant than heterogeneous cultures.

> **Teachers are expected to be "moral change agents."**

In short, the socio-cultural context for teachers' own learning and ownership for reform will change (Gallimore, Goldenberg and Saunders, 1995). The changes in school culture are part of a more fundamental change in the nature of the teaching profession itself. The role of the teacher has widened and deepened over the past decade. Teachers are expected to be "moral change agents," making a difference in the lives of students while becoming experts in managing change. How far this change will go is as yet undetermined, but there is no doubt that radical changes in the teaching profession and preforce in the principalship are in store (Fullan and Hargreaves, 1996; Hargreaves and Fullan, 1996).

Whole school reform, in other words, changes the culture of the school and the nature of the teaching profession. Principals are front and center in this transition which goes far beyond conceptions of principals as leaders of site-based management.

### School Councils

The establishment of School Councils with parent and community participation in advisory or decision making roles is an international phenomenon of major proportions. What is the principal as change agent to make of these developments? The old way of responding would be to treat it as a necessary evil—something to be tolerated, blunted—or to go about dutifully trying to make the Council work. Both of these responses are narrow and limiting as a broader conception and considerable evidence reveals.

The principal steeped in leadership for change would have a different approach. First, he or she would recognize the emergence of School Councils as part of a systemic shift in the relationship between the communities and schools that is both inevitable and that contains the seeds of a necessary realignmnet with the family and other social agencies. Put another way, the principal would not take School Councils literally, but would see them as the tip of a more complex and powerful iceberg. Systemic thinking says that boundaries need to be more permeable and operate in interaction and with mutual influence. An abstract way of putting it to be sure, but specifically meaningful in rethinking the relative roles of the family/community and the school.

Second, and to be much more specific, research and best practice are abundantly clear: Nothing motivates a child more than when learning is valued by schools and families/community working in partnership. Furthermore, you can do something to improve this relationship through deliberate action. For the same reason that site-based management (involving teachers) bears no relationship to changes in the culture and learning of the whole school, the presence of School Councils per se does not affect student learning. The establishment of a Council involving a handful of parents (not to mention matters of representation and skill) could not possibly improve the learning for the hundreds of students in the school (see Wylie, 1995) assessment of the New Zealand experience). What does make a difference is the multiple forms of particular involvement deliberately fostered, developed and supported. Summarizing over a decade of research and development of best practice, Epstein (1995) makes the case unequivocally. At least six types of involvement working in concert are needed to make a difference, namely, programs that promote greater:

1. Parenting Skills (improving home environments)
2. Communication (two-way school-to-home)
3. Volunteering or Parent Aides (recruit and organize parent help)
4. Learning at Home (specific home tutoring assistance)
5. Decision-making (involve parents and develop parent leaders)
6. Coordinating with Community Agencies (identify and interpret community services)

Note that involvement in decision-making is only one of six forms (and a skilled form at that). Moreover, these form of involvement do not happen by accident or even by invitation. They happen by explicit strategic intervention. In other words, both parents and educators need staff development in their new roles and new role relationships in order to become effective. This incidentally is one of the main reasons why programs like James Comer's School Development Program are successful, that is, they succeed in large part because they have a *parent development* component (Comer, 1992; see also the principal's parent involvement role in "Accelerated Schools," Christensen, 1994).

Third, in thinking and working through these developments, the principal's theory of change becomes much more powerful. It becomes clearer what Sarason (1995) and Ontario's Royal Commission on Learning (1994), meant when they said that school councils or parent involvement is not an end in itself. Shifts in power are involved, but it is not power in and of itself that counts, but what the new power arrangement can actually do:

> To seek power is to raise and begin to answer the question: to seek power to change *what?* Changing the forces of power in no way guarantees that anything else will change. . . To seek power without asking the "what" question is not only to beg the question but to avoid it and, therefore to collude in cosmetic changes. (Sarason, 1995: 53, his emphasis)

Both Sarason and Dolan (1994) make it clear that parents are a crucial and largely untapped resources. While there are destructive and hopeless parents, on the whole, parents have (or can be helped to have) assets and expertise that are essential to the partnership. Parents have knowledge of their child that is not available to anyone else, they have a vested interest in their child's success, they have the expertise of the customer who is paying for and experiencing a service, they have valuable knowledge and skills by virtue of their "special interests, hobbies, vocation, and community" role (see Sarason, 1995: ch. 4; Dolan, 1994: ch. 14).

Dolan draws this powerful conclusion:

> To educate children without a deep partnership of teacher parent is hopeless, and going in we have conditioned everyone to minimal interaction, indifference, maybe even suspicion. This is the Steady State in most of the country. And, it has to change. (p. 159)

Fourth (and once again we see the operational principles of leadership for change in action), ideas about diversity and conflict become a natural part of the creation of something new:

> In a school, where mistrust between the community and the administration is the major issue, you might begin to deal with it by making sure that parents were present at every major event, every meeting, every challenge. *Within the discomfort of that presence,* the learning and the healing could begin. (Dolan, 1994: 50, emphasis added)

Similarly, without knowledge for change, School Councils can easily become diversions where energy is diverted to compliance and power struggles not to capacity building. A School Council, as surprising as this may seem:

> ... is *not* primarily a decision making mechanism. This is not principalship by committee. A Site Council that focuses only on decision-making tends to make the intervention solely a power issue. It often exhausts itself on petty issues and control struggles and never gets to the main business which is *driving* the change. (Dolan, 1994: 131, his emphases)

Rather, the role of the Council is to help mobilize the forces and resources of change by developing the skills of parents, teachers, students and principals a leaders in "group problem-solving," "dealing with conflict," and "making content expertise accessible" (ibid., p. 134). This brings new, more complex meaning to the role of the principal in the middle.

### State Policy

Two related problems plague educational reform at the system level: overload and fragmentation. In a certain objective sense this is inevitable because post modern societies are non-linear, chaotic, dynamically complex (Fullan, 1993). Under these circumstances leadership for change is essentially a "coherence-making" proposition. Leithwood and his colleagues' case study of local implementation of state policy in British Columbia is instructive (Leithwood, 1995; Leithwood, Jantzi and Steinbach, 1995). They found that school leadership made the single largest contribution to school restructuring through supporting and helping develop teachers' commitments, capacities and opportunities to engage in reform—findings which are compatible with our discussion above about whole school development.

Viewed in the context of state policy, Leithwood et al.'s additional finding are noteworthy. While school people experienced state policy as lacking coherence, consistency and sustained commitment (an endemic feature of chaotic systems), some schools were able to overcome these limitations. Schools "with a coherent sense of direction essentially were able to make sense of even relatively large numbers of disparate initiatives undertaken within the school" (Leithwood et al., 1995: 34). In other words, schools with leadership that served to increase the capacity of teachers to engage in individual and collective learning were less troubled by lack of clarity in central policies and made more progress in implementing them.

This represents another example of principals operating effectively in ambiguous, complex environments by getting their own community in order and by being less dependent on the vagaries of system policies. Such principals and their staff become "critical consumers" of central policies. They see the occasion of state initiatives as representing legitimate if not well worked out concerns. They are willing to stop, think and examine the issues contained in new state policies and to "exploit" the potential resources that might be obtained.

**Educational change is neither top-down or bottom-up.**

I shall use a simple example from our files on "Vignettes of successful change" from the Ontario Teacher's Federation (1992) project "Creating a Culture of Change." In this case, a principal, faced with a newly-issued curriculum policy from that state was troubled by the prospect of carrying forward the policy to his staff. He, probably correctly, predicted that the staff would see it as yet another misguided imposition. Instead of introducing the policy, the principal, working with a facilitator, conducted a professional development session designed to identify which curriculum changes the teachers' themselves would like to see in the school. The principal and teachers then connected some of the identified themes with state policies, and began to work upwards in relation to the policies.

This is an oversimplified example because there are a great many additional contextual factors that one would have to take into account. But the example clearly illustrates that educational change is neither top-down or bottom-up. The role of leaders is to work with teachers and the local community to navigate the complex two-way relationship between the school and the state. These ideas are contained in the literature but it is only when you begin to marshall particular examples and learn from them that you can begin to build a meaningful approach to leadership for change.

## CONCLUSION

I have made the case that the literature on school leadership is misleading in some respects, and unhelpful in others. This is largely because many of the new theories of change purportedly formulated to address complex systems requiring leaders to "manage paradox," fail to provide particular examples and insights, which in turn can be linked to powerful concepts. Although much more work remains to be done to develop a meaningful action-based theory of leadership, we were able to obtain from the empirical literature a number of problem-based examples which contribute to as well as are informed by the emerging theory. They place the principal (at least in this transition period working toward a learning organization) in the role of what Dolan (1994: 94) calls a "deep coordinator" working in fundamentally interdependent ways within the school and community, and externally with the wider system.

The role of the school principal has become significantly more complex. Principals are experiencing greater stress and greater mental and physical health problems (Wylie, 1995). In the same way that some people handle stress better than others, principals who develop leadership for change capacities learn to control more of their own and their community's destiny in more healthy and productive ways.

Most of the literature and examples in this article were from North American sources, and this is a limitation. The issues, however, are consistent at least across most developed countries. Nor did I address gender differences, which by and large tend to confirm that the directions of new leadership are more congruent with women's socialization and leadership style (see Rothschild, 1990), although the main message is that all leaders need to develop the capacities that we have been discussing.

Differences across cultures are a different story still. There are bound to be major differences in the role of "school leadership for change" across Eastern and Western, and Northern and Southern cultures, but there is almost a complete absence of specific insights and examples at the level of analysis presented in this article—a gap that requires urgent attention in the literature.

Leadership for change in education is a field that has generated enormous interest over the years. It is a tribute to the complexities and dilemmas inherent in this topic to realize that much of the message remains elusive. By working in a self reflective way on real paradoxes of change we can build a more insightful set of theories and develop a richer array of skills and effective practices. There will be no shortage of opportunities to do so.

## REFERENCES

Beckhard, R. & Pritchard, W. (1992). *Changing the essence.* San Francisco, CA: Jossey-Bass.

Bennis, W. & Nanus, B. (1985). *Leaders.* New York, NY: Harper & Row.

Champy, J. (1995). *Reengineering management.* New York, NY: Harper Collins.

Christensen, G. (1994). *The role of the principal in transforming accelerated schools.* Unpublished doctoral dissertation, Stanford University.

Deal, T. & Peterson, K. (1992). *The leadership paradox.* San Francisco, CA: Jossey-Bass.

Dolan, P. (1994). *Restructuring our schools.* Kansas City, MO: Systems & Organizations.

Epstein, J. (1995). School/family/community partnerships. *Phi Delta Kappan,* Vol. 76, pp. 701–712.

Fullan, M. (1993). *Change forces.* London, U.K.: Falmer Press.

Fullan, M. (1995). Schools as learning organizations: Distant dreams. In M. Seltzer (Ed.). *Theory into practice.* Columbus, OH: Ohio State University.

Fullan, M. & Hargreaves, A. (1996). *What's worth fighting for in your school?* 2nd edition. New York, NY: Teachers College Press; Toronto, ON: Ontario Public School Teachers' Federation.

Gallimore, R., Goldenberg, C. & Saunders, W. (1995). The sociocultural context of teacher development. In M. McLaughlin (Ed.), *Research reports of the National Centre for the Study of Cultural Diversity and Second Language Learning.* Palo Alto, Stanford University.

Gitlin, A. & Margonis, F. (1995). The political aspect of reform: Teacher resistance as good sense. *American Journal of Education,* Vol. 103, pp. 377–405.

Goldring, E. & Rallis, S. (1993). *Principals of dynamic schools.* Newbury Park, CA: Corwin Press.

Hallinger, P. (1995). Culture and leadership: Developing an international perspective on educational administration. *UCEA Review,* Vol. 36, pp. 1, 4, 5, 10–12.

Hargreaves, A. & Fullan, M. (1996). *What's worth fighting for out there?* New York, NY: Teachers College Press; Toronto, ON: Ontario Public School Teachers' Federation.

Leithwood, K. (1995). *School restructuring in British Columbia: Summarizing the results of a four-year study.* Paper presented at the American Educational Research Association Annual Meeting, San Francisco, CA.

Leithwood, K., Jantzi, D. & Steinbeck, R. (1995). *An organizational learning perspective on school responses to central policy initiatives.* Paper presented at the American Educational Research Association Annual Meeting, San Francisco, CA.

Mintzberg, H. (1994). *The rise and fall of strategic planning.* New York, NY: Free Press.

―――. (1995). *Strategically speaking.* Seattle, WA: Acumen.

Ontario Teachers' Federation. (1992). *Creating a culture for change.* Toronto, ON: Ontario Teachers' Federation.

Ontario Royal Commission on Learning. *Love of learning.* Vol. I–V. Toronto, ON: Queen's Printer.

Paterson, J. (1993). *Leadership for tomorrow's schools.* Alexandria, VA: Association for Supervision and Curriculum Development.

Prestine, N. (1994). *Ninety degrees from everywhere: New understandings of the principal's role in restructuring essential school.*

Rothschild, J. (1990). *Feminist values and the democratic management of work organizations.* Paper presented at the 12th World Congress of Socioliogy, Madrid.

Sarason, S. (1995). *Parent involvement and the political principal.* San Francisco, CA: Jossey-Bass.

Senge, P. (1990). *The fifth discipline.* New York, NY: Doubleday.

Wylie, C. (1995). *School-site management: Some lessons from New Zealand.* Paper presented at the American Educational Research Association Annual Meeting, San Francisco, CA.

# Teacher's Professional Development in a Climate of Educational Reform

by Judith Warren Little

*This essay posits a problem of "fit" among five streams of reform and prevailing configurations of teachers' professional development. It argues that the dominant training-and-coaching model—focused on expanding an individual repertoire of well-defined classroom practice—is not adequate to the conceptions or requirements of teaching embedded in present reform initiatives. Subject matter collaboratives and other emerging alternatives are found to embody six principles that stand up to the complexity of reforms in subject matter teaching, equity, assessment, school organization, and the professionalization of the teaching. The principles form criteria for assessing professional development policies and practices.*

T his essay posits a problem of "fit" among five streams of reform and prevailing configurations of teachers' professional development. It argues that the dominant training model of teachers' professional development—a model focused primarily on expanding an individual repertoire of well-defined and skillful classroom practice—is not adequate to the ambitious visions of teaching and schooling embedded in present reform initiatives. Emerging alternatives to the training model, though small in scale, embody assumptions about teacher learning and the transformation of schooling that appear more fully compatible with the complex demands of reform and the equally complex contexts of teaching.

The essay begins by posing some of the ways in which current reform movements shape challenges, possibilities, and constraints for teachers' professional development. The second section frames a policy dilemma that revolves around the limitations of the dominant

From *Educational Evaluation and Policy Analysis,* 1993, Vol. 15, No. 3, pp. 129–151.
© 1993 by the American Educational Research Association. Reprinted with permission.

training paradigm for purposes of achieving the reform agenda. A third section introduces principles that seem especially congruent with reform requirements, together with examples of four options that appear to hold promise. The final section outlines selected issues that bear on the fit between reform imperatives and teachers' professional development and that inform the criteria for assessing professional development policy choices.

Two caveats preface the broader argument. First, the discussion concentrates exclusively, or nearly so, on teachers. For principled and pragmatic reasons, it places teachers at the center, even while acknowledging the ways in which entire institutions, and all the roles and relations they encompass, are implicated in any reform effort. Second, the essay reflects certain reservations about any stance that places teachers solely or largely in the role of implementors of reform. To be certain, reforms pose certain technical demands—demands on the knowledge, skill, judgment, and imagination of individuals. In that sense, the implementation problem at the level of the classroom is real. But reforms also convey certain values and world views. They communicate a vision of what it means to learn, and what it means to be educated; they communicate a vision of schools and teaching, of students and teachers. They are to greater or lesser degrees compatible with the organizational structures and cultures in which persons work. In these crucial ways, powerful reform ideas engage teachers in a broader consideration of the educational enterprise both in and beyond the classroom.

> **To be certain, reforms pose certain technical demands.**

Professional development in the service of implementation may obscure questions related to purpose and may mask the internal contradictions and tensions within and across reform initiatives. To make sensible critiques of proposed reforms requires getting at their underlying assumptions, their social and historical context, the degree to which they are congruent or not with teachers' existing beliefs, commitments, and practices, their probable consequences for students, and the ways in which they vary or converge across communities. By this argument, one test of teachers' professional development is its capacity to equip teachers individually and collectively to act as shapers, promoters, and well-informed critics of reforms. The most robust professional development options will locate problems of implementation within this larger set of possibilities.

## PROFESSIONAL DEVELOPMENT AND THE REFORM AGENDAS

Five streams of reform, both singly and in combination, present complex challenges to teachers as individuals and as members of a wider professional community. Those challenges are illustrated, though not exhausted, in the descriptions that follow. The test of different professional development strategies resides in their capacity to engage teachers in the kinds of study, investigation, and experimentation required to understand and undertake the multiple challenges described here, and to grasp the relationships among them.

**Individual teachers may be pressed to move on many fronts at once.**

### Reforms in Subject Matter Teaching (Standards, Curriculum, and Pedagogy)

Reforms in subject matter standards, curriculum content, and pedagogy increasingly aspire toward more ambitious student outcomes. Among them one would count the shift to a whole language and literature-based approach to language arts, the new mathematics standards, proposals for integrated science curricula, and the like. Among them, too, one would place conceptions of authentic achievement that require a fundamental change in the nature of students' intellectual tasks and teacher-student relations (Newmann, 1990). These reforms constitute a departure from canonical views of curriculum and from textbook-centered or recitation-style teaching. They demand a greater facility among teachers for integrating subject content and for organizing students' opportunities to learn. They represent, on the whole, a substantial departure from teachers' prior experience, established beliefs, and present practice. Indeed, they hold out an image of conditions of learning for children that their teachers have themselves rarely experienced.

In addition, individual teachers may be pressed to move on many fronts at once (see Hargreaves, 1990, 1992; Little, 1992a). Elementary teachers must absorb the changes in content and method associated with an entire spectrum of the elementary curriculum. The rotating curriculum adoption schedules for the California state frameworks, for example, could keep elementary teachers permanently in an implementation-of-innovation mode—an exhausting prospect. Secondary teachers are asked to consider possibilities for interdisciplinary curricula at precisely the time they are asked to reconsider their approaches to subject matter teaching—the latter reinforced by new state curriculum frameworks, standardized test protocols, subject-specific university admission requirements, textbook design, and the like. Meanwhile, reforms aimed at critical thinking sit in tension with the basic skills reforms that began in the 1960s and that are still a prominent part of the urban school improvement landscape (Carlson, 1992).

### Reforms Centered on Problems of Equity Among a Diverse Student Population

Equity reforms respond to the persistent achievement disparities among students from differing family backgrounds and are aimed at altering both the demonstrated achievement and school completion rates of the lowest achieving groups. Over the past decades, such reforms have centered largely on remedying individual student deficiencies. Although more recent analyses have pointed with increasing specificity and persuasiveness toward institutional structures and norms that define and contribute to student failure (e.g., Fine, 1991; Oakes, 1985, 1992), programmatic remedies continue to focus on students' individual skills (and deficits).

**Advances in professional development have centered on problems of diversity and equity in individual classrooms.**

There are a few exceptions in which reforms in school organization specifically target the structures of students' opportunity to learn; these range from the charter schools experiment in Philadelphia high schools (Fine, 1992) to a single teacher's efforts to "untrack" an Advanced Placement English class (Cone, 1992). By comparison with individualistic remedies (to what is arguably a systemic and structural problem), these efforts are few in number; most school restructuring proposals are founded on other assumptions and strategies.

Advances in professional development, too, have centered on problems of diversity and equity in individual classrooms—assisting teachers to identify and alter classroom practices that contribute to student failure and that undermine equal opportunity to learn. The most promising of these efforts engage teachers collectively in studying classroom practices in ways that sometimes lead to more systematic changes at the school level (Cochran-Smith & Lytle, 1992; Cone, 1992). They do so by building a norm conducive to the close scrutiny of well-established practices and by building a capacity for organizational change.

## Reforms in the Nature, Extent, and Uses of Student Assessment

Reform proposals argue for more widespread and rigorous use of authentic assessment. Yet the technical advances in assessment have typically lagged behind the formulation of standards and the advances in curriculum design. State and local policymakers continue to judge the success of reform efforts on the basis of standardized test scores. Components of statewide tests that strike teachers as most authentic (e.g., writing samples or open-ended math reasoning items) are also those most difficult and expensive to develop and to score. In areas other than language arts and math, they may also be relatively underdeveloped, especially where they call for synthesis across subject areas, as in the exhibitions favored by the Coalition of Essential Schools. At the local level, teachers' expressed interest in and commitment to alternative forms of assessment far exceeds their professed skill and confidence in constructing, evaluating, or incorporating such alternatives—and also exceeds the resources currently available from the research and test development communities. Yet local discussions do not and cannot wait upon the psychometricians' advances. In schools embarked upon "reinventing," "redesigning," and "restructuring" themselves, teachers wrestle with the criteria for good work and the forms in which it might be expressed.

## Reforms in the Social Organization of Schooling

The recurrent strains of criticism throughout the 1980s culminate in the widespread agreement that business as usual will not suffice. The convergence of interest (and funds) around the broad image of school restructuring has been quite astounding. The call to more systemic reform permeates initiatives in school restructuring supported by states, private foundations, and, to a lesser extent, teachers' associations in concert with local schools and districts.

The most ambitious of these initiatives have in common an orientation toward principles, not programs or specific practices. The Coalition of Essential Schools, for example, is united by a commitment to nine principles for the redesign of secondary schools (Sizer, 1992). Predictably, teachers' commitment to these principles are provisional and uneven; in that regard, we have what might appear to be a conventional implementation-of-innovation situation. But the dilemma for school leadership and for professional development goes far deeper in this instance: There is no well-developed picture of what these principles look like in practice. In the scramble to define a model, isolated cases of success become the focus of lore— Central Park East springs to mind, but few others (Meier, 1992). And no matter how persuasive the precedent set by any success story, broad principles require close attention to each local context. To fit opportunities for professional development to a campaign for the principled redesign of schooling is arguably a different matter from organizing the training and support to implement a program or a set of readily transferable practices. Yet we lack descriptions of restructuring initiatives that supply a detailed portrait of the learning demands on teachers and the corresponding professional development responses.[1]

### Reforms in the Professionalization of Teaching

The professionalization reforms at the national and state levels center on teachers' demonstrated knowledge base (as reflected in standards for teacher education program accreditation and candidate assessment), on conditions surrounding teacher certification and licensure, and on the structure of career opportunities in teaching. At the local level, professionalization tends to take the form of extended assistance to new teachers, expanded career opportunities for experienced teachers, and experiments in site-based decision making. For purposes of this article, these reforms are interesting principally for the way in which they bear upon the four reform movements discussed above—that is for the way in which they equip teachers both individually and collectively to play an informed and active role in defining the enterprise of education and the work of teaching.

This is not the place to repeat all the major arguments surrounding the professional standing of the teaching occupation, although the reforms have spawned a large and growing literature. Two comments seem germane. First, state and local policymakers seem most readily disposed to support appeals to professionalization where they see it as: (a) sustaining a reasonably well-prepared and stable teacher work force and (b) coupled with assurances of local accountability for student outcomes. Second, initiatives that promise professionalization of teaching increasingly expand opportunity and reward in exchange for increased obligation. Teachers are expected to contribute to the support of beginning teachers and to participate in other ways in the improvement of schooling and teaching.

These five streams of reform cannot be done well piecemeal, nor are they reforms that succeed if attempted only in isolated classrooms. As Fine (1992) puts it, the present ventures pursue the "big systemic, educational question" of transforming whole systems into "educationally and emotionally rich communities of learners" (p. 2). This suggests quite a different organization of learning opportunity (and obligation) than one that supplies teachers with measured increments in knowledge, skill, and judgment from a known pool of effective classroom practices.

## THE POLICY DILEMMA

Three assertions help to share the policy problem. They are derived in part from studies that reveal the dominant configurations of professional development opportunity (Little, 1989, 1992b) and in part from emerging research and other commentary on the demands that multiple reform initiatives present to teachers (Fine, 1992, 1994; Little, 1992a; Meier, 1992).

1. The well-tested models of skill development, built on the staff development and implementation-of-innovations literatures, will work reasonably well to introduce those aspects of reforms that are technical or that can be rendered as a repertoire of classroom practices. Among the possibilities generated by the five streams of reform, for example, are training programs in which outside experts or experienced colleagues introduce teachers to various models of cooperative learning, to the uses of manipulatives in mathematics instruction, or to methods for organizing portfolio assessment of students' work. On the basis of research into the conditions of teachers' skill transfer, the practices associated with skill training have demonstrated increasingly greater sophistication (e.g., Joyce, Murphy, Showers, & Murphy, 1989; Sparks & Loucks-Horsley, 1990). Effective training has come to be defined largely by its ability to provide adequate opportunities for practice and to provide for classroom consultation and coaching as teachers learn to use new ideas. All in all, then, we might make some substantial gains in some arenas if we more uniformly and consistently made use of what we have learned about the organization of training and classroom follow-up.

2. However, much of what we anticipate in the present reforms does not lend itself to skill training because it is not readily expressed in terms of specific, transferable skills and practices. Rather, the present reforms require that persons in local situations grapple with what broad principles look like in practice. In Deborah Meier's terms, we are called upon to reinvent teaching and schooling, and to do so even while in the midst of day-to-day work (Meier, 1992). This aspect of reform calls not for training, but for adequate opportunity to learn (and investigate, experiment, consult, or evaluate) embedded in the routine organization of teachers' work-day and work year. It requires the kinds of structures and cultures, both organizational and occupational, compatible with the image of "teacher as intellectual" (Giroux, 1988) rather than teacher as technician. And finally, it requires that teaches and others with whom they work enjoy the latitude to invent local solutions—to discover and develop practices that embody central values and principles, rather than to implement, adopt, or demonstrate practices thought to be universally effective. This assertion acknowledges both the uncertainty surrounding best practice and the complexity of local contexts.

3. Local patterns of resource allocation tend to favor the training model over alternative models. In the absence of a good fit between the nature of the reform task and the nature of professional development, schools and districts are nonetheless inclined to do *something* in the name of professional development (before the fiscal year ends, the state program expires, or the school board demands results). That something is likely to look very much like the existing menu of training options: workshop series, special courses, or in-service days devoted to transmitting some specific set of ideas, practices, or materials to teachers. For example, a decision to expand the available training in cooperative learning is readily defensible: The training is accessible as a well-tested program, and it has a plausible connection with efforts to improve classroom teaching. But such a decision is also problematic on two grounds. First, the investment in packaged programs of training tends to consume all or most of the available resources. The messier and more contentious forms of teachers' involvement required to examine existing practice and to invent new possibilities remain undersupported. Second, the training paradigm tends toward standardized solutions to the problem of best practice. The more ambiguous aspects of reform—what authentic assessment or integrated curricula might amount to, for example—are granted comparatively less attention.

So, we know how to do training well, and could profitably do more of it well; the training paradigm, no matter how well executed, will not enable us to realize the reform agendas; and resource allocations for professional development represent a relatively poor fit with the intellectual, organizational, and social requirements of the most ambitious reforms.

## PROFESSIONAL DEVELOPMENT PRINCIPLES AND PRACTICES

As a basis for achieving a more compelling fit, we might seek strategies or mechanisms that embody principles consonant with the complexity of the reform task. This is not to say that these practices and principles will provide the smoothest path to the implementation of reform proposals or initiatives as they are presently charted; to take these principles seriously, for example, could prolong the implementation of state level curriculum frameworks.

> **The most promising forms of professional development engage teachers in the pursuit of genuine questions, problems, and curiosities.**

### Alternatives to the Training Model

Four alternatives to the training model rest on a common implicit claim: that the most promising forms of professional development engage teachers in the pursuit of genuine questions, problems, and curiosities, over time, in ways that leave a mark on perspectives, policy, and practice. They communicate a view of teachers not only as classroom experts, but also as productive and responsible members of a broader professional community and as persons embarked on a career that may span 30 years or more.

### *Teacher Collaboratives and Other Networks*

Subject-specific teacher collaboratives in mathematics, science, and the humanities have grown in size, visibility, and influence over the past decade. Lord (1991) locates the subject collaboratives within an alternative paradigm of professional development in which the vision of teachers' professional development encompasses "(a) teachers' knowledge of academic content, instruction, and student learning, (b) teachers' access to a broader network of professional relationships, and (c) teacher leadership in the reform of systemwide structures" (p. 3; see also Lieberman & McLaughlin, 1992).

Two accounts suggest how subject collaboratives equip teachers individually and collectively to deepen their subject knowledge and to assume a more assertive role in the reform of curriculum, pedagogy, and assessment. The first is an account of Philadelphia's humanities collaborative (PATHS); the second centers on the mathematics collaborative PLUS, one of several subject matter collaboratives organized under the sponsorship of the Los Angeles Educational Partnership.

PATHS (Philadelphia Alliance for Teaching Humanities in the Schools) engages teachers directly in the modes of inquiry related to the various humanities disciplines. The project's aim to provide urban *students* a genuine curriculum in the humanities—not one that is watered down, dumbed down, or packaged—required a parallel experience for *teachers*. The former project director traces this decision about teachers' professional development in part to the general absence of humanities background in teachers' pre-service preparation or subsequent studies:

> Most teachers hold degrees in education, psychology, and related technical fields; few have been trained as historians, scientists, philosophers. Even those who do hold liberal arts and science undergraduate degrees rarely continued their pursuit of these subjects as graduate students. Advancement in teaching depends on certifications and supervisory credentials, not on learning more about arts and science subjects. (Hodgson, 1986, p. 29)

The specific program formats employed by PATHS all place teachers in direct contact with the city's rich humanities collections and with the curators and other experts who acquire, maintain, and interpret them. Mini-grants were organized to give greater incentives to collaborative work and to engage teachers with a broader array of material and human resources. "We stacked the deck quite unashamedly"—teachers could receive up to $300 for an individual classroom project, but up to $3,000 for collaborative work with other teachers, university people, museums, or libraries (p. 31). One example of a minigrant product is a slide show and teachers' guide on the Ars Medica exhibit for art, science, and social studies teachers: "All areas that can benefit from the show on the artistic images of disease and the medical arts through the centuries" (p. 31). An

outgrowth of the minigrant program is the two-week summer institute "Good Books for Great Kids," designed to

> enlarge teachers' visions about literature to a much broader range
> of genres and subjects, and to teach them how to do a search of the
> literature in a variety of fields that would take them beyond whatever
> the salesmen from textbook publishers left on their desks. (Renyi,
> 1992)

Using the children's literature collections in the Rare Book Room of
the Philadelphia Free Library and in similar collections, the teachers
"did research in these collections and were trained to seek out books
in their subject areas by children's librarians, children's literature
specialists and special collections experts." At the end of two weeks,
each teacher presented an oral defense of an annotated book list
comprising trade books, library books, and special collections
books; after the defense, the teacher received $500 to spend on trade
books in the list and on trips to bring children to the special collections.

Colloquia sponsored by PATHS meet monthly throughout the
year. In one, teachers working in Philadelphia's Rosenbach Museum
and Library concentrated on manuscripts detailing how 20th century
writers revised their work. This arrangement with the Rosenbach
permits up to 25 teachers per month to study some aspect of the
manuscript collection. The colloquia are oversubscribed, although
they offer neither credit nor stipends. Summer institutes in literature,
history, and languages (which do offer graduate credit) also are conducted on-site where relevant collections are held. These institutes,
like the colloquia, entail an altered set of relations between the
schools and other institutions (museums, libraries) and between
teachers and other experts. Through activities organized by PATHS,
teachers were able to see how curators conducted their own work
with primary materials, and to work with those materials themselves. They got behind the scenes in museums, libraries, and other
archival collections. They came to know not only the materials, but
the people who worked with (and interpreted) them. They were able
to examine (and sometimes contest) one another's interpretations.

Hodgson remarks: "[Teachers] have been starved (a metaphor
teachers themselves use) for serious stimuli, and they are immensely
enthusiastic patrons of museum and library collections" (p. 32).
When her account is read in juxtaposition with rather common
accounts of "unmotivated," "reluctant," or "resistant" teachers, one

is struck by marvelously contradictory images of teachers as intellectual beings. In PATHS, we have an oversubscribed colloquium series and avid participants in archival research, while in much of the professional development literature we find a portrait of teacher as troglodyte. Surely there is a lesson here.

In a second example, the Urban Mathematics Collaboratives in more than 15 major cities engage teachers with mathematicians in industry and higher education, with the combined aims of strengthening the caliber of math teaching and deepening teachers' commitment to all students (equity). The Urban Math Collaboratives have positioned themselves in support of the NCTM standards, though not without substantial discussion and debate, and have issued policy statements regarding equity, student assessment, and teacher professionalism (e.g., Urban Mathematics Collaboratives, n.d.)

In Los Angeles, the mathematics collaborative (PLUS) retains structural independence from the participating districts but secures a foothold in the school workplace by inviting departments rather than individual teachers to join. Observers highlight six aspects of the collaborative's strength: (a) a capacity for teacher support in subject matter teaching that exceeds that of the district or university, (b) a norm of informed and steady experimentation in mathematics teaching, (c) a system of mutual aid that compensates for uneven subject matter preparation among the district's secondary math teaches, (d) sustained involvement with a professional community of mathematicians and mathematics educators, (e) a connection to the classroom that is sustained by teachers' control over the content and format of the collaborative's activity, and (f) a broadened conception of professional knowledge and involvement that engages teachers in discussion and debate over the nature of mathematics and mathematics teaching, and also engages them in policy deliberations surrounding math teaching at the local, state, and national levels (Little & McLaughlin, 1991).

Both of these collaboratives, together with various models based on the Bay Area Writing Project, underscore teachers' involvement in the *construction* and not mere consumption of subject matter teaching knowledge.[2] They constitute a challenge to intellectual and collegial passivity. Further, they prepare teachers to make informed responses to reforms in subject matter teaching and student assessment without being linked narrowly to specific reform proposals.

*Subject Matter Associations*

The place of teachers' professional associations remains nearly invisible in the mainstream professional development literature. We know little about the role played by the largest and most prominent subject matter associations (NCTE, NCTM, NSTA, and others) in the professional lives of teachers or in shaping teachers' disposition toward particular reforms. Although it is clear that the subject associations are exerting an increasingly powerful influence in the articulation of subject curriculum and assessment standards, we have virtually no record of the specific nature or extent of discussion and debate over subject matter reform. In what ways is the ordinary classroom teacher touched by an association's involvement in state and national debate over standards? If we were to examine the agendas for state, regional, and national conferences held by these associations, what traces of reform would we encounter? How do elementary and secondary teachers experience the demands associated with subject-specific reforms? In what ways are the various subject matter reforms congruent or in conflict? (The Alliance for Curriculum Reform, sponsored by the Rockefeller Foundation, has begun to work with the major subject matter associations to trace the commonalities and differences in the reforms targeted at subject paradigms, subject-related pedagogies, curriculum policy, and assessment.)

Smaller, more informal regional associations have attracted even less policy research attention, yet may prove crucial in shaping teachers' responses to specific reform initiatives. The Curriculum Study Commission (CSC), a long-standing group of English educators spanning elementary, secondary, and higher education, provides forum for pursuing a wide range of teaching interests linked to the subject discipline. Although the CSC gives serious attention to any reform with crucial implications for teachers' work, it reserves its support for those reforms shaped fundamentally by teachers—as some of the new frameworks, standards, and assessments have been (Wagner, 1991; see also Ellwood, 1992).

In each of these examples—the NCTM and the CSC—we find an instance of teachers' professional community that extends well beyond the school walls, fundamentally independent of the employing organization, but positioned to exert considerable influence on teachers' dispositions toward reform proposals. To the extent that an association's most active members also occupy leadership roles within their schools, districts, or collective bargaining units, the association's effect is multiplied.

*Collaborations Targeted at School Reform*
Professional development is one integral feature of some collaborations targeted to school reform. School-university collaborations exhibit something of a rocky history. As instruments of reform, and as sites for professional development, they have had difficulty overcoming long-standing asymmetries in status, power, and resources. As partnerships have evolved, they have moved toward greater parity in obligations, opportunities, and rewards. The Coalition of Essential Schools offers the image of the school "friend," the insider/outsider (generally affiliated with a university) who remains attached to the school to provide support and critique of school progress. The friend, in principle, is a resource to the collective, a way of expanding access to information and other resources. In the Stanford/Schools Collaborative, certain structural mechanisms help to introduce and sustain reciprocity. Governance arrangements achieve parity not only by formal provisions for equal representation, but also by operations that ensure widespread availability of important information (especially information about resources) and provisions for exercising influence in the distribution of resources. Separate planning committees for key program components or events expand representation in decision making. The committees are a distance-closing device that is particularly crucial to the school-based participants (who have greater numbers), reducing the organizational distance from any one teacher or administrator to a node in the decision-making net. To the extent that the structure of leadership spans groups and institutions, it helps to permeate organizational boundaries. Organizational boundaries are further blurred by the development of cross-institutional roles (for example, research activities designed and led jointly by teachers and professors, Professor in Residence in Schools opportunities, and the incorporation of classroom teachers as lecturers in the teacher education programs). However, these cross-institutional roles are still small in

> **As partnerships have evolved, they have moved toward greater parity in obligations, opportunities, and rewards.**

number, low in visibility, modest in institutional salience, and perhaps too dependent on individual will.

Various other partnerships employ new conceptions of the university-school relation in the service of particular reform agendas. Faculty from National-Louis University have entered into a partnership with the Chicago schools in support of various subject matter reforms. They express the basic problem this way: "For most elementary school teachers, a very different type of instruction is described in the [Mathematics] Standards than they experienced as students." In mathematics, for example, "the professional development programs that our Best Practice leaders provide require teachers to become actively engaged in *doing mathematics*" (Chicago Project on Learning and Teaching, 1992, p. 6). The idea is to promote and provoke breakthroughs in conceptual understanding for the teachers by facilitating mathematical experiences rather than by teaching the teachers mathematical content or methods. A similar investigatory stance toward curriculum and instruction also distinguishes a partnership described by Marilyn Cochran-Smith and her colleagues at the University of Pennsylvania, university faculty, experienced and prospective teachers, and secondary school students in Philadelphia join in research on aspects of a multicultural society (Cochran-Smith & Lytle, 1992). In this instance, teachers' professional development is intricately interwoven with the daily life of the classroom—for example, as English teacher Bob Fecho (1992) engages his students in research into the relations between language and power.

Whether broadly conceived or more closely focused, these partnerships invite a re-examination of the traditionally privileged position of the university in relation to schools and of the asymmetries in the relations between professors and schoolteachers.

## Special Institutes and Centers

Among the accounts that teachers offer when they are asked to describe favorable professional development experiences, certain stories stand out. They are those that describe participation in special institutes or centers—summer institutes sponsored by NSF, for example, where teachers enjoy sustained work with ideas, materials, and colleagues, or centers such as the University of California's Lawrence Hall of Science where every activity expresses a commitment to make mathematics and science more accessible, rich, and engaging for students, parents, and teachers. Judging by teachers' accounts, such institutes and centers offer substantive depth and focus, adequate time to grapple with ideas and materials, the sense of doing real work rather then being "talked at," and an opportunity to consult with colleagues and experts. Some are grounded in a conception of systemic reform, their influence magnified by mechanisms that sustain connections among participants (electronic networks) and by explicit attention to the local and state contexts surrounding subject matter reforms.

By comparison with the volume of studies directed at district-sponsored training or school improvement projects, there is virtually no body of work directed toward these institutes and centers as a vehicle for teachers' professional growth and colleagueship. On the basis of anecdotal evidence, two policy issues stand out. The first is one of scale. Special institutes and centers concentrate resources, representing a greater cost per participant and a more restricted access than more modest local ventures. The second and related matter is scope or purpose—in a climate of reform, how might participation by a relative few achieve a ripple effect among a larger number in local schools and districts? Some institute sponsors more than others extend their agendas in ways that address the realities of reform; they understand the problem of knowledge use in context. The relevant contexts include states, where graduation standards are set and curriculum frameworks promulgated. They include districts, where curriculum policy is specified and local priorities are expressed. And, most centrally, they include schools. It is a commonplace of the school workplace literature that schools are generally not organized to exert much influence on teaching practice, that collegial norms do not admit special claims to expertise, and that the social organizational of daily work offers scant reason or opportunity for teachers to take much account of one another's interest in new ideas, materials, or methods (Bird & Little, 1986; Huberman, 1993). Some schools stand out as dramatic exceptions. They have been built through acts of leadership and organization, not legislated, mandated, regulated or coerced. The policy challenge is to enlarge their number.

> **Some institute sponsors more than others extend their agendas in ways that address the realities of reform.**

*Six Principles for Professional Development*
The strategies for professional development described above
embody, each to a greater or lesser extent, certain principles that
arguably stand up to the complexity of present reforms. Each principle represents a challenge to some aspect of present practice. Each
is manifest in one or more of the alternatives to the conventional
training model that are emerging in the context of present reform.
Although stated as design principles—that is, in normative language—they are subject to the kinds of rigorous study and evaluation by which their consequences for teachers, students, and the
nature of schooling might be demonstrated. Teachers' professional
development might reasonably be tested against these principles:

1. Professional development offers meaningful intellectual, social, and
   emotional engagement with ideas, with materials, and with colleagues both in and out of teaching. This is an alternative to the
   shallow, fragmented content and the passive teacher roles observable in much implementation training. Teachers do not assume an
   active professional role simply by participating in a "hands-on"
   activity as part of a scripted workshop. This principle also acknowledges teachers' limited access to the intellectual resources of a
   community or a subject field. Thus, the subject matter collaboratives engage teachers in the study and doing of mathematics,
   enlarge teachers' access to mathematicians or industry settings, and
   establish mechanisms of consultation and support among teachers.

2. Professional development takes explicit account of the contexts of
   teaching and the experience of teachers. Focused study groups,
   teacher collaboratives, long-term partnerships, and similar modes of
   professional development afford teachers a means of locating new
   ideas in relation to their individual and institutional histories, practices, and circumstances. This principle thus challenges the context-
   independent or "one size fits all" mode of formal staff development
   that introduces largely standardized content to individuals whose
   teaching experience, expertise, and settings vary widely. The training and coaching model, which by its nature tends to *assume* the
   importance of its training content, grants only residual status to
   questions regarding the fit between new ideas and old habits, or
   between new ideas and present circumstances.

3. Professional development offers support for informed dissent. In
   the pursuit of good schools, consensus may prove to be an over-
   stated virtue. Admittedly, deeply felt differences in value and belief
   can make agreements both difficult to achieve and unstable over
   time. At its extreme, dissent many engender a certain micropolitical

paralysis (see Ball, 1987), while shared commitments may enable people to take bold action. Nonetheless, to permit or even foster principled dissent (e.g., by structuring devil's advocate roles and arguments) places a premium on the evaluation of alternatives and the close scrutiny of underlying assumptions. To do so may alter that dynamic by which dissenters come quickly to be labeled as "resisters." Although specific examples do not abound, one might expect that close collaborations and long-term inquiry-oriented partnerships provide more opportunity than do training experiences for the kind of principled and well-informed dissent that strengthens both group decisions and individual choices (e.g., Nemeth, 1989).

4. Professional development places classroom practice in the larger contexts of school practice and the educational careers of children. It is grounded in a big-picture perspective on the purposes and practices of schooling, providing teachers a means of seeing and acting upon the connections among students' experiences, teachers' classroom practice, and schoolwide structures and cultures. This is a challenge to a narrowly technological view of curriculum reform that depends heavily on the accumulation of specific technical skills, and to the tendency to treat teachers nearly exclusively as classroom decision makers independent of larger patterns of practice. It recalls Fullan's (1991) argument that reforms or innovations are simultaneously technical and social, and underscores the balance of obligations and opportunities in teachers' professional development. Partnerships and collaboratives to a large extent engage these multiple levels and aspects of reform; special institutes do so to some extent when they help prepare teachers to assume leadership or assistance roles in their schools or districts.

5. Professional development prepares teachers (as well as students and their parents) to employ the techniques and perspectives of inquiry. Without denying that there are times when technical skill training is indeed appropriate, this principle anticipates a model based more persuasively on the pursuit of knowledge. It provides the possibility for teachers and others to interrogate their individual beliefs and the institutional patterns of practice. It acknowledges that the existing knowledge base is relatively slim and that our strength may derive less from teachers' willingness to *consume* research knowledge than from their capacity to *generate* knowledge and to *access* the knowledge claimed by others. Those teacher consortia and partnerships centered most directly on teachers' research come closest to embodying this principle.

6. The governance of professional development ensures bureaucratic restraint and a balance between the interests of individuals and the

interests of institutions. Despite some well-publicized exceptions such as the various subject matter collaboratives, the field is dominated by a district-subsidized marketplace of formal programs over which teachers exert little influence or in which they play few leadership roles. Further, few states or districts have any mechanism for evaluating the criteria on which resources are allocated; few have examined the ways in which the entire configuration of professional development obligations and opportunities communicate a view of schools, teachers, teaching, and teacher development. Evaluation and research, to the extent that they exist at all, tend to center on individual projects rather than on the policy import of whole patterns of resource allocation (for exceptions, see Little et al., 1987; Moore & Hyde, 1981; Schlechty et al, 1982). A principled view of resource allocation might more readily balance support of institutional initiatives with support for those initiated by teachers individually and collectively.

Comparison of the training model with various alternatives suggests that there are precedents worth preserving and dilemmas worth revealing. To start, it seems we must be willing to ask: Among the formal activities or agreements that make up the most common approaches to professional development, where does one find the most ambitious reflection of the six principles? Even among the alternatives described here, some principles are more clearly evident than others. Principles 3 (informed dissent) and 4 (the big picture or systematic view) prove most difficult to locate, though they are arguably central to professional development that is at once intellectually rigorous and socially responsible. What are the most challenging issues?

## EMERGING ISSUES

In the present reform context, three issues dominate policy considerations in the design of professional development:

1. The sheer complexity of the reform tasks being proposed, together with the relative absence of tested principles, policies, and practices; the contradictions across policies; and the propensity to seize upon early-stage experiments as models.

2. The problem of fit between the task of reform and the prevailing models of professional development—in particular, the dominance of a training paradigm built on knowledge consumption, and the lesser support for an inquiry and problem-solving paradigm built around knowledge production.

3. The relative inattention to teachers' opportunity to learn within the salaried work day and work year—an issue in the social organization of teachers' work in schools and their participation in a wider professional community.

## The Complexity and Uneven Pace of Systemic Reform

Complexity and ambiguity are inherent features of the more ambitious reforms, making progress uneven and difficult to detect. The picture is complicated further by the internal contradictions of the reform movement itself, for example, in the competing views of schooling and teaching inherent in the basic skills reforms that still dominate urban reform versus the more ambitious outcomes embodied in the NCTM standards and in other reform initiatives that emphasize higher order thinking. Confronted with complexities, ambiguities, and contradictions, individuals and institutions move forward in fits and starts. The professional development problem mirrors the larger problem of reform in several ways.

### *Limited Grasp of Possibilities*

Asked to participate in the redesign of their work and workplace, participants at first invent a narrow range of responses or solutions. Michelle Fine, who chronicles the progress of Philadelphia's reform effort, says simply: "The categories people have in their heads are the categories people have in their heads"(Fine, 1992, p. 20). Inertia prevails, undergirded by established ideologies that explain and defend massive student failure (see also Fine, 1991). Such explanations "block any sense of possibility" (p. 22). Even among enthusiastic teachers, Fine observes, few could imagine a "sufficiently collective effort" to produce substantial improvements in student outcomes (p. 21).

Conventional forms of professional development and support grounded in training are poorly conceived to help people expand the possibilities for learning, teaching, and schooling. Rarely do they contend with fundamental debates and disagreements about the purposes of schooling, the relationships between teachers and students, and the obligations of teachers to a wider larger community. It seems unlikely that teachers' sense of possibility will be enlarged in the absence of expanded information, deeper discussion and debate, and a tolerance for public dispute over fundamental matters. After three years, Fine considers it progress in Philadelphia "that at least now people are fighting aloud" (p. 21).

*Policy Collisions and the Legacy of Past Reforms*
Most plans for systemic reform or restructuring underestimate the sustained impact of long-standing policy and practice. Teachers and administrators witness policy collisions between present reforms and their predecessors, many still reflected in statute, regulation, policy, and local habit. Darling-Hammond (1990) reminds us that "policies do not land in a vacuum; they land on top of other policies" (p. 346). She notes with respect to California's new curriculum frameworks: "Several previous policy initiatives stand out sharply as competing with the new reform" (p. 343). Among them she names the state's standardized testing system, "which values a type of mathematical knowledge and performance very different from the conceptions embodied in the new Framework" (p. 343). She goes on to argue:

> **The professional development problem mirrors the larger problem of reform in several ways.**

> In several respects, policy accretion is a more difficult problem than the older problem bemoaned by reformers (which has not left us) of ingrained tradition. . . . This can create an Alice in Wonderland world in which people ultimately begin to nod blithely at the inevitability of incompatible events. (p. 344; see also Evertson & Murphy, 1992)

*Pressures of Fast-paced Implementation*
Systemic change is also undermined when local and state leaders attempt to reduce conceptual and practical complexities in the interest of a fast-paced implementation. The California curriculum frameworks serve as one example of a complex policy instrument that is experienced in distilled form by classroom teachers. In her introduction to a series of case studies of the math framework implementation, Linda Darling-Hammond (1990) observes:

> The cases suggest that, at least from the vantage point of the teachers interviewed, the mathematics curriculum framework consisted of a 'statement' . . . and its transmission to them occurred when they were handed new textbooks, selected by the local administration after being approved by the state as compatible with the framework. (p. 342; see also Peterson, 1990)

*The Magnitude of the Task*

Observers remind us of the sheer difficulty of the reform task and the tool that it takes on people. The work of systemic reform is enormously difficult, frustrating, slow—and rewarding. Fine (1992) says once-discouraged teachers are "back" in droves but they must contend with powerful dilemmas. They experience the frustration of doing what is, while envisioning what could be—what Debbie Meier, principal at Central Park East (New York City), is famed for describing as changing the tire on a moving car. A certain amount of "institutional schizophrenia" is generated around specific institutional routines—practices of student evaluation, for example. And the burden is felt especially by the front runners, the ones that Schlechty would call the "trail-blazers" (Cole & Schlechty, 1992). They "offend almost every vested interest, at some point" (Fine, 1992, p. 24).

> **The work of systemic reform is enormously difficult, frustrating, slow— and rewarding.**

*Political Will*

The success of the trail-blazing individuals and institutions will rest ultimately on a crucial fund of political will. Whatever the shortcomings of the knowledge base on which reform stands, we can nonetheless assert that we have sufficient knowledge to move forward; we have "the knowledge, methods, assessment strategies to transform our classrooms into engaging, critical and creative sites of intellectual growth and personal development" (Fine, 1992, p. 30). What remains uncertain is whether we have the political will to employ our knowledge in the service of public (and particularly urban) education. Professional development, in this view, will prove fruitless if it fails to cultivate and sustain political will.

The available (though rare) amounts of large-scale restructuring efforts thus underscore the *systemic* character of reform and, correspondingly, the *collective* capacity needed to achieve and sustain it. But professional development practice remains, on the whole, highly individualistic. Rates of participation vary enormously, generating "radically different profiles of professional development for teachers with comparable experience and teaching assignments" (Lanier with Little, 1986, p. 548; also Arends, 1983). These differences appear to persist even in schools formally committed to reform initiatives.

A shift to school-based initiatives does not necessarily alter the variable pattern of individual practice. Schools associated with the Illinois Writing Project showed promising changes in language arts scores, but in the urban schools "typically less than half the teachers in each building attended the voluntary, after-school workshops" (Chicago Project on Learning and Teaching, 1992, p. 1). What we do not learn is why. Were teachers opposed to the assumptions and practices of the Writing Project? Unimpressed with the quality of the workshops, or already expert in the practices? Pressed by the demands of too many projects or of too burdensome a teaching load? Committed to other activities that required time, thought, and energy? Not persuaded that participation would make a difference to the students they taught? Discouraged by failures of administrative leadership? Truly discouraged about teaching?

**As a context for professional development, reform movements place a premium on institutional perspectives.**

Here we have a tension between institutional imperatives and individual prerogatives, between the conditions necessary to attempt systemic change and the conditions that engage individual teachers in their work. At best, these are in harmony; at the least, we must learn the sources of conflict between them. We will be better served by knowing the grounds on which teachers choose to participate or not. As a context for professional development, reform movements place a premium on institutional perspectives. They may absorb all of the resources available for teachers' professional development, leaving little in the way of subsidy for individually inspired intellectual pursuits that may also, in quite different ways, make a difference to the character of schooling.

In any event, the complexities and tensions illustrated here are not resolved by any simplistic distinction between voluntary and mandatory occasions of professional development. More productive will be careful consideration of teachers' professional obligations and opportunities, of the balance and tension between individual latitude and collective endeavor, and of the resources and rewards devoted to each.

### Problems of "Fit:" Professional Development Models and the Task of Reform

Without becoming preoccupied by barriers to reform, we might highlight five issues that states and localities confront in matching professional development to the challenges surrounding systemic reform.

*Innovation on the Margins*

The training paradigm dominates the world of teachers' professional development. Short-term skill training workshops far out-number teachers' study groups and well-conceived teacher research. But the training paradigm has also come under assault: Critics charge that most training places teachers in passive roles as consumers of knowledge produced elsewhere, that the "workshop menu" is fragmented in content, form, and continuity—at precisely the time when teachers are confronted with the challenge of redesigning the way we do schooling (Little, 1989; Moore & Hyde, 1981).

**Innovative approaches to teachers' professional development— remain small in scale and number.**

Alternative approaches of the sort described above have gained the admiration of teachers, administrators, school boards, and state policymakers. Some, to be certain, have grown in stature and reach over the past decade. The history of the Bay Area Writing Project (BAWP) is a case in point; the BAWP model now guides a large number of local and regional projects in many states, and serves as the basis for comparable projects in math and science. It has attracted state and local district funding.

On the whole, however, innovative approaches to teachers' professional development—those that correspond most closely to the principles outlined above—remain small in scale and number. Most have been supported with private dollars (foundation and corporate funding) and have made relatively little impact on the configuration of publicly supported professional development. Partnerships have formed between individual activists in universities and schools or districts, or between individual consultants and schools, or between departments of education and local schools. In large institutions, however, multiple partnerships may operate in ignorance of one another's efforts or in pursuit of quite different or even conflicting goals.

Lord (1991) maintains that the subject matter collaboratives have "magnified the impact of local resources—both human and financial," but provides no detail (p. 1). Meanwhile, the risks associated with moving from the margins to the center are well known: teacher-centered programs such as the Bay Area Writing Project or the Los Angeles Educational Partnership's teacher networks risk bureaucratization when they are absorbed within district structures.

*The Limitations of Packaged Knowledge and Standardized Programs*
Given the option, district and school administrators say they will choose a well-packaged program of staff development (Little et al., 1987). Packaged programs have an understandable appeal. They are readily defended, managed, and evaluated. Most district-sponsored staff development is oriented toward the acquisition of specific knowledge and skill; assessing impact, though it is rarely done, is relatively straightforward (especially if centered on changes in observable teacher behavior).

Alternative approaches, by comparison, are conceptually pragmatically messier. The main benefits that participants derive from teacher networks, study groups, curriculum experiments, and the like may be more broadly intellectual, motivational, and attitudinal. By acknowledging the importance of teachers' intellectual curiosities and capacities, and by crediting teachers' contributions to knowledge and practice, such approaches may strengthen the enthusiasm teachers bring to their work and the intellectual bent they display in the classroom. Over the long run, teachers who participate in experiences of this sort might be expected to show higher rates of classroom innovation and to inspire greater enthusiasm for learning on the part of their students. Nonetheless, appropriate comparisons with conventional staff development are likely to prove very difficult. This is due in part to differences in program aims, content, and format, and in part to the difficulty of tracing the crucial longer term consequences of individual teachers.

The proliferation of classroom- and school-based studies over the past two decades has fed the organized professional development marketplace. "Research says" is a common preface to many workshop presentations and exercises, serving as a warrant for recommended practice. But "research says" has increasingly become a means for exercising institutional authority rather than for informing teachers' judgments or framing their own inquiries. Teachers are typically less well positioned than district specialists or outside consultants to invoke research (or challenge it) as a warrant for action—they have less routine access to sources of research, less time to read and evaluate it, and less familiarity with its arcane language.

What is inevitably hidden in the effort to translate research are all the ways in which the research findings conflict, or are limited by design flaws, or reflect particular conceptions of the phenomena under study. What is also missing is an invitation to teachers to act not only as consumers of research but also as critics and producers of research—to be participants in a more visible and consequential manner. An alternative to the formulation "research says," reads something like: "The way this question has been framed in most research is. . . ." Or: "There are three main approaches to this problem in research thus far. Here's what each has produced. . . ." These formulations leave open the possibility that the available research knowledge is incomplete and that there is room for discovery. They neither romanticize teachers' knowledge nor unduly privilege researchers' claims.[3]

**The status of the knowledge base in support of systemic reform is uncertain.**

The status of the knowledge base in support of systemic reform is uncertain. Some argue that the base is strong, others that it is more hortatory and ideological than it is theoretically coherent or empirically defensible. Advocates of reform argue that we know enough to make considerable difference in the ways that students experience school and the benefits they derive from schooling. Whatever the strength of that claim, it also seems certain none of the knowledge we assert will be adequate to account for the complexities of any specific context, and that there is no substitute for local invention and inquiry. These circumstances prompt various responses to the burgeoning teacher research movement (not the first such movement in this century). In recent symposia on the subject, debate revealed widely diverse and competing views about teachers' preparation to engage in research, the nature of research topics and methods, conventions associated with legitimation of research, and issues surrounding the political control of research agendas and products (see Hollingsworth & Sackett, 1994).

Phillip Schlechty is fond of observing that we are still confined by unworkable conceptions of school and school improvement, much as if NASA had decided that we could get to the moon by funding improvements in the internal combustion engine.[4] In the allocation of professional development resources, we find a tremendous reliance on research-based solutions, on being able to give assurances of certainty. Our own voyage to the moon may require that we abandon our reliance on the present base of consumable research and expand our support for arrangements for teachers' involvement in the explication, invention, and evaluation of local practice.

## The Dominance of Training Over Problem Solving

States and local school districts have learned—in part, anyway—the lesson of the implementation problem and the importance of inadequate local support. In the late 1970s, one could reasonably charge that "many . . . education reform efforts fell short primarily because planners seriously underestimated teacher training needs" (McLaughlin & Marsh, 1979, p. 69). An adequate supply of well-conceived training opportunities seemed a major contributor to implementation success. More than a decade later, we boast a more sophisticated understanding of the implementation problem, casting it as a complex interaction between external policy variables (clear statutes, effective authority, and the like) and the micro-contexts shaped by individuals' and groups' commitments, histories, and politics (McLaughlin, 1987, 1990; see also Ball, 1987). Our conception of implementation was evolved "from early notions of implementation as transmission or as a problem of incentives or authority to conceptions of implementation as bargaining and transformation" (McLaughlin, 1987, p. 175). Looking back at the celebrated Rand Change Agent Study (1973–1978) from a vantage point of nearly 15 years, McLaughlin (1990) expresses a certain skepticism about the power of policy mandates, especially those that take the form of special projects aimed at "discrete elements of the education policy system" instead of embracing the systemic nature of problems and the systemic character of local practice (pp. 14–15).

But districts' strategies for reform, at least with regard to teachers' professional development, do not appear to capitalize fully on what we have learned about the importance and variability of local contexts and about the transformational nature of reform. In-service activities tend to be linked to special projects or to discrete components of reform and to embody a relatively traditional conception of classroom experience. The most sophisticated of these make some provision for follow-up in the form of classroom consultation and coaching.

The training-and-coaching strategy that dominates local professional development has much to recommend it when considered as a balanced part of a larger configuration, and when linked to those aspects of teaching that are properly rendered as transferable skills. But the training model is problematic. The content of much training communicates a view of teaching and learning that is at odds with present reform initiatives. It is not at all clear, for example, that any form of training is adequate to develop the substantive conversation that Newmann (1990) envisions (see also Hargreaves & Dawe, 1990). Nor is the content of training set against the content of local belief, practice, and policy in any meaningful and detailed way. In addition, principles of good training are frequently compromised in practice. In particular, schools and districts demonstrate far less capacity for classroom consultation and support than is required by the training and coaching model. Those persons typically designated as coaches or mentors are far outnumbered by their clientele of regular classroom teachers. They are further constrained by school workplace cultures that perpetuate a norm of privacy and constrain advice-giving (Little, 1990b). Finally, to attain results from the training/coaching model requires a consistency of purpose and a coordination of effort that is not the norm in many districts. Rather, districts parade a litany of short-term goals in their response to various state mandates and incentives, local constituencies, or the individual enthusiasms of superintendents, school board members, or others.

Having launched such criticisms, I want to reiterate that the skill training and coaching model to which so many districts seem wedded has demonstrated consistent results in those cases where training content can be represented as a repertoire of discrete practices, and where classroom performance is oriented toward specified student outcomes. At their best, local activities incorporate the wealth of research on effective training and support that we can trace to the various implementation or innovation studies and to

> **Principles of good training are frequently compromised in practice.**

studies of specific professional development ventures (Guskey, 1986; Romberg & Price, 1983; Showers, Joyce, & Bennett, 1987; Smylie, 1988; Sparks, 1986; Sparks & Loucks-Horsley, 1990). Nor are these remarks in any way meant to impugn the knowledge, skill, thoughtfulness, or good intentions of those persons designated by local districts as staff development specialists, coaches, mentors, and the like. Rather, the aim is to record the dominance of the training model, the possibilities it offers, and the constraints on its effectiveness.

*Conceptions of Cost or Investment*

Policymakers require a way of making sense of costs—or more persuasively, investments. This note centers on issues surrounding the allocation of discretionary resources—the monetary expenditures that typically come to mind when persons consider staff development budgets. Direct monetary expenditures includes only those costs directly and necessarily associated with program operations; these include staff salaries, workshop presenters, substitutes, and facilities. (For a broader conception of investment and its relation to policy considerations, see Little, 1992b; and Stern, Gerritz & Little, 1989). One straightforward way to compare costs is to divide the direct monetary expenditure by the number of actual participants to arrive at a per participant cost. By this calculation, the per participant cost of some special projects may exceed $2,000.

How does this figure compare with the average per teacher investment in professional development? In relative cost terms, institutes and retreats are an expensive venture; ongoing local study groups and after-school workshops are not. The average per teacher investment of direct monetary expenditures in California in 1985–1986 (the only year for which such estimates are available) was approximately $900 (Little et al., 1987). That is, the total annual professional development of the average California teacher was subsidized by approximately $900 in public monies over a single fiscal year. A program that invites 25 teachers to a retreat for five days will invest more than 1 ½ times the resources per participant in three to five days than local districts typically invest in an entire year of a teacher's professional development.

The "average teacher" figure is, of course, something of a fiction; resources are not distributed uniformly. Experimental programs typically invest higher amounts in smaller cadres of teachers. The most prominent example in California at present is the California

Mentor Teacher Program, which allocates approximately $6,000 per
year to each teacher selected as a mentor. The mentor program's per
participant investment is thus nearly seven
times the average per teacher expenditure.
(Two thirds of that allocation goes directly to
the teacher as a stipend; the remaining one
third is allocated to the district in support of
the mentor's work). The program reflects an
implicit policy wager: that concentrating
resources on fewer than 5% of the state's
teachers will yield benefit for the remaining
95% (see also Little, 1990b). The legislative
intent attached to the mentor program outlines a set of obligations to
beginning teachers, experienced teachers, and curriculum development; to the extent that mentors meet these obligations, they generate a ripple effect that lowers the per participant cost. That is, to the
extent that the effects extend beyond the individuals who are the primary participants, the per teacher cost is appreciably lower than the
per participant cost.

> **In the past decade, tastes have assumed greater prominence in shaping reform initiatives.**

Investments beyond the ordinary (that is, narrow concentrations
rather than broad distribution of resources) are more defensible if
they can meet one of three criteria: (a) they can be credibly tied to a
ripple effect (so that per teacher cost is demonstrably lower than per
participant cost); (b) one can claim that the direct individual benefit
of this specific program is far more certain than the benefit linked to
conventional funding; or (c) the program contributes in demonstrable ways to increased organizational capacity in ways that transcend the impact on those individuals who participate directly in the
program.

*The State and Other Players*
When we consider levels of policy intervention and influence, we
quickly find the state and the district to be the most prominent players in defining and promoting reform and in sponsoring formal occasions of professional development. In the past decade, states have
assumed greater prominence in shaping reform initiatives. This is
not to say that state policy offers a coherent vision of the fit between
teacher policy and various reform ventures (Little et al., 1987). Nor
is it clear that state agencies and legislatures have given much consideration to the various possible forms that a state presence might
take—though in some of the more policy-active states, such as

Connecticut, Kentucky, California, and Oregon, the traditional impetus toward regulatory control is increasingly tempered by a role centered around the supplying of information and incentives for local experimentation.

On the whole, however, states and districts have been relatively slow to reshape professional development in ways that respond to the complexities and ambiguities of reform. Much reform legislation reflects a tension between incentives and control, between provisions that expand teachers' leadership opportunities (e.g., California's mentor teacher program) and provisions that tighten external controls over teaching and teachers (e.g., new credentialing requirements or curriculum standards). On the whole, the incentives are attached to small, voluntary, and peripheral activities, while the controls embrace the entire teacher work force and shape more central aspects of their work. In this asymmetry between support and control we may find some evidence of a pervasive skepticism among policymakers about teachers' capacities and motivations, and thus a certain reservation about professional development strategies that measurably expand teachers' collective autonomy.

Meanwhile, the responsibility and resources for teachers' professional development have for several decades (since the mid-sixties' federal social reform legislation) resided primarily with districts—that is, with the employing organization.[5] The shift to the school site brings control over resources closer to the classroom and increases the possibility that content and context might be more closely joined. Altogether, the profoundly local character of much reform activity would seem to offer substantial opportunity to create and support alternative modes of professional development—those that enable local educators to do the hard work of reinventing schools and teaching. But there is no guarantee of that. If the established marketplace of training options fits poorly with the demands of reform, it nonetheless fits reasonably well with bureaucratic structures of accountability (by providing a record of participation). If a menu of workshops fits poorly with the long-term vision and capacity required by genuine reform, it responds well to the short-term incentive structure and resource allocation scheme. Finally, staff development at the local level, despite the pervasive rhetoric of change, serves in large part as a vehicle of organizational maintenance—a point worth remembering in the surge of interest toward reform (Schlechty & Whitford, 1983).

States and districts have emerged as the most visible and powerful players on the reform landscape. Less visible but potentially influential in achieving the fit between reform requirements and teachers' professional development are the various professional associations (teachers, administrators, other specialists, and school boards) and organizations representing business and industry. Foundations have been active in the support of various reform efforts, including those devoted to teachers' professional development, but it is only very recently that they have begun to join directly with states in pursuit of a reform agenda (Lagemann, 1992). Of particular interest and import is the increasingly powerful influence exerted by teachers' subject matter associations (perhaps most prominently, NCTM) in shaping reforms in curriculum, assessment, and standards for teacher certification. Yet the place of subject matter associations in the lives and careers of teachers, and especially in preparing them to engage meaningfully and productively in reform, remains largely unexamined in the research and policy literature; recent case studies of the various mathematics collaboratives may signal a shift (Lord, 1991; Salmon-Cox & Briars, 1989). On the whole, however, available evidence suggests a weak connection between those subject associations and the main providers of professional development (the districts, private vendors, and universities).

> **States and districts have emerged as the most visible and powerful players on the reform landscape.**

The disposition of the unions toward these major reform initiatives—and particularly any response they may have made in the form of teachers' professional development—is largely undocumented. In interviews with union leaders in 30 California districts, conducted in 1986 (Little et al., 1987), we found that most locals concentrated on constraining administrators' access to teachers' time for purposes of school- or district-initiated staff development. We found no examples of a more affirmative or proactive involvement in substantive programs of teacher development although some promising exceptions have emerged since that study was completed, for example, in the form of the policy trust agreement projects established in California (Koppich & Kerchner, 1990). Nor do we know much about the relative salience of the union compared with other sources in shaping teachers' response to or involvement in reform initiatives (Bascia, 1992). One is struck by some countervailing currents. First, the unions have responded to escalating pressure to balance a concern with personnel issues (compensation and other conditions of employment) with responsible attention to matters surrounding professional practice. Second, the unions have become more frequent and prominent players in shaping the reforms in teaching at the state or national level—most often those having to do with the preparation and licensure of teachers. Their involvement at the local level is less clear, and certainly more uneven. Among the issues most germane to the major reforms discussed here are perceived constraints on teacher autonomy with regard to curriculum and instruction, and challenges to the deep-rooted egalitarianism of teachers that arise in various career ladder and mentorship schemes.

> **Colleges and universities may simultaneously foster and impede reform.**

We thus have multiple players and multiple levels of policy and practice. Two major questions seem germane. First, what fit between reform and professional development is best achieved at each level or niche in the policy system, and through what policy mechanism? To what extent does policy making in each arena rely on regulation or persuasion? Second, in what ways and to what extent are the various policy orientations congruent or in conflict? For example, university faculty have maintained an avid interest in the development of state curriculum frameworks—yet university admission requirements have also been said to exert a "chilling effect" on innovation in the K–12 curriculum (Grubb, 1992, personal communication). That is, colleges and universities may simultaneously foster and impede reform. At the local level, a district's interest in comprehensive restructuring may operate to displace small, vital pockets of initiative by teachers in individual schools.

### The School Workplace and Teachers' Opportunity to Learn

Concentration on formal programs of professional development tends to obscure issues of obligation, incentive, and opportunity in the salaried workday and work year. Investigation of teachers' instructional assignments, ratio of in-class to out-of-class time, and school-level affiliations (departments, grade levels, friendship nets) provides us both with a perspective on *motivation or pressure to learn* and with a description of those *opportunities to learn* that are embedded in the social organization of schools (Little, 1990a; see also Glidewell, Tucker, Todt & Cox, 1983; Hargreaves, 1990; Smylie, 1995).

Teachers' central reasons and opportunities for professional development begin with the teaching assignments they acquire, the allocation of discretionary time, and other work conditions encountered day by day. They begin, that is, with a teacher's experience of what it is to teach and to be a teacher—in general, and in particular circumstances. To some large degree, it is only in relation to the daily experience of teaching that one can anticipate the contributions of more structured opportunities that range from independent reading to formal course work, conference attendance, skill training workshops, leaves or sabbaticals, participation in committees or special projects, and scheduled consultation with colleagues.

Reform movements tend to orient us toward an institutional (and largely fundamentalist) perspective. By this perspective, the schools' capacity for supporting the professional development of teachers is expressed in a system of obligations, opportunities, and rewards. Teachers' obligations for professional preparation and development reside formally in certification and recertification requirements, teacher evaluation standards, and other personnel policies and practices. They are communicated informally by institutional norms regarding teachers' performance.

In according precedence to the institutional and collective view, however, the language of reform underestimates the intricate ways in which individual and institutional lives are interwoven. It underexamines the points at which certain organizational interests of schools and occupational interests of teachers may collide. Critics of reform movements stress the tendency to "de-skill" teaching and a corresponding tendency to legitimate institutional surveillance and coercion under the rubric of "vision" and "instructional leadership" (Carlson, 1992; Hargreaves, 1992). Carlson describes the principled opposition mounted by a teachers' association to the "specter of standardization" they detected in basic skills reforms built around programmed materials, prearranged objectives, and batteries of standardized tests (p. 113). Smylie and Smart (1990), examining sources of support for and opposition to merit pay and career ladders, note that "the primary beliefs and assumptions that guide the development of relationships among teachers include norms of independence and professional equality" and find it naive to suppose that such programs will generate widespread support unless they resolve "social and normative incongruities" (pp. 152, 153). Each of these cases is consistent with the observation that members of an occupational community may find that "what is deviant organizationally may be occupationally correct (and vice versa)" (Van Maanen & Barley, 1984, p. 291).

As the arena in which teaching traditions and reform imperatives confront one another most directly and concretely, the school workplace is both the most crucial and the most complex of domains in which we play out the possibilities for teachers' professional development. Teachers' motivations, incentives, and frustrations come foremost from the immediacy and complexity of the classroom: teachers' responses to the students they teach and the circumstances in which they teach them. Idiosyncratic classroom realities may take precedence over broader institutional interests, leading teachers to protect a "strategic" or "elective individualism"

**The impetus to protect autonomy may be intensified by various circumstances surrounding collegial and institutional life.**

(Hargreaves, 1993; see also Flinders, 1988). The impetus to protect one's autonomy may be intensified by various circumstances surrounding collegial and institutional life—the norms underlying peer acceptance and admiration, and the fabric of relations between teachers and administrators. The Academics and Coaches who make up the dominant cliques in Bruckerhoff's (1991) social studies department at Truman High express quite different teaching priorities, but they have in common their selective resistance to administrative pressures. Clearly, taking the workplace seriously requires more than shifting staff development resources and activities to the school site.

## CONCLUSION

Five streams of reform present a challenge of considerable complexity, scope, and ambiguity. Yet the present pattern of professional development activity reflects an uneven fit with the aspirations and challenges of present reform initiatives in subject matter teaching, equity, assessment, school organization, and the professionalization of teaching. Much staff development or in-service communicates a relatively impoverished view of teachers, teaching, and teacher development. Compared with the complexity, subtlety, and uncertainties of the classroom, professional development is often a remarkably low-intensity enterprise. It requires little in the way of intellectual struggle or emotional engagement and takes only superficial account of teachers' histories or circumstances. Compared with the complexity and ambiguity of the most ambitious reforms, professional development is too often substantively weak and politically marginal.

Professional development must be constructed in ways that deepen the discussion, open up the debates, and enrich the array of possibilities for action. Ground for optimism resides in those innovations on the margin that embody principles consonant with the complexity of the reform task and with the capacities and commitments of a strong teacher work force.

## NOTES

Preparation of this article was supported by the Consortium for Policy Research in Education (CPRE), as part of the project Evaluating Reform: Systemic Reform, with funds from the Office of Educational Research and Improvement (OERI), U. S. Department of Education (No. RR91172005).

1. Such descriptions may be in the making. For example, see Fine (1994), Evertson and Murphy (1992), and Murphy (1991).

2. Throughout these examples are references to teachers' own research and to teachers as researchers. In some important respects, teachers' expanding presence as a distinct community of educational researchers has taken on the character of a movement. Teachers' research as an intellectual and political enterprise—has been the focus of recent AERA symposia, the subject of a forthcoming NSSE volume (Hollingsworth & Sackett, 1994), and a means for investigating the nature of professional community among teachers (Threatt et al., 1994).

3. On the problems of the former, see Buchmann (1990), and for an example of a challenge to researchers' privileged standing in the reform discourse, see Nespor and Barber (1991).

4. I have recalled this example from various speeches, but Schlechty (1990) elaborates the basic argument.

5. The steady shift away from participation in university course work and toward district-centered activity can be attributed only in part to changes in

the age distribution of the teacher work force. Over the past two decades, formal staff development has become district business, conducted largely by specialists located in a district's central office (Moore & Hyde, 1981). Teachers are more likely to choose from a menu of district-sponsored workshops than they are to receive release time or other individual subsidies to attend conferences hosted by subject area associations or institutes sponsored by universities (Little et al., 1987).

## REFERENCES

Arends, R. (1983, April). *Teachers as learners: A descriptive study of professional development activities.* Paper presented at the Annual Meeting of the American Educational Research Association, Montreal.

Ball, S. J. (1987). *The micro-politics of the school: Towards a theory of school organization.* London: Mehuen.

Bascia, N. (1993). *The role of unions in teachers' professional lives* (Doctoral dissertation, Stanford University, 1992). Dissertation Abstracts International, 53, 770.

Bird, T., & Little, J. W. (1986). How schools organize the teaching occupation. *Elementary School Journal, 86,* 493–511.

Bruckeroff, C. E. (1991). *Between classes: Faculty life at Truman High.* New York: Teachers College Press.

Buchmann, M. (1990). Beyond the lonely, choosing will: Professional development in teacher thinking. *Teachers College Record, 91,* 481–508.

Carlson, D. (1992). *Teachers and crisis: Urban school reform and teachers' work culture.* New York: Routledge.

Chicago Project on Learning and Teaching. (1992). *Best practice: Teaching and learning in Chicago, 3.* Chicago: Author & National-Louis University.

Cochran-Smith, M., & Lytle, S. L. (1992, April). *Interrogating cultural diversity: Inquiry and action.* Paper presented at the Annual Meeting of the American Educational Association, San Francisco.

Cole, R. W. & Schlechty, P. C. (1992). Teachers as trailblazers. *Educational Horizons, 70*(3), 135–137.

Cone, J. K. (1992). Untracking advanced placement English: Creating opportunity is not enough. *Phi Delta Kappan, 73,* 712–717.

Darling-Hammond, L. (1990). Instructional policy into practice: "The power of the bottom over the top." *Educational Evaluation and Policy Analysis 12,* 339–347.

Ellwood, C. (1992, April). *Teacher research for whom?* Paper presented at the Annual Meeting of the American Educational Research Association, San Francisco.

Evertson, C. M., & Murphy, J. (1992). Beginning with classrooms: Implications for restructuring schools. In H. H. Marshall (Ed.), *Redefining student learning: Roots of educational change.* Norwood, NJ: Ablex.

Fecho, B. (1992, April). *Language inquiry and critical pedagogy: Co-investigating power in the classroom.* Paper presented at the Annual Meeting of the American Educational Research Association, San Francisco.

Fine, M. (1991). *Framing dropouts: Notes on the politics of an urban public high school.* Albany, NY: State University of New York Press.

————. (1992). *Chart[er]ing urban school reform: Philadelphia style.* Philadelphia: CUNY Graduate Center/Philadelphia Schools Collaborative.

————. (1994). *Chartering urban school reform: Reflecting on public high schools in the midst of change.* New York: Teachers College Press.

Flinders, D. J. (1988). Teacher isolation and the new reform. *Journal of Curriculum and Supervision, 4*(1), 17–29.

Fullan, M. (1991). *The new meaning of educational change.* New York: Teachers College Press.

Giroux, H. A. (1988). *Teachers as intellectuals: Toward a critical pedagogy of learning.* Granby, MA: Bergin & Garvey.

Glidewell, J. C. Tuck, S., Todt, M., & Cox, S. (1983). Professional support systems: The teaching profession. In A. Nadler, J. Fisher, & B. DePaulo (Eds.), *New directions in helping* (pp. 189–212). New York: Academic Press.

Guskey, T. (1986). Staff development and the process of teacher change. *Educational Researcher, 15*(5), 5–12.

Hargreaves, A. (1990). Teachers' work and the politics of time and space. *Qualitative Studies in Education 3,* 303–320.

Hargreaves, A. (1992). Time and teachers' work: Teacher preparaion time and the intensification thesis. *Teachers College Record, 94,* 87–108.

Hargreaves, A. (1993). Individualism and individuality: Reinterpreting the teacher culure. In J. W. Little & M. W. McLaughlin (Eds.), *Teachers' work: Individuals, colleagues, and contexts* (pp. 51–76). New York: Teachers College Press.

Hargreaves, A., & Dawe, R. (1990). Paths of professional development: Contrived collegiality, collaborative culture, and the case of peer coaching. *Teaching and Teacher Education, 6,* 227–241.

Hodgson, J. (1986, June). Teaching teachers: Museums team up with schools and universities. *Museum News,* 28–35.

Hollingsworth, S., & Sackett, H. (Eds.). (1994). *Teacher-research and educational reform* (yearbook of the National Society for the Study of Education). Chicago: University of Chicago Press.

Huberman, M. (1993). The model of the independent artisan in teachers' professional relations. In J. W. Little & M. W. McLaughlin (Eds.), *Teachers' work: Individuals, colleagues, and contexts* (pp. 11–50). New York: Teachers College Press.

Joyce, B., Murphy, C., Showers, B., & Murphy, J. (1989). School renewal as cultural change. *Educational Leadership, 47,* 70–77.

Koppich, J., & Kerchner, C. (1990). Redefining teacher work roles through the educational policy trust agreement. In S. C. Conley & B. S. Cooper (Eds.), *The schools as a work environment: Implications for reform.* Boston: Allyn & Bacon.

Lageman, E. (1992). Philanthropy, education, and the politics of knowledge. *Teachers College Record, 93,* 361–369.

Lanier, J. E., with Little, J. W. (1986). Research on teacher education. In M. Wittrock (Ed.), *Handbook of research on teaching* (3rd ed., pp. 527–569). New York: MacMillan.

Lieberman, A., & McLaughlin, M. W. (1992). Networks for educational change: Powerful and problematic. *Phi Delta Kappan, 73,* 673–677.

Little, J. W. (1989). District policy choices and teachers' professional development opportunities. *Educational Evaluation and Policy Analysis, 11,* 165–179.

———. (1990a). Conditions of professional development in secondary schools. In M. W. McLaughlin, J. Talbert, & N. Bascia (Eds.), *The context of teaching in secondary schools: Teachers' realities* (pp. 187–223). New York: Teachers College Press.

———. (1990b). The "mentor" phenomenon and the social organization of teaching. *Review of Research in Education, 16,* 297–351.

———. (1992a). *Stretching the subject: The subject organization of high schools and the transformation of work education.* Berkely, CA: University of California at Berkeley, National Center for Research in Vocational Education.

———. (1992b). Teacher development and educational policy. In M. Fullan & A. Hargreaves (Eds.), *Teacher development and educational change* (pp. 170–193). London: Falmer.

Little, J. W., Gerritz, W. H., Stern, D. S., Guthrie, J. W., Kirst, M. W., & Marsh, D. D. (1987). *Staff development in California: Public and personal investment, program patterns, and policy choices.* San Francisco: Far West Laboratory for Educational Research and Development.

Little, J. W., & McLaughlin, M. W. (1991). *Urban Mathematics Collaboratives: As the teachers tell it.* Stanford, CA: Stanford University, Center for Research on the Context of Secondary School Teaching.

Lord, B. (1991, April). *Subject-area collaboratives, teacher professionalism, and staff development.* Paper presented at the Annual Meeting of the American Educational Research Association, Chicago.

McLaughlin, M. W. (1987). Learning from experience: Lessons from policy implementation. *Educational Evaluation and Policy Analysis, 9,* 171–178.

———. (1990). The Rand Change Agent Study: Macro perspectives and micro realities. *Educational Researcher, 19*(9), 11–16.

McLaughlin, M. W., & Marsh, D. D. (1979). Staff development and school change. In A. Lieberman & L. Miller (Eds.), *Staff development: New demands, new realities, new perspectives* (pp. 69–94). New York: Teachers College Press.

Meier, D. (1992). Reinventing teaching. *Teachers College Record, 93,* 594–609.

Moore, D., & Hyde, A. (1981). *Making sense of staff development: An analysis of staff development programs and their costs in three urban school districts.* Chicago: Designs for Change.

Murphy, J. (1991). *Restructuring schools: Capturing and assessing the phenomena.* New York: Teachers College Press.

Nemeth, C. J. (1989). *Minority dissent as a stimulant to group performance.* Invited address, Conference on Group Processes and Productivity, Texas A & M University, College Station, TX.

Nespor, J., & Barber, L. (1991). The rhetorical construction of "the teacher." *Harvard Educational Review, 61,* 417–433.

Newmann, F. M. (1990). *Linking restructuring to authentic student achievement.* Paper presented at the Indiana University Annual Education Conference. Madison, WI: University of Wisconsin, National Center on Effective Secondary Schools and National Center for Educational Research.

Oakes, J. (1985). *Keeping track: How schools structure inequality.* New Haven, CT: Yale University Press.

Oakes, J. (1992). Can tracking research inform practice? Technical, normative, and political considerations. *Educational Researcher 21*(4), 12–21.

Peterson, P. (1990). Doing more in the same amount of time: Cathy Swift. *Educational Evaluation and Policy Analysis, 12,* 261–280.

Renyi, J. (1992). Description of "Good Books for Great Kids." Included in a compilation of "Best Practice Examples" prepared by the Rockefeller Foundation.

Romberg, T. A., & Price, G. G. (1983). Curriculum implementation and staff development as cultural change. In G. Griffin (Ed.), *Staff development, 82nd yearbook of the National Society for the Study of Education* (pp. 154–184). Chicago: University of Chicago Press.

Salmon-Cox, L., & Briars, D. J. (1989, March). *The Pittsburgh Mathematics Collaborative: Staff development for secondary teachers.* Paper presented at the Annual Meeting of the American Educational Research Association, San Francisco.

Schlecty, P. C. (1990). *Schools for the twenty-first century.* San Francisco: Jossey-Bass.

Schlechty, P. C., Crowell, D., Whitford, B. L., Joslin, A. W., Vance, V. S., Noblit, G. W., & Burke, W. I. (1982). *The organization and management of staff development in a large city school system: A case study.* Chapel Hill, NC: University of North Carolina.

Schlechty, P. C.., & Whitford, B. L. (1983). The orgnanizational context of school systems and the functions of staff development. In G. Griffin (Ed.), *Staff development, 82nd yearbook of the National Society for the Study of Education* (pp. 62–91). Chicago University of Chicago Press.

Showers, B., Joyce, B., & Bennett, C. (1987). Synthesis of research on staff development: A framework for future study and a state-of-the-art analysis. *Educational Leadership, 45*(3), 77–87.

Sizer, T. (1992). *Horace's school: Redesigning the American high school.* Boston: Houghton Mifflin.

Smylie, M. (1988). The enhancement function of staff development: Organizational and psychological antecedents to individual teacher change. *American Educational Research Journal, 25,* 1–30.

Smylie, M. A. (1995). Teacher learning in the workplace: Implications for school reform. In T. R. Guskey & M. Huberman (Eds.), *Professional development in education: New paradigms and practices.* New York: Teachers College Press.

Smylie, M. A., & Smart, J. C. (1990). Teacher support for career enhancement initiatives: Program characteristics and effects on work. *Educational Evaluation and Policy Analysis, 12,* 139–155.

Sparks, G. M. (1986). The effectiveness of alternative training activities in changing teaching practices. *American Educational Research Journal, 23,* 217–225.

Sparks, D., & Loucks-Horsley, S. (1990). Models of staff development. In W. R. Houston, M. Haberman, & J. Sikula (Eds.), *Handbook of research on teacher education* (pp. 234–250). New York: Macmillan.

Stern, D. S., Gerritz, W. H., & Little, J. W. (1989). Making the most of the district's two (or five) cents: Accounting for investment in teachers' professional development. *Journal of Education Finance, 14*(Winter), 19–26.

Threatt, S., Buchanan, J., Morgan, B., Sugarman, J., Strieb, L. Y., Swenson, J., Teel, K., & Tomlinson, J. (1994). Teachers' voices in the conversation about teacher research. In S. Hollingsworth & H. Sackett (Eds.), *Teacher research and educational reform.* Chicago: University of Chicago Press.

Urban Mathematics Collaboratives (n.d.) *Policy statement on teacher professionalism.* Newton, MA: Educational Development Center.

Van Maanen, J., & Barley, S. R. (1984). Occupational communities: Culture and control in organizations. *Research in Organizational Behavior, 6,* 287–365.

Wagner, J. (1991). *Teacher professionalism and school improvement in an occupational community of teachers in English.* Paper presented at the Ethnography and Education Forum, University of Pennyslvania, Philadelphia.

# Section 3

# School and Community Change

There is increasing consistency in the research literature about what kinds of school cultures make a difference in the professional learning of teachers, how they teach, and what students learn. Wholstetter and Peterson et al. present compelling evidence and analysis that schools are successful when they develop professional learning communities with a school-wide focus on pedagogical practices linked to the examination of student learning, which in turn feeds back on school improvement.

It is one thing to conduct research on what is out there, but quite another to engage in action that would actually alter schools. As Donahoe observes, it is extremely difficult to change structures, cultures, and the use of time in schools. Yet it is precisely reculturing and retiming that is needed along with restructuring. Most attempts fall short because, at best, they change the structure (a site-based team, new roles, and timetable) without affecting teaching and learning. The articles in this section focus on teaching and learning in an organization-wide context.

Parallel arguments can be made about school-community relationships. Epstein argues that it is not the decision-making "structure" that must change, but the development of new *capacities* in communities and schools and how they relate. The most powerful forms of family/community and school relationship are those in which parents and teachers develop new skills, resources, and abilities to work independently and collaboratively on student learning. These ideas are all the more crucial given the analysis in Section 1 indicates the context of schools has radically changed—with much more need for boundary spanning alliances.

# Getting School-Based Management Right
## What Works and What Doesn't

by Priscilla Wohlstetter

*What conditions in schools promote high performance through school-based management? From research in 44 schools, Ms. Wohlstetter extracts four basic reasons why school-based management fails and six strategies that lead to success.*

A fter years of waiting for solid evidence that school-based management (SBM) leads to improved school performance, educators and policy makers are questioning the wisdom of using decentralized management to reform education. Many people say that the best decisions about education are those made closest to the students, but few realize the extent of systemwide change that SBM entails. Often an SBM system is implemented simply by setting up a council at the school site and giving the council at least some responsibility in the areas of budget, personnel, and curriculum. It is assumed that individual school councils understand their new roles and responsibilities and will take appropriate action to improve school performance.

For more than three years, my colleagues and I at the Center on Educational Governance at the University of Southern California in Los Angeles have been studying schools and school districts in the United States, Canada, and Australia to find out what makes SBM work.[1] The purpose of the research was to identify the conditions in schools that promote high performance through SBM. We defined "high-performance SBM" as occurring in schools that were actively restructuring in the areas of curriculum and instruction; these were schools in which SBM worked well. We compared this group of

From *Phi Delta Kappan,* September 1995, pp. 22–26. © 1995 by Phi Delta Kappa. Reprinted with permission.

successful schools to schools that were using SBM but with less success in making changes that affected teaching and learning.

We visited a total of 44 schools in 13 school districts and interviewed more than 500 people, from school board members, superintendents, and associate superintendents in district offices to principals, teachers, parents, and students. All the schools were studied—which included elementary, middle, and high schools—had been operating under SBM for at least four years, and some of them much longer.[2]

In brief, we found that successful SBM requires a redesign of the whole school organization that goes far beyond a change in school governance. For SBM to work, people at the school site must have "real" authority over budget, personnel, and curriculum. Equally important, if SBM is to help improve school performance, that authority must be used to introduce changes in the functioning of the school that actually affect teaching and learning.

> **Successful SBM requires a redesign of the whole school organization.**

The school's strategy for using its new power must include strategies for decentralizing three other essential resources: 1) *professional development and training* for teachers and other stakeholders in managing, in solving problems, and in curriculum and instruction; 2) *information* about student performance, about parent and community satisfaction, and about school resources to help schoolpeople make informed decisions; and 3) *rewards* to acknowledge the increased effort SBM requires and to recognize improvements in school performance. Our research also pointed out the importance of *leadership* on the part of the principal and of having some sort of *instructional guidance mechanism*—e.g., a curriculum framework—at the school site to direct reform efforts.[3] Here I present the knowledge we gained in our research in the form of four basic reasons why SBM fails and six strategies that lead to success.

## WHY SBM FAILS

1. *SBM is adopted as an end in itself.* As a form of governance, SBM will not in itself generate improvement in school performance. Instead, SBM is simply a means through which school-level decision makers can implement various reforms that can improve

teaching and learning.[4] In the schools we visited that were struggling to implement SBM, there was little connection between SBM and the reform of curriculum and instruction, and school councils often got bogged down in issues of power—who can attend meetings, who can vote, and so on—and had no time or energy left to confront issues of school improvement.

2. *Principals work from their own agendas.* In struggling schools, many principals were perceived as too autocratic by their staff, who reported that the principals appeared to have agendas of their own and to dominate all decisions.[5] Such principals typically identified, on their own, a vision for the school and then presented it as a fait accompli to the staff. Such tactics often led to power struggles between the teachers and the principal over who controlled the school, and in some cases the faculty rejected the principal's unilateral plan for change. Teachers felt little sense of ownership or accountability to the plan. In schools where the leadership was autocratic, teachers frequently referred to "the principal's vision."

3. *Decision-making power is lodged in a single council.* Schools that were struggling with SBM tended to concentrate power in a single school council that often was composed of a small group of committed teachers who were painfully aware that they did not have board representation. These councils tended to get bogged down in establishing power relationships. One struggling school spent almost a year developing a policy manual that specified who had power and under what conditions. There were also strong feelings of alienation among faculty members, and often factions developed between "them"—the empowered—and the rest of "us."[6] Subcommittees and other decision-making bodies (if they existed at all) did not have wide participation, and so the committed few often felt exhausted and burned out.

4. *Business proceeds as usual.* Too many schools have assumed that SBM can be put in place successfully with just average levels of commitment and energy. Our research found that SBM is a time-consuming and complicated process that places high demands on all individuals involved.[7] Schools struggled with SBM when they simply layered it on top of what they were already doing. Meetings ended up being held after school, and frequently they were poorly attended. Such schools did not redesign their schedules to encourage teachers to interact during the regular school day. Furthermore, there

were strong feelings of isolation among teachers because of the absence of meetings that allowed them and other stakeholders to discuss specific projects or tasks.

## STRATEGIES FOR SUCCESS

1. *Establish many teacher-led, decision-making teams.* In schools where SBM worked, many teacher-led, decision-making teams were created that involved a broad range of school-level constituents in the decision-making process. Many of these groups were designed to facilitate interaction across the traditional boundaries of departments and grade levels.

Common structures included subcommittees of the school council that were open to membership by interested teachers or parents and teacher teams that were actively included in building consensus for school decisions. The decision-making groups, set up to address such topics as curriculum, assessment, and professional development, also helped focus participants' energy on specific tasks rather than on abstractions such as "culture" or "empowerment." The net effect was that in schools where SBM worked there was lots of communication and reflective dialogue about specific projects.

The most effective school councils were those that served largely to coordinate and integrate the activities of the various decision-making groups operating throughout the school. These councils provided the direction for the changes taking place and allocated resources to support them; they focused on the needs of the school as a whole rather than on the needs of individual academic departments or teaching teams. Because entire faculties were involved in the decision-making process, the multiple teams and subcommittees also reduced the workload on individual teachers and broadened the commitment to reform.

2. *Focus on continuous improvement with school-wide training in functional and process skills and in areas related to curriculum and instruction.* In schools where SBM worked, professional development was a very high priority. Staff members regularly participated in training opportunities. Professional development at these schools was used strategically and was deliberately tied to the school's reform objectives.[8] At many schools, the council or a separate decision-making body assessed professional development needs and planned and coordinated activities to meet those needs.

Professional development activities were oriented toward building a schoolwide capacity for change, creating a professional community, and developing a shared knowledge base.[9] The schools where SBM worked had greater proportions of the staff taking part in professional development. In particular, training in the area of decision-making skills was not limited to members of the school council. At successful SBM schools, sources of training included the district office, local universities, and even such nontraditional providers as businesses that offer training in management and group decision making. These successful schools also expanded the range of content areas for training beyond the typical areas of curriculum and instruction to include participation in decision making, leadership responsibilities (e.g., running meetings, budgeting, interviewing), and the process of school improvement.

3. *Create a well-developed system for sharing school-related information with a broad range of constituents.* The schools where SBM worked used many communication mechanisms to share information. In these schools, information flowed to the school from the central office but it also circulated within the school and flowed out from the school to the community. Multiple decision-making groups collected and dispensed information within the school and informed parents and the community. In addition, more kinds of information were regularly disseminated in successful SBM schools, including information about innovations going on in other schools, districts, and states and information about school performance.

Most of the successful SBM schools were systematic and creative in their efforts to communicate with parents and the community. They relied as much on face-to-face communication as on formal documents. These schools also had a strong "customer service" orientation. Many conducted annual parent and community surveys and used the results to help set priorities for the following year. The principals in schools where SBM worked often attended many different types of meetings at which external constituents, such as representatives of local businesses, were present to discuss school activities. Another common practice in successful SBM schools was regular dissemination to parents of data on daily attendance and tardiness. Parent/teacher conferences and newsletters were also used as information channels. Several schools used grant money to install voice mail for classroom teachers, while one school hired a part-time ombudsman to serve as a liaison between the school and the parents.

4. *Develop ways to reward staff behavior that helps achieve school objectives.* Where SBM worked, the school community rewarded effort and recognized improved performance. Many principals at successful SBM schools regularly recognized individuals for work done well; in other effective schools, principals preferred to recognize group efforts. The principals used various extrinsic reward strategies, including "pats of the back" and notes of appreciation. The principal of one high school began every faculty meeting with a "thank you" list. We also heard about teachers recognizing one another's efforts informally and about parents holding "thank you" luncheons for teachers.

A few schools used monetary rewards. Such rewards took a variety of forms, including differented staffing positions that provided extra compensation for administrative responsibilities, funding for professional development, and grants to reimburse teachers for extra time spent on management.

Where SBM worked, many teachers were excited and motivated by the climate of professional collaboration and learning in their schools. However, some teachers who had been working with SBM for longer than four years were tired and wondered whether they could maintain their level of involvement. The argument that intrinsic rewards, such as opportunities to innovate and to be effective with students, are sufficient to motivate and reinforce teachers for engaging in SBM over the long haul may be too optimistic. The use of extrinsic rewards, in combination with other incentives, might help reduce the fatigue factor and sustain the reform effort.

5. *Select principals who can facilitate and manage change.* The schools where SBM worked had principals who played a key role in dispersing power, in promoting a school-wide commitment to learning, in expecting all teachers to participate in the work of the school, in collecting information about student learning, and in distributing rewards. The principals were often described as facilitators and managers of change, as strong supporters of their staffs, and as the people who brought innovation to their schools and moved reform forward.

Such principals tended to delegate to subcommittees such responsibilities as the selection of materials, the development of budgets, and the scheduling of professional development activities. What emerged was leadership shared by a broad range of individuals throughout the school. For example, in some cases teachers took the lead in introducing ideas about new instructional practices. The most successful principals were the ones who worked to coordinate the efforts of teacher leaders so that they involved entire faculties and so that all efforts were oriented toward the school vision. Aside from formal collaboration, principals in schools where SBM worked also fostered informal communities by scheduling common lunch periods for students and staff members and common break time for teachers.

6. *Use district, state, or national guidelines to focus reform efforts and to target changes in curriculum and instruction.* School-based management exerted more leverage for change when adopted in the context of a set of curricular guidelines. Developed variously at the district, state, and national levels, such guidelines provided direction for the reform of curriculum and instruction.[10] Many of the people we interviewed said that guidelines—in the form of performance standards, curriculum frameworks, or assessment systems—specified the "what" of the curriculum, leaving the "how" up to them. The guidelines also set boundaries within which schools could create their own visions or improvement plans outlining the instructional direction of the school. These documents articulated what the school was all about and served as a focus for its reform activities.

## IMPLICATIONS FOR POLICY AND PRACTICE

We have described the conditions that make schools effective or ineffective in using SBM to improve teaching and learning. SBM is a large-scale change that requires long-term process. When policy makers adopt SBM, they need to plan for change at all levels of the education system. The lessons about what makes SBM work suggest a set of action steps or initiatives that district and state administrators can take to help schools implement SBM in ways that enhance school performance.

- Work together with union officials to remove as many constraints as possible to give school-level decision makers greater flexibility in the areas of budget and personnel. Strategies might include providing schools with lump sum budgets, allowing schools to recruit and select staff members, and giving schools the authority to design their own decision-making apparatus.
- Offer direction for curriculum and instruction reform through the creation of an instructional guidance system that includes standards,

curriculum frameworks, and assessment components. Within this context, schools must be allowed considerable discretion to determine how to deliver the curriculum.

- Create a set-aside for professional development and training at both the district and school levels. Such set-asides amount to from 3% to 5% of each budget. In addition, administrators can promote alternative modes of professional development that allow for training in usual topics, conducted by different service providers, at nonschool training sites, and using unusual instructional approaches.
- Invest in building a district-wide computer network to allow schools access to information from the central office regarding resources, student performance, and teacher performance. This network will enhance each school's capacity to monitor its own performance. Districts could also conduct an annual or biennial survey of parents and other community members regarding satisfaction with the schools.
- Promote the sharing of information across levels through the establishment of state-level office of reform assistance and dissemination and an electronic communications network.
- Encourage experimentation with compensation systems that connect rewards with desired behaviors. For example, trying innovative instructional practices, helping to design new curricular modules, and becoming actively involved in school decision making are the kinds of behaviors that might be rewarded.[11]

SBM requires new roles and responsibilities for schools. But an equally important requirement is that district and state administrators move away from telling schools what to do and instead offer services and provide incentives for school-level change.

Our findings suggest that the creation of school-site councils—typically the first step in implementing SBM—will not automatically result in improved performance. SBM must be augmented by a range of school-, district-, and state-level strategies that facilitate interactions involving various stakeholders and that provide a direction for those interactions. SBM can act as the facilitator of school improvement. But when it is implemented narrowly as a political reform that merely shifts power from the central office to schools, SBM is an inadequate effort to improve school performance.

## NOTES

1. The international work was supported by grants from the Carnegie Corporation of New York and the Finance Center of the Consortium for Policy Research in Education. I would also like to thank members of the research team from the University of Southern California (Kerri Briggs, Susan Albers Mohrman, Peter Robertson, Roxanne Smyer, and Amy Van Kirk) and from the University of Wisconsin, Madison (Allan Odden, Eleanor Odden, John Smithson, and Paula White).

2. A comprehensive discussion of the design, methods, and results of our study is provided in Susan Albers Mohrman, Priscilla Wohlstetter, and Peter J. Robertson, *Reforming Schools Through School-based Management: Lessons from Research* (forthcoming).

3. Priscilla Wohlstetter and Susan Albers Mohrman, *School-based Management: Promise and Process* (New Brunswick, N.J., Consortium for Policy Research in Education, Rutgers University, 1994); and Eleanor R. Odden and Priscilla Wohlstetter, "Making School-Based Management Work," *Educational Leadership,* February 1995, pp. 32–36.

4. See also Helen Marks and Karen Seashore Louis, *Does Teacher Empowerment Affect the Classroom? The Implications of Teacher Empowerment for Teachers' Instructional Practice and Student Academic Performance* (Madison: Center on Organization and Restructuring of Schools, University of Wisconsin, 1995).

5. For additional information about the changing role of the principal in restructured schools, see Priscilla Wohlstetter and Kerri L. Briggs, "The Principal's Role in School-Based Management," *Principal,* November 1994, pp. 14–17; and Kent Peterson and Valli Warren, "Changes in School Governance and Principals' Roles," in Joseph Murphy and Karen Seashore Louis, Eds., *Reshaping the Principalship: Insights from Transformational Reform Efforts* (Thousand Oaks, Calif.: Corwin Press, 1994), pp. 219–36.

6. Anthony Bryk et al., "The State of Chicago School Reform," *Phi Delta Kappan,* September 1994, pp. 74–78. This article also makes the point that adversarial politics can lead to unfocused reform and make systematic change unlikely.

7. David Marsh, "Change in Schools: Lessons from the Literature," in Susan Albers Mohrman et al., Eds., *School-Based Management: Organizing for High Performance* (San Francisco: Jossey-Bass, 1994), pp. 215–51; and Susan Albers Mohrman and Priscilla Wohlstetter, "Understanding and Managing the Change Process," in Mohrman et al., pp. 253–68. See also Joseph Murphy and Lynn G. Beck, *School-Based Management as School Reform: Taking Stock* (Thousand Oaks, Calif.: Corwin Press, 1995) for a detailed discussion of the costs associated with SBM.

8. Ann Lieberman, "Practices That Support Teacher Development: Transforming Conceptions of Professional Learning," *Phi Delta Kappan,* April 1995, pp. 591–96. Lieberman offers interesting approaches for structuring professional development in ways that support learning.

9. Jane David, *School-Based Decision Making: Linking Decisions to Learning* (Palo Alto, Calif.: Bay Area Research Group, 1994). In this third-year report to the Prichard Committee, David stresses the importance of giving schools lots of opportunities to learn and time to learn, if SBM is to work.

10. Susan Fuhrman, *Politics and Systemic Education Reform* (New Brunswick, N.J.: Consortium for Policy Research in Education, Rutgers University, 1994).

11. For some interesting ideas about this topic, see Sharon Conley and Allan Odden, "Linking Teacher Compensation to Teacher Career Development," *Educational Evaluation and Policy Analysis,* vol. 17, 1995, pp. 219–37; and Allan M. Mohrman, Jr., Susan Albers Mohrman, and Allan Odden, "Aligning Teacher Compensation with Systemic School Reform: Skill-Based Pay and Group-Based Performance Rewards," *Educational Evaluation and Policy Analysis,* in press.

# Learning from School Restructuring

by Penelope L. Peterson, Sarah J. McCarthey, and Richard F. Elmore

*We analyzed cases of restructuring experiments in three elementary schools, each with ethnically diverse populations, located in large urban school districts in different parts of the United States. Over two years, we gathered data on views and classroom writing practices of two teachers in each school through on-site interviews and observations. We also interviewed the principal and other support personnel. We found that these three schools did successfully restructure; changes included new student grouping patterns, new ways of allocating time for subject matter, teachers meeting together as a whole school or in teams, and access to new ideas through professional development opportunities. Through close analyses of teachers' classroom practices, we learned that changing teachers' practice is primarily a problem of learning, not a problem of organization. While school structures can provide opportunities for learning new practices, the structures, by themselves, do not cause the learning to occur.*

In the late 1980s, *restructuring* became a key word in the language of contemporary education reform to characterize changes needed in the organizational structure of schools. The purpose of restructuring was to transform the nature of teachers' work and to recognize governance systems (Elmore & Associates, 1990; Tyack, 1990). At the center of debate on school reform is the idea that, by changing ways in which schools are organized, educators can change how teachers teach and increase the opportunities for student learning. On the face of it, this seems plausible, especially because impediments to good teaching have been located in the lack of supportive school contexts (Sarason, 1982, 1990; Sirotnik, 1986).

From *American Educational Research Journal,* 1996, vol. 33, no. 1, pp. 119–153. © 1996 by American Educational Research Association (AERA). Reprinted with permission.

For example, the traditional organization of the school day into short periods of time designed to cover a multitude of subjects and unrelated topics makes the job of an elementary teacher demanding. The traditional division of labor with one teacher responsible for 25–30 students for the entire day also seems to prevent the sharing of knowledge and contributes to teacher isolation (Little & McLaughlin, 1993). Additionally, teachers have felt little influence over the substantive decisions that affect their classrooms—such as, curricula, class size, and testing (Cuban, 1984). This lack of influence over larger issues may result in an expression of authority and control and fragmentation of knowledge at the classroom level (McNeil, 1986). It seems entirely plausible that changing the features of school organization to reorganize the school day, reduce teacher isolation, and increase teacher decision making would result in better teaching and learning for students. This article explores that seemingly straightforward connection between school organization and classroom practice through the cases of three schools' restructuring efforts.

### Issues in Restructuring

Restructuring rests on the assumption that changes in school organization and the workplace conditions for teachers will result in changes in teachers' and students' roles and the provision of new opportunities for student learning in the classroom. For example, Kentucky's plan to restructure schools opens with the ideas that schools ought to provide instructional programs that are tailored to individual learning styles and abilities of students and that

> teachers cannot adapt their teaching to the unique learning needs of children unless they have flexibility in the selection of teaching methods and instructional materials, in the use of both student and teacher time, and in the use of space and other school resources (Wilkinson, n.d., p. 1)

The plan implies a direct connection between structural changes, teachers' practices, and student learning by asserting the need to change a "top-down bureaucratic organization into one based on professional practice" and suggesting that such change "involves altering long-standing patterns of decision-making, resource allocation and work" (p. 2).

Sympathetic critics of restructuring conceptions have focused on four problems. The first problem is the lack of consensus about a definition (Elmore & Associates, 1990; Tyack, 1990). Restructuring efforts vary from changes in governance structures, such as parent choice plans, to changes in districts and schools reflected in school-based management plans, to changes in curriculum and instruction such as collaborative learning (Murphy, 1991; Newman, 1992). A second problem in the talk about restructuring is isolation from any specific purposes. While advocates embrace the goals of "depth of understanding" and "new roles for teachers" (Newman, 1992), they often fail to specify how these practices operate in particular school contexts.

> **Efforts at reorganization—despite prevailing rhetoric—often have more to do with politics than with greater efficiency and enhanced quality.**

Third, although an implicit assumption of restructuring efforts is the causal connection between organization and teaching and learning, this connection is relatively unspecified. Advocates suggest that teachers should have more collaborative planning time, students should work together in groups, and schools should have more opportunities for increased contact between teachers and students. However, Murphy (1991) states, "efforts at reorganization—despite prevailing rhetoric—often have more to do with politics than with greater efficiency and enhanced quality" (p. 76). Fourth, critics have noted that the process of going from structural changes to enhanced teaching and learning is not clearly understood. While schools need to be staffed by teachers and principals who already possess the vision and capability of leading change efforts, they cannot postpone change until most of the staff demonstrates commitment or no change would ever occur (Newman, 1992). These criticisms highlight the dilemmas that accompany efforts at school change.

### Research on Innovation and Teacher Change

A continual dilemma in research on school change is that, although schools are constantly engaging in activities designed to effect change in response to external pressures, they seldom change their essential patterns of organization (Sarason, 1982, 1990; Sirotnik, 1986). When schools do change, the changes are seldom sustained, and teachers do not attribute change to external forces (Elmore, 1991). Fullan (1991) provides an explanation for why this might be the case: "It is possible to change on the surface by endorsing goals, using specific materials, and even imitating the behavior without specifically understanding the principles and rationale for change" (p. 40). Building on the work of other researchers examining change (Cuban, 1984; Little & McLaughlin, 1993; Sarason, 1982, 1990), Fullan has identified many of the problems in achieving successful change. He has suggested that educators must "redesign the workplace so that innovation and improvement are built into the daily activities of teachers" (p. 353). However, the nature of the relationship between these efforts to redesign the workplace and teaching practice and student learning remain elusive. Richardson (1990) suggested that while

> teacher-change literature provides a way of thinking about systemic change, and the importance of the organization and its norms in the change process . . . the conceptual framework within which the research is conducted does not include a conception of individual teacher change. (p. 13)

She argued for the need for researchers to focus on individual teachers' cognitions, knowledge, and actions and to consider the content of the change being advocated.

In the late 1980s, reformers advocated major innovations and changes in classroom practice aimed at teaching for understanding or ambitious teaching (Marshall, 1992; Cohen, McLaughlin, & Talbert, 1993). Advocates subscribe to more student-centered pedagogy, in which students' ideas and understandings are the focus of concern in the classroom. They are committed to engaging students in active learning using a more constructivist approach. They also want students of diverse abilities and backgrounds to work together and to have equal access to learning and literacy previously reserved for only the gifted or a privileged few (Bereiter & Scardamalia, 1987; Resnick, 1987).

Nowhere are these ideas about teaching for understanding and ambitious teaching more evident than in current reform efforts aimed at improving classroom practice in the area of writing. Derived from cognitive and transactional views of rhetoric (Berlin, 1987), these approaches advance the notion of the writing process as a recursive set of practices including prewriting, drafting, and revising (Emig, 1971; Flower & Hayes, 1981). Educators, including those associated with the National Writing Project (see Gray, cited in Gomez, 1988; Calkins, 1986; Graves, 1983), have transformed these ideas into applicable classroom suggestions such as writing conferences, in which the teacher or peers meet with the author, and the *author's chair,* in which all students share their work with others. These efforts are directed toward encouraging teachers and students to spend more time composing original, purposeful texts in a variety of forms.

In this study, we address the problem of trying to understand the nature of restructuring in relation to its effects on teaching practice in writing within the context of three schools in different parts of the United States.

> **Educators must "redesign the workplace so that innovation and improvement are built into the daily activities of teachers."**

## METHOD

Over two years, we gathered data on the restructuring experiments in three elementary schools, each with ethnically diverse student populations, located in large urban school districts in different parts of the United States. In a more complete report of this project (see Elmore, Peterson, & McCarthey, 1996), we provide case analyses of the literary, scientific, and/or mathematical practices of four individual teachers at each school in relation to the school-wide restructuring efforts. Here, we briefly present the ways in which writing is taught by two teachers from each school and examine how these changes in practice are linked to school-level changes.

### Participants

The three schools were selected based on their undertaking school-wide restructuring. After an initial site visit to each school, teachers volunteered to be interviewed and observed three times over the course of two years. Participants at each school included the principal, classroom teachers, and support staff, such as the school psychologist, librarian, or art teacher. The two teachers at each school studied for this article each taught writing; each school considered changing writing practices an important feature of their restructuring efforts.

### Observations

We conducted full-day classroom observations in which the teacher wore a wireless microphone, supplemented by "dish" microphones which provided data on student-student interactions. Observations focused on the tasks teachers assigned and interactions between teacher and student and among students. We also collected samples of student writing and made copies for later analysis. We attended at least one staff meeting at each school, spent time in the teachers' lounge, and attended assemblies or other relevant activities to get a picture of the school culture.

> To probe teachers' underlying conceptions of learning, we developed questions and scenarios.

### Interviews With Classroom Teachers

We interviewed the principal, classrooms teachers, and support personnel at each school. Before visiting the schools for the first time, we interviewed each of the teachers by telephone for approximately one hour. Questions focused on teachers' goals, specific concepts they were teaching, and examples of activities and materials used. We attempted to get as much contextual detail about teachers' classrooms as we could before entering their rooms.

We developed two interview protocols for the classroom teachers: (a) new roles and (b) post-observation formats. The new roles protocol focused on three main areas: (a) decision making, (b) collegiality and collaboration, and (c) conceptions of teaching and learning literacy. In the first interview, we asked teachers to describe their personal histories, their roles within the school, and the types of influence they had over decisions at the school level such as resources, curriculum, and evaluation. The second interview focused on teachers' interactions with their colleagues. In the third interview, we asked teachers to reflect on their own learning by asking about their strengths, involvement in staff development activities, and their beliefs about a school-wide philosophy. To probe teachers' underlying conceptions of learning, we developed questions and scenarios. Beginning with the lesson we observed that day, we asked teachers to reflect on students' engagement, interest, and learning. We then asked teachers about students' learning in the beginning of the year and at the end of the year, continually requesting specific examples of student learning. We then presented several literacy scenarios describing the practices of three different hypothetical teachers, each enacting literacy practices consonant with either an information-processing, Piagetian developmental, or social constructivist approach to learning (see McCarthey & Raphael, 1992). Teachers were asked a series of questions about which hypothetical teacher was the most like themselves and why. Follow-up probes consisted of questions about teacher roles, tasks, and opportunities for student learning.

> **Much of the interview focused on curricular goals, changes, and teacher's pedagogical strategies.**

Postobservation interview questions focused on the specific lessons observed. We asked about materials, tasks, and representations that the teacher had used, specific events that had occurred, and individual children. Our goal was to get as much insight as possible about the teacher's intentions, conceptions of teaching and children, and rationale for selection of tasks.

### Interviews With Principals and Support Personnel

We conducted two-hour interviews with each principal on several occasions. At Lakeview School, we held one two-hour interview in person with the first principal, Laurel Daniels, and a two-hour telephone follow-up interview in the summer.[1] We interviewed the second principal, Cathy Channing, on two occasions, for two hours each time. At Webster, we interviewed Cheryl Billings for two hours, on two occasions. We interviewed Northeastern's principal, Luisa Montoya, on two occasions for two hours.

The first interview consisted of questions about the school's restructuring efforts such as the school history, philosophy, structure, schedule, student grouping, decision making, staff development, and evaluation. Much of the interview focused on curricular goals, changes, and teacher's pedagogical strategies. In the second interview, we asked the principals to respond to the same scenarios we gave the teachers to probe their beliefs about student learning. These interviews provided lengthy descriptions of the principals' viewpoints about school level and classroom level changes.

We interviewed support personnel such as the art teacher, psychologist, and others from each school who worked with teachers and students to provide their perceptions of school changes. At Webster, we also interviewed classroom teachers who acted in particular roles such as the writing specialist and the cooperative learning specialist. Questions focused on issues of school restructure, roles, goals, curriculum, decision making, and collaboration among teachers. We were interested in how the support personnel fit into the overall restructuring efforts.

### Analyses

All interview and observational data were transcribed verbatim. Using analytic induction (Goetz & LeCompte, 1981), our analyses began by gathering and comparing demographic data about schools, teachers, and students. Looking for emergent patterns, we read the interviews several times and wrote summaries of the school histories and school level changes. We developed the categories of physical workplace, collegiality, teacher roles within the school, decision making, and opportunities for professional development to compare the three schools' practices.

To examine the classroom level practices, we drew from both interview and observational data. We looked for overall patterns and key events in teachers' writing practices and then looked to the postobservation interview data for ways in which the teachers made sense of those events. Each researcher independently summarized the event and the significance and then discussed it with the others, looking for alternative explanations. We then looked for patterns within individual teachers, and then within a school, and finally we compared practices across schools.

We recognize that it is difficult to capture the complexity of teaching writing over time and to compare the practices of different teachers in a few pages. Therefore, in presenting the vignettes from the teachers' cases, we selected the ones that were most representative of the entire set of observations. We provide only glimpses of teachers' practices because of space constraints but also in an effort to balance presentation of data with analysis of larger patterns.

The process of within- and between-school comparison was somewhat iterative as we compared and contrasted teachers and schools throughout our analytical process. Triangulation (Lincoln & Gruba, 1985) occurred through the use of several sources of data and continual comparisons and challenges to each other's assertions. Observational data is limited because we only have three collection points. Although we only draw from two teachers' data from each school here, support for our conclusions is increased by having at least six teacher participants from each school contributing to the overall picture (see Elmore et al., 1996).

## CASES OF THREE SCHOOLS' RESTRUCTURING EFFORTS

We found that these three schools did successfully restructure in accordance with the school's own vision of restructuring. The restructuring efforts of the three schools shared four key features.[2] First, all three schools had some type of vision or philosophy related to student learning that was enacted through structural changes. These structural changes which included new patterns of student grouping and new ways of allocating time for subject matter, were significantly different from the ways in which most schools are organized. Second, teachers met together to discuss curriculum and instruction, either as a whole school or in teams. Third, teachers at the three schools were all involved in shared decision making about personnel, resources, and curriculum and instruction. Fourth, teachers had access to new ideas about instruction either through staff development or through ongoing discussions about teaching.

> **All three schools had some type of vision or philosophy related to student learning that was enacted through structural changes.**

Although these features were reflected in school level changes at all three schools, the ways in which they were enacted differed from one another, and the responses at the classroom level also differed significantly. In the next section, we explore these changes on a school-by-school basis. Within each school, we consider two teachers' literacy practices in the area of writing as a site for investigating how restructuring efforts played out within classrooms.

### Lakeview School: Facilitating Expression and Esteem— Is It Enough?

Lakeview School is an urban elementary school composed of an ethnically diverse group of approximately 245 students located in the northwestern United States. About 55% of the students are classified as minority students (including African American, Asian, Latino, and Native Americans), and 30% of the students receive free or reduced lunch. Many students were bussed to the school as part of the district's desegregation plan, and, during the 1989–1990 school year, Lakeview became a "school of choice" because the district had moved to implement a new choice plan.

Over five years, restructuring efforts at Lakeview School took
the form of changes in organizational structures, new roles for teachers, and the introduction of curricular reforms. Organizational
changes involved teachers becoming part of one of three teams: a K-first
grade team, a second-third grade team, and a fourth-fifth grade team.
Each team consisted of three or four classroom teachers and specialists. The school eliminated all pull-out programs for Chapter 1 and
special education and, instead, organized students according to
achievement levels for instruction in reading and math. Within
classes, students were grouped heterogeneously for theme units and
other subjects. The school day was restructured to accommodate
teachers' sharing of instructional time blocks and meeting together
in teams for planning instruction. Teachers participated in shared decision making about personnel, resources, curriculum and instruction.

The original principal, Laurel Daniels, supplied the vision
behind the restructuring efforts of Lakeview and introduced three
major curricular innovations. Her vision included grouping students
in flexible ways to go through the curriculum at their own pace and
to learn in their own styles. Curricular innovations included implementing the "whole book approach," based on a whole language
philosophy in reading; adopting the innovative textbook, *Real Math*
(Willoughby, Bereiter, Hilton, & Rubenstein, 1987), for the teaching
of elementary mathematics; and using theme units for integrating
science and social studies. Writing was emphasized and all teachers
were expected to involve students in daily writing activities. Greg
Crandall, a primary grade teacher, was the key figure in providing
information about whole language and process writing to the school
because he was involved in a master's program at a nearby university where these approaches were stressed.

Staff development occurred through a series of school-wide
mini workshops exploring different topics including cooperative
learning and students' learning styles (McCarthy, 1980). The principal and teachers also participated in retreats to develop faculty
morale and school-wide themes.

These restructuring efforts resulted in a strong sense of team
spirit and increased morale. Teachers valued Lakeview's emphasis
on self-esteem and personal support. Laurel Daniels was the key figure in providing a supportive environment for two teachers who had
personal problems affecting their professional lives. In the cases of
Peg Ernst and Lynn Horn, Daniels made changes in the organizational

structure to accommodate the needs for teachers. For Peg Ernst, who had suffered from what she called "teacher burnout," Daniels helped negotiate a reduced contract after her leave of absence before Peg assumed full-time teaching responsibilities. The reduced contract served as a transition period for Peg to regain her confidence in teaching children and conducting other professional activities. Peg credits Laurel with having developed an open, encouraging, and trusting school environment that allowed her to become a successful teacher who recovered from burnout. Peg attributed changes in her own teaching to the former principal, Laurel, by saying, "We have to give her credit; she's just been a wonderful person to work with. I think a lot of these changes that we've made are due to her."

In the case of Lynn Horn, who suffered from cancer, Laurel developed the teacher's personal and professional strengths by setting up a situation in which Lynn taught one section each of mathematics and writing in the morning and art in the afternoons so that Lynn would not have the full-time responsibilities of a self-contained classroom. A European-American woman in her fifties, Lynn Horn felt that she had been, for most of her life, a square peg in a round hole. She saw herself as having been constrained from personal self-expression for much of her life because of the social community in which she lived. She had been a nun and lived in a convent where she was "just bashed and bashed and bashed" until she finally realized that she "could be destroyed." After these experiences, Lynn felt she was suffering from burnout, and, even after she came to Lakeview, she was just a "little island" unto herself until Laurel came to the school. Lynn credited Laurel with having created a professional work situation that was adapted to her and allowed her to express her own special needs, interests, and strengths. Lynn also felt that Laurel had attempted to create a feeling among the staff that was like that of a family where individuals cared about one another and valued individuals' strengths.

Lakeview staff members had come to believe that it was essential to provide a supportive, collegial environment because it would promote risk-taking and personal growth for both students and teachers. Teachers' self-esteem, nurtured by a supportive school setting, would then result in the provision of a safe environment where students could take risks in their own learning.

How did these ideas play out in practice in the classroom? We investigate this question by analyzing one selected writing episode from each teacher's classroom. These episodes reflect general patterns consistent with the teaching for the classroom. Perhaps because of their own personal experiences, both Ernst and Horn focused on students' self-esteem and on providing students with opportunities for self-expression through the writing curriculum in their classrooms.

### Writing in Peg Ernst's Classroom: Supporting Students' Self-Esteem

The atmosphere in Ernst's K–first grade classroom was both lively and comfortable. Students freely walked about the room for materials and asked other students for help. Ernst dashed around the room helping students get organized, putting her arms around her young students, and listening to their stories, problems, and questions.

Ernst introduced students to the writing topic, balloons, by bringing in a balloon for children to feel and discuss. Ernst gathered students at the back of the room and explained that she would give everyone a chance to touch the balloon. She asked students to think about how it would feel to be a balloon, to pretend the balloon had eyes and think about the things it could see, or to imagine what could happen to the balloon as it floated by when the wind came up. Ernst then asked students to provide ideas about what might happen to the balloon. After students responded and touched the balloon, Ernst told students that for their "journaling" (writing or drawing on paper), they were to get a piece of paper and with crayons or felt pens draw a picture of a balloon and write about what it would be like to be a balloon or write about how a balloon feels. When students began to draw and write on paper, Ernst circulated among individuals talking briefly with them. Her style of interaction was supportive—she praised students, got additional materials such as pens for them, and wrote words on the paper for them.

Excerpts from the classroom dialogue illustrate how Ernst worked with individual students. Ernst leaned down beside one child, Sammy, who told her that he had made a balloon. Ernst responded, "Oh, you made a hot air balloon. What a good idea. I didn't think of that. You're so creative." To Sean, Ernst commented, "Well, that's beautiful, yeah. Tell me what yours says? I want . . .?" Sean completed the sentence: "to be a balloon." Ernst responded,

"Oh, a balloon! Isn't that neat?" She continued to circulate around the room encouraging students with brief, supportive comments.

Ernst's interactions in the classroom reflected her personal concerns with self-esteem and building confidence as expressed in her interviews. She talked with many students about their writing in a short period, and she talked with students in ways that encouraged them. Yet her interactions were limited to continued praise of students' work; she did not attempt to extend or question their ideas or have students elaborate on them. Instead, she accepted everyone's idea without consideration of effective communication or idea development. Student work reflected Ernst's concerns. Because Ernst had selected the topic, students' writing seemed uninspired and was not elaborated. It appeared constrained by the necessity of writing about balloons. However, students did have opportunities to write daily, and they were supported in their efforts by Ernst.

### Writing in Lynn Horn's Classroom: "Facilitating" Self-Expression

In her teaching of fine art and language, Horn was guided by her belief that her role was to facilitate children's self-expression; she taught poetry as a means of encouraging it and enriching the lives of her students. She volunteered that, while some Lakeview children had "enriching experiences," with books and poetry at home, for example, other children didn't. LaShaunda, a fourth-grade African-American girl, was an example of a child who didn't. Horn described LaShaunda as "very stilted creatively" although she had "written a lot of darling stories."

We observed Horn teach poetry to a class of third and fourth graders. During that lesson, the students worked on writing concrete poems at their seats with Horn worked with individual students to correct the clerihew poems they had written on a previous day. Horn described the clerihew as a "simple poetry form—a form of couplet." The following dialogue occurred when LaShaunda brought her clerihew to Ms. Horn for correcting. Ms. Horn (H.) began by reading the first line of LaShaunda's (L.) clerihew aloud:

> H: "Little Annie found a dog." Alright. Big dog, little dog, puppy dog, describe your dog.
> L: It's a puppy dog.

H: Oh. "Found a little puppy dog." *(On LaShaunda's paper, Ms. Horn rewrote the first line of the clerihew to read: "Little Annie found a little puppy dog!")*

H: *(reads from LaShaunda's paper):* "Then she found a little hog." That's cute, but let's put some cute little words in there with it. Well, "then she"—those aren't exciting words. Here—you found this little puppy dog, and you're cuddling it and taking it home, and you heard these little . . . oink, oink, oink, oink, oink, oink, oink, oink. My golly! We're not alone! I not only have a little puppy dog for a pet, but a . . .

L: A cute . . .

H: Piglet hog. We'll call it a piglet hog because it's tiny, huh? Was the piglet following you?

L: Yeah.

H: Mmm, 'kay.

L: I had to carry them home.

H: Was it close behind you, or was it a block down the street?

L: It was close . . .

H: Alright, "then close behind her," *(Horn wrote this on LaShaunda's paper as she said it.)* Did she hear it before she saw it?

L: Yeah.

H: She saw a piglet hog. *(Horn wrote this as she said it.)* We'll put piglet hog; that sort of sounds silly, but don't want to, unless you want a great big one?

L: No, not a big one.

H: *(reading from what she had written):* Little Annie found a little puppy dog; then close behind her she saw a piglet hog."

In interviews, Horn described herself as a *facilitator*. As a facilitator, she didn't want to push her values or her words on her students. Rather, she would "drop little subtle hints to get the mind working." She wanted to enhance students' vocabulary skills and, for example, to get rid of the words like *nice* and *good*. And from her own perspective, Horn *was* a facilitator in this interaction because she began the interaction by questioning LaShaunda about her ideas and her words. Horn asked LaShaunda to describe the piglet, its size, and its location, and then she used LaShaunda's ideas in the subsequent rewriting of the poem. She proceeded by giving LaShaunda hints about what words might fit into the poem. Consistent with her perspective on teaching vocabulary skills in context, Horn turned the words *little hog* into the "more exciting words" *piglet hog.*

But from another perspective, Horn appeared less supportive and facilitative than she thought. For example, Horn took the pen, crossed out LaShaunda's words, and rewrote the poem in her words and in her own writing. Further, without querying LaShaunda about what ideas she was trying to express, Ms. Horn suggested that LaShaunda's words and ideas were lacking or insufficient when she said, "Those aren't nice words," and "No, no. You don't give a bone to a pig," and "You don't want to feed her a mouse." LaShaunda did little talking, and her talking was directed by Ms. Horn. The discourse was convergent and followed a course determined by Ms. Horn with scant influence from the student. Horn did both the thinking and the expressing in this episode, not LaShaunda.

### Reflections on Esteem and Expression: The Cases of Ernst and Horn

These two cases suggest that school level changes related to classroom changes in complex and interactive ways. In the case of Ernst, school level norms were reflected more obviously at the classroom level—she felt valued at the school level, and, in turn, she strove to support her students' self esteem and written expression. In the case of Horn, school level changes were reflected less apparently in her classroom practice. Horn was supported by Daniels; she had regained lost morale and self-esteem, and she herself had achieved a greater fit for her own creativity at Lakeview than in previous settings. Her own experiences of regained self-esteem and support for individual expression were reflected in the goals she embraced for students—increased confidence and ability and willingness to express themselves. Yet it could be argued that Horn failed to inspire confidence or support students' own expressive efforts. In responding to student's writing, Horn negated their ideas and imposed her own ideas and style.

What might explain the different relations among the espoused beliefs and classroom practices of these two teachers? An important difference was apparent between Ernst and Horn in what led them to revise their classroom practice and their different approaches to learning. Although both teachers endorsed the need to change their practices on an ongoing basis and they provided evidence of having made specific changes in their own practices, they differed in their reflectivity on their own teaching practice and, specifically, in their reports of what led them to revise their classroom practice. Both Ernst and Horn felt that growth was highly valued at Lakeview. But for Peg Ernst, changes in her teaching came about through growth in her own learning. Ernst believed that "the way you grow is to look at what you're doing, and you have to tear it apart. You can't be afraid to look at everything." Ernst described how she learned by reflecting on her teaching practice. She focused particularly on her relationships with students and their relationships with one another. She also stressed the importance of analyzing critically her own teaching in terms of its effects on students' self esteem and on her relationships with students. Although Horn also viewed revision of her practice as important, she described a different process of revising her practice than her colleague did. In her own teaching of writing, Horn focused considerably less on students' abilities and dispositions to express themselves than did Ernst. Rather, Horn focused on her own expression, and her teaching reflected her own desire to express herself: "I think poetry is a lost art and want to enhance my own expertise by experimenting."

> **Ernst and Horn felt that growth was highly valued at Lakeview.**

Although on the surface, Horn's classroom practice appeared less consistent with school level reforms than did Ernst's, deeper analyses revealed more coherence than was apparent initially. From Horn's point of view, Lakeview was engaged in innovation, growth, and change. This orientation toward experimentation and creativity fit with Horn's own learning and teaching styles. Horn also was supported by Daniels for her "strengths" of expression and creativity.

### Learning from the Case of Lakeview

Both Ernst and Horn believed they had created new classroom practices in response to school level reforms. Both Ernst and Horn had changed their classroom practices in having students write much more than they ever had before. Written production and fluency of expression are worthy goals of schooling. Yet are written production and expression sufficient if they are not learned and taught within contexts of disciplined discourse with teachers who explicitly consider standards, quality, and norms?

One insight we gain from our analyses of Lakeview and the practices of Ernst and Horn is that how teaching and learning occur may be more a function of teachers' and students' beliefs, under-standings, and behaviors in the context of specific problems of class-room practice than a function of specific structures. As a result of school-wide structural changes, these two teachers entered into dif-ferent relationships with each other and with their students. These new arrangements for teaching students created new demands on the teachers to consider their work in different ways. Yet because teach-ing practice is tightly bound by the context of the classroom, in the sense that what is real for teachers and students is what goes on in the classroom, changing structures did not necessarily make substan-tial differences in practice.

To have meaning and to be useful, the reforms must have mean-ing in terms of the daily work of teachers. If code words and phrases embodied in reform (e.g., "teacher as facilita-tor") are not discussed among teachers and with reformers, then individual teachers con-struct different meanings of these terms and carry out different, related practices in their classrooms. Moreover, Lakeview teachers explicitly embraced the idea that each of them would have different beliefs and prac-tices because teachers had different "learning styles" and "teaching styles." These stylistic differences were a valued part of the principal's restructuring and professional development efforts at the school level.

> **To have meaning and to be useful, the reforms must have meaning in terms of the daily work of teachers.**

Lakeview teachers met in teams. However, team meetings gen-erally served as a place for discussion of school routines and proce-dures rather than for discussion or sharing of ideas about curriculum and learning. Although teachers participated in a series of profes-sional development workshops organized by Daniels, the "real" teacher learning at Lakeview seemed to be more of an individual affair that took place in different ways for each teacher. Peg Ernst was attempting to learn and reflect on her own practice, but she did not have access to other practitioners with whom she might discuss substantive issues of writing or ways to extend students' work. Her knowledge of the writing process was superficial, and she had lim-ited access to ideas about writing because she depended on Greg, her colleague, whose own understandings were partial and incomplete (see Peterson & McCarthey, 1991). Lynn Horn focused on the free-dom of developing her own style, which was not necessarily concerned with student learning. For both teachers, their reflection occurred in isolation, and their opportunities for learning within the context of their practices were restricted.

In the case of Webster School, to be described next, we saw teachers also valuing and respecting their own and others' different styles and beliefs. Yet the reform took a slightly different turn because of teacher learning that occurred within the teams and with the support of a district liaison.

*Webster: What Is the Role of Community and Teams*
*in Literacy Learning?*
Located in a major metropolitan area in the central southern United States, Webster is a large elementary school with approximately 500 students in kindergarten through fifth grade. Children are bussed to the school from other areas within the county as part of the school district's desegregation plan. As a result, children in the school represent the ethnic and socioeconomic diversity of the urban metro-politan area with 26% of the school's children coming from African-American families and 25% of the children receiving free or reduced lunch.

The principal, Cheryl Billings, saw the school restructuring captured in Webster School's motto, "Expect the best, achieve suc-cess!" The slogan meshed well with the county school district's vision: "Every leader a teacher; every teacher a leader; every student a success." The county began major restructuring efforts in 1985 when a group of district administrators and principals came together to develop a shared vision for education reform aimed at restructur-ing rules, roles, and responsibilities in the school.

Beginning in 1987, teachers had access to a Professional Devel-opment Center funded by the school district in collaboration with a local private foundation. The center included a professional develop-ment library, curriculum resource center, materials center for special education students, computer education unit, and grants assistance office. During the 1989–1990 school year, the school district pro-vided the Webster School with a staff member, Jay Ross, from the Professional Development Center and the district's restructuring team. Because Jay's special area of expertise was writing and because he had worked on the City's Writing Project (an offshoot of the National Writing Project that began in the San Francisco Bay area), he served as a resource for teachers in the school who wanted to learn new ways of teaching a process approach to writing.

Restructuring efforts began at Webster School in the fall of 1988 following a summer retreat in which the teachers and the principal decided to begin restructuring by piloting two major organizational changes— teaming and multi-age grouping—with two teams of teachers in the school. By the 1990– 1991 school year, staff at the school had chosen to expand teaming and multi-age grouping to include all teachers and students in the school. Teaming meant that four teachers shared responsibility for all the students, approximately 120 children, on their team and, within each team, teachers had a common time to meet and plan together. Multi-age grouping meant that students on each team spanned several grades (e.g., 1st–3rd). A purpose of multi-age grouping was to allow for adaptation to students' learning needs and abilities and to promote success by eliminating the possibility of grade-level retention of students. Although each teacher still taught within a self-contained classroom, students within a team moved from classroom to classroom during the day, and each team's classrooms were grouped next to each other in corners of the school building. Within teams, teachers chose to specialize (i.e., teaching the subjects regarded as their areas of expertise).

> **Multi-age grouping meant that students on each team spanned several grades.**

During the first year of study, the "Snoopy Gang" consisted of four teachers responsible for first, second, and third graders. The next year, the team included three members: Julie Brandt, who taught writing, reading, and science; Joyce Hancock who taught reading, writing, and social studies; and Melissa Benton who taught mathematics and writing. The teachers decided within their team who would be responsible for what subject areas and how to arrange their schedule. We focus here on Brandt and Hancock who shared some common goals in writing but differed in their approaches.

Joyce Hancock had been teaching at Wheeler since it opened 21 years ago. She described herself as the prototypical basal teacher before restructuring; this mean she used the basal reader as the only text, followed the teacher's manual closely, and focused on skills instruction. For the last two years, however, Joyce saw herself as a

convert to literature-based instruction who could never return to her
old ways. Having been at Webster School for four years, Brandt had
assumed the role of leader for the first pilot team when the school
began restructuring. She described herself as having been a traditional teacher who used workbooks and basals prior to restructuring,
although she acknowledged that, when she was a middle-school science teacher, she used many discovery-oriented materials. When we
looked inside Brandt's classroom, we saw her efforts to build a liter-
ate community.

### Writing in Brandt's Classroom:
### Building a Literate Community

During one of the observed sessions that Brandt held with her primary grade classes, she introduced the writing topic by explaining to
students that many of them had discussed their fears during *teacher-
based guidance* (a time each day where students and the teacher discussed important issues in their lives). She then wrote *fear* on the
board and asked students to close their eyes and think of a time they
had felt frightened. She asked students to generate other feelings,
and, after they offered ideas, the students closed their eyes and
remembered some incident in their own lives where they experienced that feeling. Brandt later explained to us that she had students
write about feelings as a topic because she wanted students to write
from their own experiences. Brandt then told students they could use
these ideas to generate written stories.

Students dispersed to write stories on the floor, in the special
writing area, or at tables while Brandt circulated around the room,
assisting individuals or partners. She responded to students according to where they were in their own writing development, focusing
on different aspects of their writing, including getting an idea, story
development, or mechanics such as punctuation. For instance, Matt
was having difficulty getting started, saying that he had no fears. So
Brandt queried him by saying, "You have no fears?" When Matt
replied in the negative, Brandt suggested that he write about another
feeling, "Oh, don't write about fears then; go to another one. What
else could you write about? Have you ever been angry with someone? Have you? Tell me, about . . . what happened. What made you
angry? Something that she did or said?" When he seemed resistant
to responding, she gently probed him, built on his response of, "It
happened at eight o'clock," and provided suggestions without being
intimidating. She ended by expressing interest in the story, "It was at

eight o'clock. Start your story that way; tell me what happened at eight o'clock last night. I'll probably be back to pick up yours first because I'm very curious to see what happened at eight o'clock last night."

Brandt described her role as "a facilitator to encourage them to write." She showed interest in Matt's story and continually tried to elicit information from him. Even though he was not forthcoming, she asked him questions to get him started. When another student, Joe, wrote about a television show that scared him, she not only acknowledged what he had written and the parts she liked but also asked him to relate it back to his own feelings by saying, "That's a good story. I like the way you wrote, 'based on a true story' too;

> **Brandt described her role as "a facilitator to encourage them to write."**

that sounds good. Does it make you feel like a part of that story when you watch it? Do you feel like it's really happening? How do you feel when you read the story? Or when you watched the story?"

Brandt focused on encouraging her young children in their writing, but she also expected them to elaborate and to construct a narrative. Rather than merely accepting their work, she set high expectations consistent with the student's abilities. Depending on their prior writing experiences and where they were in the composing process of a piece, Brandt focused on different aspects of writing with different students. Rather than using a textbook or an outside source, Brandt believed it was important to use the children's own writing. She then selected some aspects such a capitalization, punctuation, or quotation marks to emphasize and involve students in proofreading one another's work.

Not only did students work together by editing one another's work, but many students chose to collaborate by writing stories together. When we observed, two girls composed a story about their bikes together by taking turns writing each sentence. They explained, "This was fair, and then one person's arm would not get too tired." They continually negotiated not only the content but mechanics and word choice with each other. For instance, after Amanda had written, "We got our bikes on our birthdays," Lucy said, "We *have.*" Lucy then asked how to spell *our* and, when Amanda told her *a-r-e,* she knew it was wrong and corrected her. When Amanda wrote, "Our bikes have the same colors," after she had written, "And they

have a lot of colors," Lucy told her not to start sentences with *and.*
Showing audience awareness she told her, "They already know that
because you wrote they were the same." In the interview, Brandt
expressed how pleased she was at this partnership, explaining that
one girl was very bright and the other had a learning disability, yet
they had chosen each other.

Brandt's classroom was filled with activity and a sense of community. She developed this community by providing students with
opportunities to hear one anothers' ideas and work together in a
variety of formats. During writing time, students could choose to
write with partners as in the case of Lucy and Amanda, or they could
talk to peers to get ideas or proofread their work. In the "author's
chair" (Graves & Hansen, 1983, p. 176), students read their work
aloud, thus having an opportunity to share work with a larger audience than the teacher.

While Brandt's goals focused on encouraging students to write,
she also provided instruction in her comments during the conferences and author's chair. The skills she taught came from students'
own writing; she emphasized student expression primarily and then
had students focus on particular mechanics within the context of
their own writing. She started with the students' experiences and
built on those rather than beginning with an outside curriculum,
allowing students opportunities to participate as readers and writers
in a particular community. Students' work reflected Brandt's goals
as they wrote well-developed pieces that were revised, edited, and
shared with others on a daily basis.

### Writing in Hancock's Classroom:
### Mixing Skills With Self-Expression

When we observed in Joyce Hancock's classroom, we saw a teacher
in the midst of change. Filled with excitement and commitment to
her new view of literacy teaching and spurred by Brandt, Joyce
sought to foster critical thinking and children's self-expression.

One observation occurred in late September as Hancock was
establishing her writing program with kindergarten, first, and second
graders. Before students wrote, Hancock involved her students in a
series of seemingly disconnected activities about the "long *i* sound"
and then introduced the "capital *I*" to indicate first person. She
expressed in an interview that, "It is a skill they will be tested on;

that's a skill they need to know—that the *I* stands in place of their name." She chose this particular skill from an English book and believed it was a good time to introduce it, especially because students often wrote sentences that started with *I*.

To extend this concept, Hancock had pre-cut ice cream scoops for each student and used what she called a "story starter"—"I like" was written on the blackboard. First, students glued a pre-made capital *I* onto a picture of themselves; then, they completed the sentence with their own ideas. For instance, Jerry wrote "I like Mom" on one scoop, "I like Dad" on the second scoop, and "I like god [*sic*]" on his third scoop.

Students were allowed to talk to one another during their writing, but each student worked on individual projects. As students wrote on their scoops, Hancock circulated around the classroom helping students focus and encouraging their work. Her interactions were limited to giving directions, and she did little to encourage them to elaborate:

| Hancock: | How you doing? |
| Adam: | Can I draw a picture? |
| Hancock: | Adam, you have to write it first, and, if you would like to put a little picture with your writing when you finish, you may. Okay, what do you put after your *K*? Good. Let's see. Point to what you like. |
| Adam: | I like playing kick ball. |
| Hancock: | You're very good at kick ball too. |

Hancock seemed to be at a transitional point. She was expressing new ideas, trying them out in the classroom, while experiencing a new sense of success and enjoyment of teaching. Yet, Hancock was not quite ready to give up some of her traditional practices or change her role in the classroom. Manifested in her practices of selecting topics for students, controlling the discourse during writing class and assigning activities for them, she was not ready to fully negotiate with students; Hancock embraced new ideas and practices while holding onto some of the old. She provided students with some opportunities to write; however, she continued more traditional practices such as the use of story starters and more traditional skills instruction. Students' writing reflected this orientation as the pieces tended to be brief and limited in development; they all started out the same way and looked like colorful worksheets.

In only two years of multi-age grouping and literature-based instruction, Hancock had come a long way in her own estimation. She attributed her changes to connections with her colleague, Julie Brandt, and Julie's mentor, Jay Ross.

**Differing Stages of Teacher Development Within One Team**

Because Julie was team leader and viewed by her peers as the source of innovation within the school, it is not surprising that she appears to be further along in her development than her teammate, Joyce. The two teachers had much in common: they provided a literature-based reading program; believed that students could work together; and established similar features in their writing programs such as providing some direction in topic selection, allowing students opportunities to write, and encouraging sharing through the author's chair. However, subtle differences emerged that demonstrated different understandings of literacy and differences in degree of implementation of process approaches to writing.

> **In only two years of multi-age grouping and literature-based instruction, Hancock had come a long way in her own estimation.**

Although Julie's students were encouraged to talk together at all writing stages, Joyce's students were permitted to talk only to the person sitting near them. The result in Julie's class was that students seized the opportunity to bounce ideas off one another as well as to proofread. Several pairs of children, such as Amanda and Lucy, actually constructed text together, producing something different from a single-authored paper. Joyce's students, on the other hand, each created their own scoops, interacted with one another, but did not help others or nurture their ideas. The two teachers also differed in how they approached skills instruction. Brandt examined students' work to find out what they needed and built her instruction around those needs. In contrast, Hancock did not look specifically at student work but found materials she thought were interesting and drew from the list of skills the team had developed using textbooks and curriculum guides as sources. Brandt seemed more comfortable taking her cues from the students, whereas Hancock looked to outside authorities or to her teammates. In sum, Brandt's practices appeared much more coherent and developed than Hancock's.

What role did the teams play in teachers' development and learning? How did teachers interact with one another? How had the teams developed over time?

## The Role of Team and Liaisons in Teacher Learning

Brandt and Hancock believed that the organization into teams was the essential ingredient in success for both the children and teachers. Students felt part of a larger group, and, because they stayed in a team for 2–3 years, teachers believed they got to know students well. Brandt saw the team as offering opportunities to share ideas and specialize in subjects.

One person who helped the Snoopy Gang become cohesive was Jay Ross, a liaison among a large local university, the Professional Development Center, and the school. His role within the university involved placing and supervising student teachers, and his directive from the Professional Development Center was to go out and create change in whatever form he chose. Because Ross's expertise was in writing and he had participated in the National Writing Project, he chose to create change by serving as a resource for the Webster teachers who wanted to learn new ways of teaching writing. Drawing on his own philosophy of learning, which included engaging students in authentic writing tasks and having students use their own experiences a writing topics, Ross modeled writing with students in classrooms where he was invited. Not wanting to impose programs on teachers, he described his approach to staff development as "invitations to learn." He spent many hours demonstrating in Julie Brandt's room and occasionally taught in Hancock's classroom when invited.

Brandt reported that Ross was the most influential person in her change process. By demonstrating with children, giving her particular materials, such as a book about how to teach spelling, and talking with her, Ross influenced her writing program enormously. Hancock was also influenced, although to a lesser degree, by the overall support that Ross provided.

Not only did Ross play a key role in introducing new ideas to the teachers, but he also played a role in their development as a team. Teachers knew the approaches to teaching and underlying philosophies of their teammates. Although they knew about one anothers' styles of teaching, teachers clearly stated that they respected the others' ways and did not want to impose their own beliefs about teaching reading and writing on one another. This working together while maintaining a respectful distance may account for why Brandt and Hancock had different enactments of the same curricular ideas and seemed to be in different "stages of development." Although they shared ideas, Brandt was clearly the leader in innovation, while Hancock's teaching was less developed and Hancock still depended on some of her more traditional skill-oriented practices. Yet the sharing of ideas within the team seemed to be a significant factor in both teachers' learning.

> **We did see changes in the organization and structure of the school which did affect events at Webster.**

### Learning From the Case of Webster

We gained an important insight from our analyses of classroom practice in the context of school organization and structure at Webster. We learned that changing practice is primarily a problem of learning for teachers, not a problem of school-based organization. We did see changes in the organization and structure of the school which did affect events at Webster. For example, teachers met in teams, and Julie herself took on a leadership role that she wouldn't have had in a traditional school organization. But for Julie, the changes in her classroom practice occurred as a result of her own learning, which was only indirectly related to restructuring. For Julie Brandt, the most important learning was situated within the context of her own classroom where, inspired and supported by her colleague, Jay Ross, she tried out new ideas and practices in the teaching of writing. What was important about this was that it was ongoing over the course of year. Julie was in charge of her learning, but she also had access to new ideas and other discourse communities through Jay Ross, who not only supported her experimentation but also gave her substantive feedback about writing from the standpoint of a disciplinary community. Standing at the intersection between structure and content, Jay Ross's most important roles turned out to be as both a facilitator of teacher learning and a mediator between discourse communities that shared ideas about curriculum and instruction.

In contrast to Peg Ernst at Lakeview, who was struggling on her own and seemed to value students' responses without extending the content or considering features of effective writing, Julie Brandt had the support to examine her practice with another person who was knowledgeable about purposes and expectations of good writing and pedagogical strategies to support them. Jay Ross played a key role, not only because he was supportive of the teachers but because he was connected to larger ideas and norms from the discourse community of the National Writing Project and could enact those ideas within the context of a specific classroom.

If we compare Webster with Lakeview, we can see that restructuring teachers into teams led to learning for Julie and Joyce at Webster, but the team structure alone was only part of the explanation. More important were the relationships that had developed between Julie and Jay, and between Julie and Joyce. Although Joyce did not feel comfortable having an outsider come into her classroom, she did admire her colleague who had the opportunity to develop a close professional relationship with the district liaison. These relationships allowed professional growth to develop not only within the individual but also within the team. From our comparison of Webster and Lakeview, we began to see that, while school structures can provide opportunities for the learning of new teaching practices and new strategies for student learning, the structures alone do not cause the learning to occur.

**Northeastern: How Do Learners Construct a Coherent World?**
Northeastern is an elementary school on a busy street in a poor neighborhood in a densely populated urban area in the eastern United States. Designated as a school of choice, Northeastern serves children whose parents have applied to send their children to the school. Northeastern I Elementary School (grades pre-K–6) is located in a large brick building that includes Northeastern Secondary School. About 250 students from ethnically diverse backgrounds (90% minority) attend Northeastern Elementary School. Nearly 80% of students in the school qualify for free or reduced lunch.

Based on ideals of an open education philosophy, Northeastern had been involved in its own brand of restructuring for almost two decades. Teachers did not refer to their efforts as restructuring but,

rather, believed they were enacting a vision of schooling that
reflected the ideals of the open education movement. Although the
teachers did not use the term *restructuring* to
describe their efforts at Northeastern, the
school had several features consistent with
restructuring efforts in other places (cf.
David, 1990). The staff was committed to
creating stimulating environments for both
teachers and students; had established roles
for teachers that involved shared decision
making, collegial interactions, and substantive discourse among professionals; and had
used alternative forms of accountability, in-
cluding innovative assessments and reporting of student progress.
Northeastern also had a well-articulated philosophy of student learning that pervaded the school climate and the curriculum, a strong
linkage with the community, and substantive discussions by staff
members about individual students which were called *staffings*.

> **Northeastern teachers continued to develop their knowledge of their students' learning of the elementary subjects.**

Northeastern teachers' conceptions of professional development
were framed by the context of how they viewed their school and
their professional practice—as a community of learners and teachers. Northeastern teachers participated in professional development
workshops and retreats they developed together as a professional
community within their own school or with teachers in two other
schools with which they shared the same philosophy of teaching and
learning. As a professional community, Northeastern teachers continued to develop their knowledge of their students' learning and
their learning of the elementary subjects. They continued to work
on developing and refining their classroom practice guided by their
well-developed vision of learning as the active construction of
knowledge by the individual and of teaching as the facilitation of
that process for individual students.

Curriculum consisted of a whole language approach to reading
and writing based on the writings of Frank Smith (1983), an emphasis on teacher-designed thematic units for use in individual teachers'
classrooms, and mathematics instruction in which teachers drew on
multiple sources and texts and worked with students individually or
in small groups. Influenced by the ideas of Smith, who suggested,
"In writing, not only can we create worlds, but we can change them

at will" (p. 129), two of the upper grade teachers, Brian Kramer and Alexis Brezinski, were committed to using writing as means of opening up new worlds for their diverse students.

**Writing in Brian's Classroom:**
**Facilitating Conversations About Texts**

Brian, a nine-year veteran teacher, embraced a constructivist philosophy that started with the student rather than the curriculum: "I want to use the kids' own work as the starting point, their interactions with other students." He also supported a literacy philosophy consistent with many whole language and process writing proponents. He considered writing a "natural process" and saw his role as helping "kids to express their own ideas in different ways." Students had free choice of topics, and his role was to "build on the individual's own writing." Besides believing students should select their own topics, Brian also had some group lessons about writing. Writing occurred both at a separate time of the day and throughout the day as it related to other projects, such as studying the surrounding community and writing about it to pen pals in Vermont. Students kept journals where they "created their own stories" and met with Brian or with one another in self-selected peer response groups. As one student explained it, students gave their opinion of the story, and if the kid liked their opinion he or she would put that part in the story or change the story.

As an example of these informal peer groups, two girls, Erin and Gloria, read their stories to each other and responded. At Gloria's request, Erin read aloud Chapter I of the lengthy book she was writing entitled *Life and Problems.* The story included dialogue between a mother and her daughter (called Spike because of her spiked hair) about a baby that Spike was going to have. Expressed through the dialogue between the mother and the child, the story contained some details about the anger and confusion the character felt toward her pregnancy. After hearing what Erin had written so far, Gloria responded, "That's good. I like it. So you want me to read my story?" Gloria realized she had not completed her own story and did not want to read it. Erin urged her to read it. Gloria, however, deferred, and Erin read Gloria's story aloud until she mispronounced a word at which point Gloria took over and read as much of the story as she had composed. Erin continued to encourage Gloria despite Gloria's reluctance.

The girls then turned back to Erin's story. Erin's story described how her main character continued to have babies and needed to put them up for adoption. When Erin described her character's becoming older and finishing high school, Gloria inserted, "So that means she can keep them." Erin acknowledged this comment and explained how the character met a friend who also had a baby. Gloria then commented, "God, this story is getting full of babies it seems." The girls continued their conversation with Erin providing details about the apartment shared by her main character and a friend. Erin continued to construct her story aloud with Gloria asking questions.

> Erin:    Then they get married. No, they start going out with this boy.
>
> Gloria.  But the boy knows it?
>
> Erin:    No. The boy sees two girls at the same time.
>
> Gloria:  But the boy doesn't know that they're friends and they live together?
>
> Erin:    Right. The boy doesn't know that they know each other. So then he asks Spike to marry him . . .

Of interest here was how the two girls sustained the conversation over most of the class period. Erin constructed her narrative orally, as a way of rehearsing the text she was going to write. Gloria was clearly engaged in the story, asking questions and occasionally pointing out places where the meaning was not clear to her. The girls were so engaged in the story that they did not want to be interrupted even when Brian needed to make an announcement to the whole class. Gloria and Erin initiated and sustained the written and oral story construction without help from the teacher. Gloria did not focus on explicitly helping Erin revise or, as is often the case in "process writing classrooms," merely edit her written work. Rather, she acted as an audience who was very involved in the story itself and helped Erin by asking questions in places where she did not understand the narrative.

Students in Brian's class responded to one another's work without focusing explicitly on changing the content or editing the mechanics of their work. Students felt free to initiate conversations about writing out of interest or friendship. These conversations fit with Brian's ideas about writing as a natural process in which students could express their ideas freely and converse with students of their choice. Students' work reflected the multiple opportunities that Brian provided them to write on topics of their own choice or topics connected to group projects. Most students' daily journals contained lengthy pieces, many of which had been developed and revised. Their letters to pen pals and expository pieces connected to projects also demonstrated how closely writing was tied to all content areas.

In his own conversations with students, Brian continually tried to negotiate, finding a topic that might be of interest to the student, yet giving his own ideas if the student did not respond. In one incident with Latoya (who was reluctant to write), he asked what she wanted to write about, provided examples from other students' stories, and related his own concerns about an upcoming class trip to Vermont. Brian then tried to elicit Latoya's feelings about the trip. When this failed, he suggested they make a list of possible writing topics. When Latoya responded that each topic was "boring," Brian provided a more specific structure for doing a character sketch. Despite Latoya's resistance, Brian did not give up; his tone remained supportive and gentle as he suggested ideas. Through these conversations, Brian revealed his constructivist approach to the teaching of writing—allowing students to choose their own topics and then develop them. When met with students' lack of interest, Brian provided alternatives before suggesting specifics.

> **Students felt free to initate conversations about writing out of interest or friendship.**

### Writing in Alexis' Classroom:
### Developing the Author's Own Ideas

In Alexis' classroom, writing occurred in the morning when children were free to choose reading, writing, or both. Free writing occurred every day in Alexis' class as children wrote in their own journals. Then every two weeks, Alexis read the journal and wrote back to the child about what he or she had been thinking and writing. Alexis corrected a child's journal only if she saw some value in the child's revising a piece that he or she had written. Then she helped the child revise by pointing out ways of expanding or extending what he or she had written. The student put the piece on the classroom computer, revised it, and printed it out. This work was formally acknowledged by putting it up on the bulletin board, sharing it with other children, or reading it aloud to the teacher and class next door.

In the following italicized descriptions, Alexis reflected on her practice and her children's learning by annotating a transcription of the discourse from a particular writing episode. In this episode, Alexis worked with Jason to turn the draft of a story into a formal piece that would be shared with others. She began by filling in some of the context of what was happening:

> The context is sustained, silent reading for all the kids; I'm with Jason at the computer, helping him revise the story he's been working on in his journal . . . Jason is not an enthusiastic writer, and the whole process is a struggle for him. He has real problems with spelling—many of the words he writes aren't even close approximations, beyond the first and last letter. His handwriting is small, with letters tightly squeezed together and very difficult to read. In general his ideas outstrip his skills, so that he tends, I think, to oversimplify rather than grapple continuously with words he can't spell and linguistic structures he can't manage. Often, in his writing, he moves from one idea to another omitting crucial transitional ideas; the bridges from one thought to another are often missing. My intentions in working with him at this point were: get the actual recopying done more quickly; help him identify those missing bridges, confusing transitions, awkward phrases, and so forth; provide some practice with mechanics of punctuation—I had been working with him, on and off, on punctuating dialogue.

Alexis began her interaction with Jason by having him read aloud to her what he had written. The story was entitled, "The Boy Who Wanted to Fly."

Jason:   *(Begins reading from his text.)* Once upon a time there was a boy that wanted to learn how to fly. His name was Roy. He watched birds and how they land.

Alexis:   He watched birds do what? *(I want to point out the awkwardness of " . . . how they land.")*

Jason:   He watched birds land. *(Jason self-corrects.)*

Alexis:   That's all? *(I want a more elaborate statement—more description.)*

Jason:   And he also watched how they fly.

Alexis:   Ok, so describe that a little bit. Let's fill the ideas in. *(Here restate and expand my "That's all?")* He watched birds . . .

Jason:   Fly and glide in the air and . . .

Alexis:   *(Reading from Jason's handwritten journal.)* He wanted to know.

Jason:   *(Makes several different tries at articulating his ideas before he puts them in this form.)* He wanted to know how come the birds could fly, and he can't . . . He even got a book on flying.

Alexis:   He even got a book on flying. Now I think there's something confusing about this. When you say "There was a boy who wanted to learn how to fly," it sounds as if it's about learning how to fly an airplane. That's what it usually means—you know, they take flying lessons, and they go to flying school. That isn't flying like a bird. That's flying like an airplane, so how could we make this first sentence a little clearer? *(There's a lot here about how Jason thinks and how he expresses ideas in language. He means learn to fly literally, and getting a book on flying presumably means a book about how birds fly, not how to fly an airplane. In other words, the boy wanted to teach himself how to fly the way birds do. So a lot of meaning is packed into very few words, but not stated clearly.)*

Jason:   Without any machine, any machinery?

Alexis:   Okay.

This dialogue with the teacher's reflections reveals how Alexis helped her children elaborate and develop their ideas in their writing and how she saw her role as their teacher. Alexis viewed her role as a teacher here as helping Jason articulate and elaborate his ideas in his writing. The text was not hers; it was Jason's story. The annotations of the transcript by Alexis reveal how she elaborated and developed her understanding of particular students and their ideas and how she used this understanding in an ongoing way in her interactions with students about their work.

In her conversation with Jason, Alexis revealed a coherence between her thoughts and actions—a reflexivity of her pedagogical beliefs and practice. Alexis indicated that, in writing, her most important goal was for her children to "write freely." She felt that, if her students were comfortable putting words on paper, then she could help "fill in mechanics" at some point. In Jason's case, Alexis succeeded; Jason moved from a reluctant writer and "resistant" student at the beginning of the year to one who, at the end of the year, was conversing fluently with his teacher about his writing and engaging in expressing his ideas orally and in writing.

**Alexis: The Teacher as Knowledgeable Learner**

How was Alexis able to carry this off so successfully? One reason
may be that, like Brian, Alexis had a great deal of subject matter
knowledge, pedagogical knowledge, and knowledge of learners. In
addition, Alexis saw herself as a learner who was continuing to
develop her own knowledge in the same way her students were
developing their knowledge.

Alexis herself was a reader and a learner of literature, taking a
course in English literature at a nearby university. She also saw herself as a writer who was as comfortable and articulate with writing
text as she was with speaking and reading text. Alexis had written
and published two articles on her own teaching. She knew what it
meant to struggle with putting ideas into writing as Jason was doing.

Like her constructivist colleagues, Alexis was able to teach the
way she did because of the in-depth knowledge and understanding
she had of her students. Over the year, she continued to develop her
understanding of her students. Alexis kept track of much of this
knowledge in her head, but she also wrote it down and talked with
her Northeastern colleague about individual students during
staffings. Additionally, Alexis kept a journal in which she wrote her
developing understanding of each individual student and her reflections on her own practice.

**Northeastern Teachers: Coherence, Integration, and Nuance**

Compared with traditional teachers and teachers at the other two
schools, Brian's and Alexis's teaching are strikingly similar to each
other and to their Northeastern colleagues. In both classes, the
coherence of philosophy and practice was apparent. These teachers'
constructivist views of learning framed their practices. They saw
learners as sense makers and were continually striving to understand
their students' developing understandings. The teachers had in-depth
knowledge of their students, and they used this knowledge in their
conversations with students and in their teaching. For example,
Brian and Alexis had a similar approach to the teaching of writing.
They followed students' interests in the choice of topics; during dia-
logues with the writer, the teacher helped the author elaborate his or
her ideas, focusing more on content than on form. One difference
between the teachers was Brian's additional use of peer response
groups.

The differences between Brian's and Alexis's classrooms seemed to be differences of degree rather than kind. Like the Eskimos, who have a hundred different words for snow, enabling them to talk about the nuances among different types of snow, so, too, Northeastern teachers had developed multiple nuances of constructivist teaching, allowing them to converse about their practices. This development among teachers is consistent with a constructivist perspective. Just as learners construct their own meanings, so, too, do teachers. In Brian Kramer and Alexis Brezinski, we see teachers who had constructed slightly different versions of constructivist teaching and thereby created their own uniquely coherent practices.

## Learning From the Case of Northeastern

Our analysis of Northeastern allowed us to explore a case in which there were close relationships among school structures, teaching practices, and opportunities for student learning. What we learned from this case was that these close relationships occurred because teachers shared common beliefs about student learning, a common view of their purposes, and shared ideas about the principles of good practice and how these principles might be enacted in the classroom. These shared understandings had come about, in part, because of recruitment and selection of teachers who shared a common view and were committed to a common purpose, but also, in part, through continued discussions and learning during staffings and conversations in school and out. Because the structural changes grew out of the shared norms, values, and understandings of what constitutes good practice, a tight fit existed between the structure of the organization and teachers' classroom practices. Although the influence of organizational structure appeared to be more subtle in Northeastern than at Lakeview and Webster, it was potentially more powerful because structure at Northeastern was so tightly bound up with beliefs, understandings, and practices.

Northeastern was also a place where teachers took seriously the notion that they, as well as their students, were ongoing learners. Teachers created school structures and classroom practices that supported and encouraged their children's learning, and, with the school's director (who was herself a teacher), they created informal and formal situations in their school to support their own learning. They learned through talking with colleagues in the hallways and lounge at Northeastern; they learned by participating in study groups and literature groups with other teachers and adults in the community or university; they learned from reflecting on their own practices and from the students in their classrooms; and they learned from their own formal and informal writings.

## DISCUSSION

At the level of classroom practice, we demonstrated how different teachers enacted selected reform efforts that have been directed towards changing the ways in which teachers teach writing (see Applebee, 1986). As we examined the practices of the six teachers across the schools, we saw that all of the teachers provided students with much more time to write and share their ideas than is common in traditional schools (see Goodlad, 1984). Yet the differences that we saw when we compared their practices were striking and linked in an indirect and complex way to the opportunities afforded by each school's restructuring efforts.

> **We saw that all of the teachers provided students with much more time to write and share their ideas than is common in traditional schools.**

From our close inspections of teachers' practices in the three schools, we raise the following hypothesis: *Teaching and learning occur mainly as a function of teachers' beliefs, understandings, and behaviors in the context of specific problems in the classroom.* If classrooms practices are largely created within the context of specific problems in the classroom and are a function of teachers' beliefs and understandings, then how are new practices created? These cases allowed us to consider this question.

Our analyses of the cases revealed that new practices clearly evolved as teachers learned but that teacher learning did not necessarily follow from the provision of opportunities for staff development workshops. Lakeview School was virtually overrun with brief, one-shot workshops covering a variety of topics. Teachers were both grateful for and exhausted by these persistent efforts of the principal to bring outside knowledge into the organization. But teachers at Lakeview had scant opportunity to transform this plethora of ideas into classroom practice or to be connected in an ongoing way to new ideas in the larger writing community. Peg and Liz's only sources of knowledge about writing were their colleague, Greg and the one workshop given for Lakeview teachers. Thus, the teachers had little direct access to well-articulated sets of ideas that might have developed their understandings of writing in a deeper way. While Greg had greater access to ideas through university courses he had taken for his master's degree, he, like all the Lakeview teachers, did not have ongoing relationships with university personnel or with district curriculum specialists to encourage and support his further learning about writing. Teachers also did not have access to a knowledgeable support group of teachers outside their school. Lacking these, Lakeview teacher were left to their own devices, and, while they may have shared their ideas with one another, both their ideas and their sharing were minimal compared to what would be needed to create and sustain major innovations in teachers' classroom practices in writing.

In contrast, Brandt was linked to several supportive communities within and outside of Webster School and had opportunities to engage in conversations at a variety of levels. She had conversations about teaching with Ross, her team, and university professors through the courses she took. Through these conversations, Brandt was also linked to larger professional and academic discourse communities. Ross's intensive work in Brandt's classroom played a large role in linking her to these communities, which led to Brandt's sharing of information with her colleague, Joyce Hancock. As a liaison among the school, the district, and the university, Ross drew on his own knowledge and expertise in writing to demonstrate in Brandt's classroom and support her efforts, while reporting back weekly to the district restructuring team.

In contrast to Lakeview, Northeastern provided very little in terms of formal staff development. Rather, Northeastern set up certain expectations for entering teachers to share a constructivist-based, open classroom philosophy; they established the norm that every teacher should have a consuming intellectual interest to pursue; and they formed both internal and external communities of like-minded professionals who were available to discuss problems of practice. These shared understandings had come about because of the recruitment and selection of teachers and were sustained through continued discussions in school and out.

Northeastern was also a place where teachers took seriously the notion that they, as well as their students, were ongoing learners.

Teachers created school structures and classroom practices that supported and encouraged their children's learning and created situations to support their own learning. This case, in particular,
exemplifies our second emergent hypothesis: *Changing practice is
primarily a problem of learning, not a problem of organization.
Teachers who see themselves as learners work continuously to
develop new understandings and improve their practices.*

Alexis and Brian, at Northeastern, were teachers who had a
great deal of subject matter knowledge, pedagogical knowledge, and
knowledge of learners. Alexis, for example,
saw herself as a learner who was continuing
to develop her own knowledge and as a
writer who was grappling with ways to
express her own ideas. Similarly, Julie
Brandt at Webster, and Peg Ernst at
Lakeview, considered themselves learners
who sought to open up their practice and find new ways of teaching
writing. Certain support structures provided the opportunities to the
Northeastern teachers and to Brandt and Hancock to a greater extent
than to Ernst or Horn. This observation suggests a third hypothesis:
*School structures can provide opportunities for the learning of new
teaching practices and new strategies for student learning, but
structures, by themselves, do not cause the learning to occur.*

**Teachers felt a
sense of pride and
professionalism.**

The major structural changes at the school level involved creating a vision through changes in the workplace environment, encouraging teachers to meet together as a team or whole group, engaging
teachers in decision making, and providing access to new knowledge. In all three schools, some benefits accrued from these school
level changes. Teachers felt a sense of pride and professionalism;
they valued the collegiality developed with other teachers; they felt a
strong sense of responsibility for all students in their team or, in the
case of Northeastern, for all students in the school. In all schools, the
opportunities for teaming and shared decision making contributed to
increased feelings of empowerment by the teachers.

At Lakeview and Webster, the teaming structures facilitated
teacher interactions and provided the time and possibilities for
teachers to discuss important issues in teaching and learning. However, merely providing the time and situation did not guarantee
classroom changes. Whereas at Webster, teams were beginning to
discuss ways to implement curriculum and to talk about individual

students, at Lakeview, discussions were limited to talk about generic themes, activities related to a topic, or procedural matters. The most substantive meetings occurred at Northeastern where teachers met together to discuss individual students' learning and to give ideas to other staff members about how to help the student. Teachers and the principal took advantage of these meetings to connect teaching practice and student learning and to develop a deeply shared vision. This observation suggests a fourth hypothesis: *Successful relations occur among school structure, teaching practice, and student learning in schools where, because of recruitment and socialization, teachers share a common point of view about their purpose and principles of good practice. School structure follows from good practice not vice versa.*

While the three schools shared some core ideas of ambitious teaching—child-centered pedagogy, active learning, and equal access for all students—there were distinct differences in the ways the schools enacted their visions of teaching and learning. Northeastern teachers articulated a common developmental theory based on Piaget, and the teachers' writing practices were consistent with this view. Webster teachers seemed to be groping toward a common view of practice, in which teachers would specialize in certain content areas within their teams for the purposes of bringing new content into the school. They had not yet achieved the same kind of coherence as Northeastern, in part, perhaps because the ideas were new to teachers like Joyce Hancock. Lakeview teachers expressed the ideas of ambitious teaching in diverse ways, connected only by a common belief that teachers and students were characterized by their different learning styles and these differences would determine how teachers would teach and students would learn.

All the teachers in our study were struggling—some more actively than others—with how to make their classroom practices approximate more closely their own ideas, and the ideas of others, about what a more student-centered, active, and equal approach to learning would look like. Realizing that some of her children had greater access to certain literacy events and written works than others, Lynn Hord had the laudable goal of giving her students experience reading and writing poetry. But her student, LaShaunda, struggled with coming up with words and ideas to fit the poetic form, and Lynn did not know how to facilitate her expression without putting words (and ideas) in her student's mouth and into her

poem. Even Brian, who had more years of experience than Lynn in
this constructivist role, was struggling when one of his students,
Latoya, failed to respond to his coaxing to
generate some text. Indeed, while all six
teachers claimed to be facilitators of
children's learning, they did it in very different ways. Yet how does a teacher facilitate a
student's understanding if he or she cannot
establish a shared understanding initially?
Also, how does a teacher like Lynn move
from her established practice, which is more
directive and teacher-centered, toward a practice that is more facilitative and student-
centered like that of Brian, Alexis, and Julie? And how did Brian,
Alexis, and Julie get where they are today?

> **Our study
> reaffirms how
> extraordinarily
> complex and
> demanding
> the work of
> teaching is.**

If we were to advise researchers, based on our study, we would
urge that they give more attention to understanding the ways in
which learners create new ways to do established tasks and the
ways in which the contexts in which they work influence how they
acquire new knowledge and skill. Advocates of restructuring have
assumed that teachers will discover new pedagogies and practices by
being exposed to new ideas and by working in organizations that
promote more collegial interaction. We question this premise
because we believe that the problem of how teachers acquire new
knowledge and skill is considerably more complex than researchers
or reformers have assumed. For example, part of what Julie Brandt
was learning was not only a new way to teach but also a new way of
thinking about knowledge and about her relationship to knowledgeable people in her field. She became willing to have her practice
scrutinized by others and to think critically about her own practice.
In other words, Brandt changed not only her view of how to teach
but also her view of how knowledge about teaching is developed,
understood, and communicated to others.

Some of what Julie Brandt was learning was what Northeastern
teachers already knew, because Northeastern teachers were not only
connoisseurs of their own particular brand of teaching for understanding but also active participants in communities of other teachers who shared their views. What these teachers knew, in other
words, they knew as a consequence of an extensive set of social and

disciplinary relationships around the practice of teaching, not just as their own personal knowledge. One way for researchers to come to understand and change teaching practice would be to focus on understanding and creating such communities of practice (Lieberman, 1992).

Our study reaffirms how extraordinarily complex and demanding the work of teaching is. It also reveals how teachers' practice is situated within the day-to-day demands and needs of particular children in a particular class dealing with particular curricular issues. These participants make it apparent that neither reformers' restructuring attempts nor their sweeping directives to "teach for understanding" go nearly far enough for the teacher who is confronted with figuring out what these directives mean for teaching writing in an actual classroom to a real group of second-grade children of diverse backgrounds, abilities, and understandings.

While some might read our cases of teaching in restructured schools as stories that confirm that "structure doesn't matter," we read these cases quite differently. If researchers, reformers, and teachers understood and agreed on what kind of teaching practices they wanted and if they understood what would need to be learned to create these practices, then they might create structures that would support this learning and these practices. While some might continue to map forward from structural changes in schools to changes in teaching practice, we prefer to map backward. Why not begin by attempting to understand teaching practice? Then researchers might try to understand what learning would need to occur to create such practices and what school structures might support this learning and these practices.

## NOTES

The research reported in this article was supported by a grant to the Consortium for Policy Research in Education (CPRE, at Rutgers University, Michigan State University, and Harvard University from the Department of Education, Office of Educational Research and Improvement, Grant No. OERI-G008690011-89). The opinions expressed in this report do not necessarily represent the position, policy, or endorsement of the OERI. We thank the teachers and principals at the three schools for their willingness to participate in our study. We also thank David Cohen for his thoughtful comments on an earlier draft and Michelle Parker for her assistance with data collection in one school.

1. In this report, all names of schools, teachers, and students are pseudonyms.

2. All three schools recognized as important several goals that Lieberman and Miller (1990) have called the "building blocks of restructuring." These include a rethinking of the structure of the school as well as a rethinking of curriculum and instruction to promote quality for all students, a focus on rich learning environments for students and professionally supportive work environments for adults, a recognition of the importance of partnerships and networks, and a recognition of the need for parent and community participation.

## REFERENCES

Applebee, A. N. (1986). Problems in process approaches: Toward a reconceptualization of process instruction. In A. R. Petrosky & D. Bartholomae (Eds.), *The teaching of writing* (pp. 95–113). Chicago: National Society for the Study of Education.

Bereiter, C., & Scardamalia, M. (1987). An attainable version of high literacy: Approaches to teaching higher-order skills in reading and writing. *Curriculum Inquiry, 17*(1), 9–30.

Berlin, J. A. (1987). *Rhetoric and reality: Writing instruction in American colleges, 1906–1985*. Carbondale, IL: Southern Illinois Press.

Calkins, L. M. (1986). *The art of teaching writing*. Portsmouth, NH: Heinemann.

Cohen, D. K., McLaughlin, M. W., & Talbert, J. E. (Eds.). (1993). *Teaching for understanding: Challenges for policy and practice*. San Francisco: Jossey-Bass.

Cuban, L. (1984). *How teachers taught: Constancy and change in American classrooms 1890–1990*. New York: Teachers College Press.

David, J. L. (1990). Restructuring in Progress: Lessons from pioneering districts. In R. F. Elmore & Associates. (Eds.). *Restructuring schools: The next generation of educational reform*. San Francisco: Jossey-Bass.

Elmore, R. (1991). *Paradox of innovation in education: Cycles of reform and the resilience of teaching*. Unpublished manuscript, Harvard University. Cambridge, MA.

Elmore, R. & Associates (Eds.). (1990). *Restructuring schools*. San Francisco: Jossey-Bass.

Elmore, R., Peterson, P. L. & McCarthey, S. J. (1996). *Restructuring in the classroom: Teaching, learning, and school organization*. San Francisco: Jossey-Bass.

Emig, J. (1971). *The composing process of twelfth graders*. Urbana, IL: National Council of Teachers of English.

Flower, L., & Hayes, J. (1981). A cognitive process theory of writing. *College Composition and Communication, 32,* 365–387.

Fullan, M. (1991). *The new meaning of educational change* (2nd ed.). London: Cassell.

Goetz, J., & LeCompte, M. (1981). Ethnographic research and the problem of data reduction. *Anthropology and Education Quarterly, 12,* 15–70.

Gomez, M. L. (1988). *The National Writing Project: Creating community, validating experience, and expanding professional opportunities* (Issue Paper No. 88–2). East Lansing: Michigan State University, National Center for Research on Teacher Education.

Goodlad, J. I. (1984). *A place called school.* New York: McGraw-Hill.

Graves, D., & Hansen, J. (1983). The author's chair. *Language Arts, 60,* 176–183.

Lieberman, A. (1992). The meaning of scholarly activity and the building of community. *Educational Researcher, 21*(6), 5–12.

Lieberman, A., & Miller, L. (1990). Restructuring schools: What matters and what works. *Phi Delta Kappan, 71*(10), 759–764.

Lincoln, Y., & Guba, E. (1985). *Naturalistic inquiry.* Beverly Hills: Sage.

Little, J. W. & McLaughlin, M. W. (Eds.). (1993). *Teachers' work: Individuals, colleagues, and contexts.* New York: Teachers College Press.

Marshall, H. (Ed.). (1992). *Redefining student learning: Roots of educational change.* Norwood, NJ: Ablex.

McCarthey, S. J., & Raphael, T. E. (1992). Alternative research perspectives. In J. W. Irwin, & M. Doyle (Eds.), *Reading/writing connections: Learning from research* (pp. 2–30). Newark, DE: International Reading Association.

McCarthy, B. (1980). *The 4Mat system: Teaching to learning style with right/left mode techniques.* Arlington Heights, IL: Excel.

McNeil, L. (1986). *Contradictions of control: School structure and school knowledge.* New York: Routledge & Kegan Paul.

Murphy, J. (1991). *Restructuring schools: Capturing and assessing the phenomena.* New York: Teachers College Press.

Newman, F. M. (1992). Beyond common sense in educational restructuring: The issues of content and linkage. *Educational Researcher, 22*(2) 4–13.

Peterson, P. L., & McCarthey, S. J. (1991, April). *Reflections on restructuring at Lakeview School: Looking in classrooms at teachers' literacy practices.* Paper presented at the Annual Meeting of the American Educational Research Association, Chicago.

Resnick, L. B. (1987). *Education and learning to think.* Washington, DC: National Academy Press.

Richardson, V. (1990). Significant and worthwhile change in teaching practice. *Educational Researcher, 19*(7), 10–18.

Sarason, S. B. (1982). *The culture of the school and the problem of change.* Boston: Allyn & Bacon.

———. (1990). *The predictable failure of school reform: Can we change course before it's too late?* San Francisco: Jossey-Bass.

Sirotnik, K. (1986). *Critical perspectives on the organization and improvement of schooling.* Boston: Kluwer.

Smith, F. (1983). *Essays into literacy.* Portsmouth, NH: Heinemann.

Tyack, D. (1990). "Restructuring" in historical perspective: Tinkering toward utopia. *Teachers College Record, 92*(2), 170–191.

Wilkinson, W. G. (n. d.). *A plan to restructure schools in Kentucky.* Frankfort, KY: Office of the Governor.

Willoughby, S., Bereiter, C., Hilton, P., & Rubenstein, J. (1987). *Real math.* LaSalle, IL: Open Court.

# Finding the Way: Structure, Time, and Culture In School Improvement

by Tom Donahoe

*To Mr. Donahoe's mind,* restructuring *means the formal rearrangement of the use of time in schools to allow them to create and sustain the kind of interactive culture and supporting infrastructure they need to improve student learning.*

A s I worked in the field of school improvement during the past four years, I became increasingly struck by the failure of those who write about and those who are directly involved in school restructuring to confront a critical question: How does a school generate and sustain the characteristics of effectiveness?

During my immersion school reform I have read about, been told of, and seen firsthand the inadequacy of the factory model, the egg crate, the cellular structure of schools. I am familiar with the characteristics of effective schools as identified by research—strong leadership, clear and ambitious goals, strong academic programs, teacher professionalism, and shared influence. I have seen lists of desired states, such as school-based management, shared decision making, schools-within-schools, integrated curriculum, interactive/cooperative learning, authentic assessment, performance-based testing, and parent involvement. But I have not read about, heard, or seen how a school takes on these features and, in so doing, differs from the traditional school in the way it functions—in the way it's organized, in the way it structures time, in the roles and interrelationships of its staff. What has been missing, I think, is an adequate consideration of the crucial relationship in schools between structure, time, and culture.

From *Phi Delta Kappan,* December 1993, pp. 298–305 © 1993 by Phi Delta Kappa. Reprinted with permission.

To be fair, the literature and practice of school restructuring nips at the heels of these factors. When a school implements the programs of Theodore Sizer, James Comer, or Henry Levin, something has to change in the way the school functions. But those changes, in Joseph Schumpeter's terms, tend to be adaptive responses—major changes that stay within the range of current custom rather than creative innovations that go beyond existing practices and procedures.[1] Maybe an evolving series of adaptive responses will get schools where they need to go eventually, but the more likely result is what Yevgeny Yevtushenko calls "fatal half-measures." As long as the responses only bend, rather than break, the traditional model, any changes brought about in a school are living on borrowed time. It is easier to go back than to go forward because the system that envelops the school was created to support the traditional model and is thoroughly inhospitable to any other form.

> **I noticed that teachers did not talk about themselves as belonging to an organization.**

It has taken me some time to put these three elements—structure, time, and culture—together. When I began thinking about school improvement four years ago, my attention was attracted by the way schools were formally organized. Gradually, however, I found that time and culture had stronger roles to play in school effectiveness than I was accustomed to seeing in other settings. The best way to bring the roles of structure, time, and culture into focus is by describing my own progression of experience and thought.

## SCHOOL ORGANIZATION

In the fall of 1989, the Pacific Telesis Foundation, of which I was then president, began working with three California elementary schools in a comprehensive restructuring project. By January 1990, I had formed what I thought at the time was an original insight into school organization. I began saying that schools had no organization, describing them as just convenient locations for a bunch of individual teachers, like independent contractors, to come to teach discrete groups of children. I noticed that teachers did not talk about themselves as belonging to an organization; they were more likely to think of themselves as being at the outer reaches of a large bureaucracy. Nevertheless, I expected them to take offense at my description of schools. But no one did—in fact, every educator I spoke to agreed rather enthusiastically. Then I found that my insight was not at all original. It permeated the literature. Here, among many writers on the topic, we find John Goodlad saying that there are no "infrastructures designed to encourage or support either communication among teachers in improving their teaching or collaboration in attacking schoolwide problems. And so teachers, like their students, to a large extent carry on side by side similar but essentially separated activities."[2]

It is only necessary to envision the organizational chart of the traditional school to understand the issue. The chart would show a box for the principal at the top and, below that, one long, horizontal line of boxes for teachers. There may be other positions and roles, especially in high schools, such as assistant principal, counselor, department head. But they don't add depth to the chart; if anything, they extend the horizontal line. The way an organization is configured affects the behavior of those who are in it, minimizing some kinds of behavior, maximizing other kinds. The traditional school organization minimizes collective, collegial behavior on the part of teachers. It maximizes two conflicting behaviors. It leads to bureaucratic, rule-prone direction from the top, since the school is not set up to determine its own direction and rules, but then it creates autonomous teachers who, behind their classroom doors, can readily ignore much of the top-down direction.

There is a scene in Tracy Kidder's *Among Schoolchildren* in which the principal of Kelly School is meeting with his teachers on the day after the local newspaper has printed the results of the statewide standardized test—flunked by more than 30% of Kelly School's sixth-graders. Almost all the students who failed came from families below the poverty line. "I don't want to hear the test scores anymore. I know what kids we got here," the principal told his teachers. "We can't bring them all up to grade level no matter what we do. But we can improve instruction here? You bet we can. But we're doing a good job. We really are."[3] And that was that. The problem at Kelly School is not just a principal who is failing to provide academic leadership, and it's not incompetent teachers. This is a group of people without the support and resources of an infrastructure that enables them to work together on schoolwide problems.

Although that issue is pointed to again and again in the literature, I have yet to find any effort to run its implications completely
to ground. I believe that when we talk about school-site councils,
school-based management, or shared decision making, we think we
are talking about structural change. However, those forms of school
management tend to be appliquéd on to the traditional school organization, not woven into its organizational fabric. They don't necessarily break up the horizontal row of boxes.

When the Pacific Telesis Foundation project began, the schools
were organized into teams, each of which was to develop a strategic
plan in one of four areas. Every member of
both the teaching and the classified staff

**Schools are
accumstomed
to ad hoc
arrangements.**

signed up for the team of his or her choice—
curriculum, teaching and learning, leadership
and management, or parent and community
involvement. The schools were encouraged
to invite parents to join a team. Each team
elected a leader; the whole school staff
elected a project coordinator. The principal, coordinator, team leaders, and, in some instances, others, such as grade-level representatives, formed a leadership council.

During that first year, as I observed the schools struggle with
the process of change, I formed a number of conclusions about
schools restructuring. The first conclusion was that the process
needed to be undertaken as a formal reorganization of the school. It
could not be perceived by the school staff as an informal or ad hoc
arrangement for the purpose of carrying out one more project.
Schools are accustomed to ad hoc arrangements for the administration of seemingly discrete operations such as the school improvement program, Chapter 1, and special education. It was not at all
apparent to the schools we were working with that they now had a
new school organization that should embrace and integrate everything they did. The idea that the schools were undertaking a formal,
comprehensive reorganization—that this was not just one project
among many—needed continuous reinforcement.

The second conclusion I reached was that there was another
reason for the reorganization to be formal and comprehensive: if it
were not, the schools would remain vulnerable to changes in leadership and staff. Informal or ad hoc ways of doing things are ephem-
eral unless, as in many private schools or some small schools in

small communities (or districts), tradition has made them inviolable. We all know examples of schools that became immensely effective through the leadership of an innovative, risk-taking principal and then, when the principal moved on, collapsed back to the ordinary.

My third conclusion, which grew out of the second, was that schools are too dependent on their principals. The plain fact is that there simply aren't enough good principals to go around. Thus a critical objective of school restructuring has to be the development of a school organiza- tion that can generate good school perfor- mance when the principal is not an effective leader or that can sustain good performance when an effective leader leaves. On the other hand, it also became clear to me that the lead- ership skills of the principal are critical, at least in the early years, to the success of an effort to create a formal environment of shared influence. Teachers who have just emerged from their individual boxes are not yet ready to assume leadership roles in a shared- influence setting. Schools are trapped by a leadership dilemma: they require skilled, effective principals in order to outgrow their utter dependency on those principals.

> **Schools need an external change agent to help them through the traumas of change.**

That observation led me to a fourth conclusion. In order for schools to outgrow their dependency on the principal, every member of the administrative, teaching, and classified staff—as well as some parents—must have an active role in the formal organization. Schools are small enough to function as a form of direct, rather than representative, democracy. Schools that restructure by forming a representative executive committee or leadership council, however those bodies are chosen, do not significantly change the isolated role of teachers within the organization. The effectiveness of such schools is as vulnerable to changes in staff as is the effectiveness of the principal-dominated school.

The fifth conclusion was that schools need an external change agent to help them through the traumas of change. We had organized the staff into four strategic planning units and virtually every staff member was involved in one of those units. A leadership council provided overall coordination, and the foundation bought time (by giving stipends and paying for substitutes, released time, and retreats) so that this new organization could function. Still, we were

asking the school to change in unspecified ways—to change in any
way that would improve student learning. We know how enormously painful, hard, fragile, and prolonged
change is for individuals, and the collective

**Change is a never-
ending proposition
under conditions
of dynamic
complexity.**

behavior of people organized into institutions
doesn't seem much different from—or less
intransigent than—individual behavior. Just
as for individuals, the help of a change agent
eases organizational change and, like rebar in
concrete, keeps the process from cracking
and crumbling.

Among the factors that made change traumatic in our schools
were a lack of leadership skills, unfamiliarity with recent research
and practice, inexperience in consensus building, staff discord, the
inability to prioritize and focus, the tendency to think in terms of
staff problems rather than in terms of student needs, and a reluctance
to step off into the unknown (or, rather, an inclination to take, once
again, fatal half-measures). Without a change agent, only schools
with an extraordinary staff or exceptional leadership will achieve
meaningful change and even for them it will be a long, long road,
highly vulnerable to changes in staff.

Having arrived at these convictions and then making use of
them to guide the effort, I believed for some time that the project,
which in its third year had grown to six elementary and two middle
schools, had the needed elements for change in place and that it was
only a matter of time and patience before the process began to have
an impact on student learning. As I prepared to leave the project at
the end of 1991, each of the schools had its own obdurate set of
issues, impediments, and problems, but I also became aware that,
to varying degrees, all of them were suffering from organizational
stress.

## THE STRUCTURE OF TIME

This was the source of the stress: we could buy time for the school
staffs, but they had no space to install it. Organizational activities
were crammed into every available corner of the day. It wasn't just a
matter of finding time for meetings; there had to be time for all the
additional interaction, assignments, and emotional energy that stitch
an organization—a culture—together. For those teachers who

thought a lot about what they did, we were crowding the time they would otherwise have spent thinking about their children and their classrooms by giving them the additional responsibility of thinking about the whole school.

This issue first surfaced in the project's second year, when Louise Bay Waters, a change agent for one of the schools, wrote a short paper on the promises and pitfalls of shared decision making. She wrote, "Time is the final, and most worrisome, potential problem with shared decision making. Teachers may become so involved with school management that they actually end up less effective in the classroom, or even burnt out." At the time, I thought that the problem was real but confined to a few especially active teachers and that is was caused primarily by the extra turmoil of the project's early stages. As the new ways of doing things became routine, even the most active teachers would find ways to balance their activities; in the meantime, we simply needed to be alert to the problem and to deal with it on an individual basis. But, following some meetings with teachers and principals in the fall of 1991, I began to think that the problem was more serious, if not endemic, and was linked to the issue of infrastructure.

> **Like most people in any other job, teachers don't necessarily work at 100% capacity, whatever that is.**

It makes sense, after all. The traditional school organizes the school day so that teaching itself, including the preparation and the paperwork, both administrative and academic, is a full-time job. Still, like most people in any other job, teachers don't necessarily work at 100% capacity, whatever that is. There is some room for most teachers to become more engaged with their schools. However, like a factory—but unlike most other organizations—a school doesn't have much flexibility for structuring into the schedule the kind of time that teachers need to make schools a collegial effort.

The tension between teaching and school leadership activities cannot be resolved by suboptimizing both. If restructuring is to make any difference, teachers need to be able to perform at their best in each role, and the roles need to be complementary, integrated, and synergistic.

According to the cross-national study Harold Stevenson and his colleagues conducted in the United States and Asia, in schools in China, Taiwan, and Japan where students seem to perform better academically than their U.S. counterparts, an eight-hour school day is structured so that teachers are in charge of classes only 60% of the time they are at school, and teaching itself is a group endeavor. Stevenson reports

**The school simply cannot continue to function traditionally.**

that, "Asian teachers are able to engage children's interest not because they have insights that are unknown in the U.S. but because they take well-known principles and have the time and energy to apply them with remarkable skill."[4]

I'm certain that the most radical and politically difficult element of school restructuring is what needs to be done with the use of time in schools so that teachers can expand their role. The barriers to establishing an eight-hour school day, for example, are probably insurmountable. Cost is certainly a major impediment, but parents and the community are also serious obstacles to change (which doesn't bode well for school choice as a change agent). A school in Southern California set aside Wednesdays for teachers to work together outside the classroom. The other four school days were slightly extended and on Wednesdays, the students worked on interactive, cooperative learning projects under the guidance of a permanently-assigned substitute teacher. A group of parents concerned about the use of substitutes ended that promising experiment after one year. Members of Theodore Sizer's Coalition of Essential Schools run into trouble with parents who resist change for a variety of reasons. Interschool athletics, beloved by parents and the community, are an overwhelming barrier to any significant change in the structure of time in high schools. Afternoons, after all, are needed for practices and games.

Nevertheless, no matter how unthinkable radical change in the school day may be, the school simply cannot continue to function traditionally, with a compressed academic day during which each teacher sticks to his or her own room and duties, as the sociologist Dan Lortie described it.[5] I believe that this factory model has never been in the best interests of teaching and learning, for the reason that Susan Moore Johnson expressed, "A lone teacher can impart phonics, fractions, the pluperfect tense, or the periodic table, but only through teachers' collective efforts will schools produce educated graduates who can read and compute; apply scientific principles; comprehend the lessons of history; value others' cultures and speak their languages; and conduct themselves responsibly as citizens. Such accomplishments are the product of a corporate venture."[6] We simply didn't know what schools were missing, but since the 1960s the social changes and expectations that have overpowered our schools and teachers have created huge cracks in the inherently faulty structure of our schools.

Those changes seem to fall into four categories: growth, diversity, inclusion, and social dislocations. First is the mismatch between growth and resources. Classrooms, schools, and, sometimes, districts are too large. They have grown beyond human scale for effective teaching, learning, and the management of these activities. Second is the phenomenal expansion of ethnic, linguistic, and cultural diversity in the classroom and the school. Third is the expectation of full inclusiveness. We have come to believe that all children can learn and should stay in school to do so.

> **Unfortunately, the traditional school does not have the organizational capacity to formulate goals.**

Fourth is a set of social changes or dislocations that have occurred over the past three decades: single-parent families, latchkey children, poverty, poor health, drugs, gangs, and violence.

Traditional schools and large bureaucratic districts cannot cope with these changes because they do not have a structure that supports an environment capable of change. The educational system is a series of closed containers—classrooms, schools, central office fiefdoms (which is what we mean by the egg crate or cellular model)—all of which are surrounded by competing special interests. Change requires a dynamic, open, self-examining, interactive system.

## CULTURE

The qualities just listed described a culture, not a structure. But the creation and life of a desired culture depend on a compatible supporting structure. Fred Newmann wrote that the restructuring movement is going about the process of change in the wrong way, by "trying to design organizational structures before clarifying purposes and reaching consensus on the educational ends that organizational structures should serve."[7] Unfortunately, the traditional school does not have the organizational capacity to formulate goals, desired outcomes, and strategies. Schools need to change their organization in order to change their culture. I would modify Newmann's observation by substituting the word "governance" for "structures" or by saying that the restructuring movement is trying to design organizational structures without sufficient regard for the culture the schools need in order to clarify purposes, to reach consensus, to ratchet student learning to a higher level.

We take for granted that the function of organization is to create levels of authority for the purpose of moving decisions and direction downward. Based on that assumption, we have made an enormous investment in maintaining a bureaucracy whose directions teachers can simply ignore behind the closed doors of their classrooms.

The kind of culture and supporting structure schools now need reduces both top-down bureaucratic direction and classroom autonomy. In the Telesis Foundation schools, the team leaders and project coordinators do not in any sense supervise units or teams of teachers. Rather, they are elected volunteers from among the staff whose role—in addition to teaching, counseling, or administering—is to facilitate the upward (and lateral) movement of influence through the organization. Schools require a very special nexus of culture, time, and structure, in which a certain kind of culture assumes the function that authority plays in traditional organizations, classic bureaucracies. A diagram of the formal organization of a school restructured in this manner might show overlapping circles representing spheres of influence, rather than boxes representing areas of responsibility and levels of authority.

When a school practices shared influence, it does not mean the decisions—and, therefore, power—are simply delegated to, or even vested in, an individual or a committee. Rather, through some consensus-building process established by the school, everyone in the school community has at least an opportunity to influence outcomes. Decision-making power that resides in one person or group may change other people's behavior but not their preferences. Influence has the more difficult task of changing preferences and therefore behavior. Or, perhaps more realistically, an accepted, collective process of shared influence realaxes the grip that personal preference has on individuals. In a shared-influence setting, teacher have less individual autonomy because the pressure to do things differently comes from a source that they need to respond to—their peers. The loss of individual autonomy is offset, however, by the collective ability to do things on behalf of student learning that the teacher was not able to do in isolation.

These thoughts clicked into place in my mind as I listened to the principals of the schools in the Pacific Telesis Foundation project air their frustrations with shared decision making. Initially, most of the principals thought that this process meant outright delegation. Finally, Bruce Baron, principal of Los Naranjos School in Irvine, said that he'd dropped the term in favor of "shared influence," because he realized that he too, after all, was still a member of the staff and in his role had valuable things to bring to the consensus-building process. The delicate skill the principal needs is the ability to bring those things to the process without cloaking them in robes of authority. The principal's suggestions, like everyone else's, must be able to stand on their own merits. The operative word is *culture*—not governance, not positional authority.

> **Culture is organic to its community. If culture changes, everything changes.**

In recent years, many organizations have been convinced that they needed to change their culture. But culture—the values, beliefs, behaviors, rules, products, signs, and symbols that bind us together—is not something we can change like a flat tire. Culture is organic to its community. If culture changes, everything changes. For schools to become organically different, it isn't nearly enough to repeat like a mantra, "Every child can learn." What psychoanalyst Allen Wheelis says about individual change seems equally true of organizational change, "Since we are what we do, if we want to change what we are we must begin by changing what we do." He adds, "We are wise to believe it difficult to change, to recognize that character has a forward propulsion which tends to carry it unaltered into the future, but we need not to believe it impossible to change." Although a change agent may be a critical enabling factor, the responsibility for change obviously lies with those whose behavior determine whether change has taken place. The plastic surgeons of organizational behavior— those with copyrighted paradigms to push—cannot do the work for us. "We are," Wheelis says, "no more the product of our therapists than of our genes: we create ourselves. The sequence is suffering, insight, will, action, change."[8]

## FINDING THEIR OWN WAY

As we think about how schools should change, we hamstring ourselves by our labored and distracting efforts to find an analogue or
metaphor for how they ought to work. We have not been properly
discouraged by the disastrous results of turning the factory metaphor
into reality.

Thomas Timar suggests that a baseball team, which "exemplifies a dynamic organizational culture that reconfigures itself to be
competitive in new situations," is a better
metaphor for schools than a factory.[9] Among
other difficulties with his metaphor, I just
can't find any trace of a analogue for students on a baseball team—nor, in the routines of teachers, do I find anything
comparable to spending half the work day
sitting together rather idly in a dug out. Still,
Timar has come up with a good description
of what a school culture ought to be. He
knows the difference between metaphor and
analogue and is only suggesting that, as organizations and cultures,
schools ought to be the polar opposite of a factory. But we need to
say that in another way.

> "Each school will have to find its own way, because everywhere the talents and the possibilities are different."

There simply isn't any other organized, human activity, either
in metaphor or in reality, that is anything like the collective effort of
a community to impart learning and character to children, to enable
them to become active, productive citizens. We need to set aside the
metaphors like "smart machines," concepts like the marketplace, and
questions like "who is the customer?"—because all of them, drawn
from other kinds of organized activity, narrow our ability to come to
terms with, to capitalize on, to envision the uniqueness of schools.

Schools are not only different from other organizations, but
they are profoundly individual in their specific circumstances. One
of the Telesis Foundation schools is located in a dysfunctional urban
area and has a student population that is 95% black; another has
seven significant groups of children whose first language is not
English; another has a student population that is 95% Latino, with
many students whose parents are migratory laborers; another is
stratified about equally into three social groups: children from
upper-middle class families, children whose families live in low-cost

housing, and children of enlisted military personnel; another is an
ethnically diverse suburban school that is taking on urban characteristics; another is a brand-new school with a magnet program and a
hand-picked faculty; another is an urban middle school with 400 students, 95% of them black, for whom safety going to and from school
is the number-one concern; another is a middle school serving more
than a thousand youngsters about equally divided among whites,
blacks, Latinos, and Asians, 20% of whom are not native English
speakers and, combined, speak 12 different languages. Two of the
schools operate year-round, one with four tracks and one with a
single track. The faculties, too, differ in many ways from school to
school. As David Kirp wrote recently in a critique of school choice,
"Each school will have to find its own way, because everywhere the
talents and the possibilities are different."[10]

## MAKING CHANGE POSSIBLE

Saying that each school must find its own way, however, does not
mean that it will not need a little help from its friends. Whether that
help is from the state, the district, or the change agent, the form that
is should take is the creation of an environment that is both enabling
and motivating—providing sanction, protection, capacity, knowledge, resources, and the opportunity to change—combined with a
set of expectations and the sensitivity to know when, where, in what
direction, and how hard to push.

The function of the change agent is to prepare and organize the
school for change; to identify the areas in which staff members are
weak, such as leadership skills and group decision making, and to
provide the training that they need; to help the principal adapt to a
new management style; to assist in the vision, mission, goals, objectives, measurements, and timetables; to identify the impediments
that are peculiar to the school and help the staff recognize and overcome them; to keep the focus of activity on improved student
achievement; to recognize when schools are attempting too little or
too much and then to help them establish the right pace of change;
to enable schools to circumvent district and state bureaucracies and
provide them air cover against interference from the district; and to
create networks within which teachers and principals can interact
with their peers from other schools and districts. Ideally, the change
agent would have experience as a teacher and an administrator;

skills in group facilitation; political savvy; a good knowledge of current research and practice in the areas of teaching, curriculum, and assessment; and a personal vision of and commitment to school improvement.

A change agent can work effectively with as many as five elementary schools within a district but with only two or, at most, three high schools. In the initial stages, it would be preferable if change agents were not district employees, but—unless the district obtains a corporate, foundation, or state grant—it is hardly likely that it could afford a corps of outside change agents. To build up its internal capacity for assisting change, a district should retain one outside person who would train, oversee, and back up a cadre of change agents who have been recruited from within the district. To make room for the change agents, the district would begin its own restructuring by eliminating such positions as curriculum coordinator and other school support roles that will be assumed by the schools. District change agents should hold the same rank as school principals and should be allowed by the district to approach their job objectively and independently. If the agents are district employees, they, as well as the schools, need to be shielded from overbearing district rules and procedures.

> **It is the principal who has the most crucial and sensitive role.**

As schools move through the process of change, the role and involvement of the agent diminishes, though not at the same rate or in the same way for every school. Nor does it ever entirely go away. Because schools must be dynamic organizations, identifying and adapting to changing circumstances and improved teaching methods and curriculum, they need someone who stands outside and looks at their culture and effectiveness with a cold eye and a warm heart, who would not be tempted to let difficult circumstances limit what the school believes it can achieve, who will not allow the school ever again to be a static organization, who cannot be co-opted by either the district or the school.

The change agent is an indispensable figure, but it is the principal who has the most crucial and sensitive role. Within the Telesis Foundation project, even the best principals—those who had an innate talent for managing a shared-influence environment—were not sufficiently prepared for the change in their role. But once they had weathered some initial stress, their lack of preparation did not hinder the process from moving forward. If a principal cannot manage well in a shared-influence setting, however, any change or improvement in the school will be marginal at best. Most districts will have very many principals who are up to the job. Shared influence requires principals who are intuitive, risk-taking, visionary, self-confident, empathetic, and trusting. These are the implied qualities of the best kind of leader, summed up about 2,600 years ago by Lao Tzu, who wrote, "When his work is done, the people say, 'Amazing: we did it, all by ourselves!'"[11]

The number of schools that a district can initially undertake to change will be limited by the number of available change agents and by the number of qualified principals, so districts must find a way rather rapidly to develop and enlarge the pool of both. That talent pool will come largely from teachers who experience the process and come forward to take leadership roles in their schools. While leadership academies for principals may be helpful for setting the stage, management skills and styles are learned primarily by experience, access to on-the-job consultation, and interaction with peers who are working through the same process of change.

## FINDING THE TIME

A culture can't change and an organization can't function unless they can make use of time in a way that sustains their life, like oxygen to the blood. Somehow, we need to find a way to provide teachers with the time they need to make productive use of their collective energy.

A basic requirement for all schools is that the full staff meet for at least three days before the start of school to set the agenda and the calendar for the year, to organize teams, and to elect leaders. Nearly as vital is a full staff meeting for a couple of days at the end of the school year to assess results, to set preliminary objectives for the next year, and to designate staff members who will do those things that need to be done over the summer, such as compiling research or receiving training. Year-round schools need to make time in their calendars at some point for these full staff conferences.

Time also needs to be found during the year. The Pacific Telesis Foundation schools have lengthened some days and shortened others in various ways to make time available for collective

effort. At Will C. Wood Middle School in Sacramento, which has
divided its 1,000 students and its faculty into eight houses, students
come to school 1 ½ hours later than normal
every Wednesday so that the house faculties

**Because teachers
make the calendar,
teachers can
also change it.**

can meet. But other team configurations,
such as house leaders, the leadership council,
subject-area teachers, and special groups like
the technology team, simply meet when they
can—usually after school, some on a regular
schedule, others not. Will C. Wood also takes

advantage of the eight days that California allows for school to be
out of session so that teachers can come together to plan for school
improvement.

The modifications of the school schedule at Will C. Wood and
the other Telesis Foundation schools are rather modest and don't
break the mold of the traditional school. They are, in other words,
adaptive responses. The schools are trying to make a new organization and culture work without sufficient time, which is surely a
recipe for organizational stress. Los Naranjos Elementary School,
however, has combined its modified schedule with a disciplined
planning and scheduling process. Beginning in May, the whole staff
agrees on the school improvement activities for the next year. These
are then developed into strategies by teams. (Every staff member is
on a team and teams may change from year to year. In 1992–93, the
four teams were devoted to instructional strategies, language arts,
technology, and assessment.) The whole staff decides what the
school's priorities will be, how much time will be spent on each
strategy, and who will be responsible for development and implementation. A steering committee then puts together a full-year calendar that includes all team meetings, grade-level meetings, and full
staff meetings, along with the subject of each meeting. The calendar
is completed in June before school is out.

Because teachers make the calendar, teachers can also change
it. But if new venture is added, some other strategy or activity must
be eliminated or diminished, which requires the agreement of the
full staff. "The mistake most schools make," says Principal Baron,
"is that they plan their use of time month by month, and they keep
tossing in new things to work on." At the beginning of the 1991–92
school year, when the district asked all schools to undertake a self-
esteem strategy, Los Naranjos was able to say no, wait until next

year, because it could show the district a full school improvement calendar and agenda for the year.

In order to create time, Los Naranjos makes use of its eight school improvement days and has also slightly lengthened four weekdays and shortened Wednesdays, dismissing students at 1 p.m. The calendar includes the specific use of all Wednesday afternoons by teams of teachers.

The school worked with parents to gain support for both the eight school improvement days and the short Wednesdays, convincing parents that, if they wanted the improvements they were beginning to see to continue, they must give the teachers time. During this outreach process, parents themselves chose to schedule the school improvement days immediately following holidays.

The formula Los Naranjos has adopted in order to make maximum use of the time available in a traditional schedule—that is, disciplined planning and scheduling combined with concentration on a limited number of strategies—is an approach that should be used no matter how radically a school is able to restructure its schedule. As Baron points out, Los Naranjos budgets time just as it budgets money. It itemizes what the time is for, how much time is needed, when it will be used, and who will use it.

The Los Naranjos year-long calendar is an effective mechanism for husbanding both time and the number of issues the school chooses to address during the year—creating a sharp staff focus and making certain there is a match between time and activities. The teachers can prepare themselves to balance teaching responsibilities and collegial activities. "Teachers have a real solid feeling they will get something done during the year," Baron says.

Nevertheless, the modifications of the schedule at both Los Naranjos and Will C. Wood amount to adaptive responses rather than creative, formal innovations. Although schools can find ways to rearrange their schedules to make some time for collective effort, these modifications do not provide enough time for the adequate involvement of every staff member and all internal interests. The problem of time is greater for large middle and high schools because they are more complex than elementary schools and need more structured planning time to attack their issues from different angles.

Collective time needs to be treated, Baron says, as a valuable and scarce commodity that is formally scheduled and rigorously allocated to specific aspects of the school's agenda. Just as the state requires a certain number of classroom minutes and a certain number of teaching days a year, it (or the districts) should find a way to formalize a certain amount of collective staff time, as the Asian schools do, leaving it up to the schools and their communities to determine how best to reconfigure the school day. Until that happens, all collective time is ad hoc, vulnerable to shifts in leadership, and most likely thought of as an add-on rather than as an integrated activity.

## TURNING UP THE HEAT

Like the Pacific Telesis Foundation schools, hundreds of other schools across the country are engaged in school reform activities. Even though each school must find its own way, it needs a system that is supportive and also willing to change itself. When only one or two or a few schools within a district are changing, the district can tolerate, or even encourage, that activity without changing its own practices, procedures, organization, staffing, and role—that is to say, its own culture. But until the district culture becomes aligned with that of the school, any changes an individual school makes are vulnerable. In addition, individual schools may be able to show the way, but they can't collectively create a critical mass for change. Samuel Johnson wrote that a scattered people resemble "rays diverging from a focus. All the rays remain, but the heat is gone. Their power consist[s] in their concentration; when they are dispersed, they have no effect."[12] Once, while walking along a Santa Barbara coast road on a starry but moonless night, I walked right into a tree. Change throughout the system will not come about through a thousand points of light but from the steady increasing, concentrated light and heat of one sun.

Turning up the heat is a district responsibility. When all the schools within a reasonably-sized district have undergone culture change and the district administration has aligned itself with its schools, the system itself will have something to build on. In most districts, however, a diversity of interests scatters any effort to coalesce around the best interests of schools. A restructuring effort that begins with special-interest politics will end the same way.

A district capable of cultural change must have certain characteristics: a supportive, patient school board; a superintendent who is a skilled leader with a vision for change; a cooperative, unthreatened middle management; a reasonable relationship with the union. These characteristics suggest that, in the beginning, the successful districts will most likely be small- to medium-sized, with not much more than 25,000 students, and they will be part of fairly cohesive communities whose special interests are not extremely divergent. When districts of this size are manifestly successful, then perhaps the larger districts, which are more grievously plagued with special interests, will be able to motivate those interests to come together. However, I suspect that the very largest districts are simply beyond human scale and need to be broken up before comprehensive change can take place.

> **The reform of structure, time, and culture does not ensure school improvement; it only makes it possible.**

The reform of structure, time, and culture does not ensure school improvement; it only makes it possible. Schools will continue to vary in quality—but, in general, from wherever they start, they will have the capacity to raise themselves to another level. In California the schools have some reliable guides for putting their collegial capability to work on school improvement: the reports of the state task forces on school improvement at the elementary, middle, and high school levels (*It's elementary, Caught in the Middle,* and *Second to None*); the state curriculum frameworks; and the revised, performance-based California achievement tests.

Without the reform of structure, time, and culture, school improvement projects can be propped up for some time with grant money and the efforts of external organizations. But unless all the elements of change become inherent within the school and the district, enabling the school to stand substantially by itself, school improvement efforts will eventually collapse.

Michael Kirst has said that *restructuring* has no objective meaning; it means whatever the speaker has in mind at the moment. To my mind, *restructuring* means something literal; the formal rearrangement of the use of time in schools to allow them to create and sustain the kind of interactive culture and supporting infrastructure they need to improve student learning—to bring about the creation of truly new American schools.

# NOTES

1. Joseph A. Schumpeter, "The Creative Response in Economic History," *Journal of Economic History,* November 1947, pp. 149–59.

2. John I. Goodlad, *A Place Called School* (New York: McGraw-Hill, 1984), p. 188.

3. Tracy Kidder, *Among Schoolchildren* (Boston: Houghton Mifflin, 1989), p. 199.

4. Harold W. Stevenson, "Learning from Asian Schools," *Scientific American,* December 1992, p. 76.

5. Dan C. Lortie, *Schoolteacher* (Chicago: University of Chicago Press, 1975).

6. Susan Moore Johnson, *Teachers at Work* (New York: Basic Books, 1990), p. 149.

7. Fred M. Newmann, "Linking Restructuring to Authentic Student Achievement," *Phi Delta Kappan,* February 1991, p. 459.

8. Allen Wheelis, *How People Change* (New York: Harper Torchbooks, 1973), pp. 13, 101, 102.

9. Thomas Timar, "The Politics of School Restructuring," *Phi Delta Kappan,* December 1989, pp. 264–75.

10. David L. Kirp, "What School Choice Really Means," *Atlantic,* November 1992, pp. 119–32.

11. Lao Tzu, *Tao Te Ching,* trans. Stephen Mitchell (New York: Harper & Row, 1988), poem 17.

12. Samuel Johnson, *A Journey to the Western Islands of Scotland* (1775; reprint, London: Oxford University Press, 1970), p. 119.

# School/Family/Community Partnerships
## Caring for the Children We Share

by Joyce L. Epstein

*Ms. Epstein summarizes the theory, framework, and guidelines that can assist schools in building partnerships.*

T he way schools care about children is reflected in the way schools care about the children's families. If educators view children simply as *students,* they are likely to see the family as separate from the school. That is, the family is expected to do its job and leave the education of children to the schools. If educators view students as *children,* they are likely to see both the family and the community as partners with the school in children's education and development. Partners recognize their shared interests in and responsibilities for children, and they work together to create better programs and opportunities for students.

There are many reasons for developing school, family, and community partnerships. They can improve school programs and school climate, provide family services and support, increase parents' skills and leadership, connect families with others in the school and the community, and help teachers with their work. However, the main reason to create such partnerships is to help all youngsters succeed in school and in later life. When parents, teachers, students, and others view one another as partners in education, a caring community forms around students and begins its work.

What do successful partnership programs look like? How can practices be effectively designed and implemented? What are the results of better communications, interactions, and exchanges across these three important contexts? These questions have challenged

From *Phi Delta Kappan,* May 1995, pp. 701–712. © 1995 by Phi Delta Kappa. Reprinted with permission.

research and practice, creating an interdisciplinary field of inquiry into school, family, and community partnerships with "caring" as a core concept.

The field has been strengthened by supporting federal, state, and local policies. For example, the Goals 2000 legislation sets partnerships as a voluntary national goal for all schools; Title I specifies and mandates programs and practices of partnership in order for schools to qualify for or maintain funding. Many states and districts have developed or are preparing policies to guide schools in creating more systematic connections with families and communities. These policies reflect research results and the prior successes of leading educators who have shown that these goals are attainable.

Underlying these policies and programs are a theory of how social organizations connect; a framework of the basic components of school, family, and community partnerships for children's learning; a growing literature on the positive and negative results of these connections for students, families, and schools; and an understanding of how to organize good programs. In this article, I summarize the theory, framework, and guidelines that have assisted the schools in our research projects in building partnerships and that should help any elementary, middle, or high school to take similar steps.

## OVERLAPPING SPHERES OF INFLUENCE: UNDERSTANDING THE THEORY

Schools make choices. They might conduct only a few communications and interactions with families and communities, keeping the three spheres of influence that directly affect student learning and development relatively separate. Or they might conduct many high-quality communications and interactions designed to bring all three spheres of influence closer together. With frequent interactions between schools, families, and communities, more students are more likely to receive common messages from various people about the importance of school, of working hard, of thinking creatively, of helping one another, and of staying in school.

The *external model* of overlapping spheres of influence recognizes that the three major contexts in which students learn and grow—the family, the school, and the community—may be drawn together or pushed apart. In this model, there are some practices that schools, families, and communities conduct separately and some that they conduct jointly in order to influence children's learning and development. The *internal* model of the inter-action of the three spheres of influence shows where and how complex and essential inter-personal relations and patterns of influence occur between individuals at home, at school, and in the community. These social relation-ships may be enacted and studied at an *insti-tutional* level (e.g., when a school invites all families to an event or sends the same com-munications to all families) and at an *indi-vidual* level (e.g., when a parent and a teacher meet in conference or talk by phone). Connections between schools or parents and community groups, agencies, and services can also be represented and studied within the model.[1]

> **The model of school, family, and community partnerships locates the student at the center.**

The model of school, family, and community partnerships locates the student at the center. The inarguable fact is that students are the main actors in their education, development, and success in school. School, family, and community partnerships cannot simply produce successful students. Rather, partnership activities may be designed to engage, guide, energize, and motivate students to pro-duce their own successes. The assumption that, if children feel cared for and are encouraged to work hard in the role of student, they are more likely to do their best to learn to read, write, calculate, and learn other skills and talents and to remain in school.

Interestingly and somewhat ironically, studies indicate that stu-dents are also crucial for the success of school, family, and commu-nity partnerships. Students are often their parents' main source of information about school. In strong partnership programs, teachers help students understand and conduct traditional communications with families (e.g., delivering memos or report cards) and new com-munications (e.g., interacting with family members about homework or participating in parent/teacher/student conferences). As we gain more information about the role of students in partnerships, we are developing a more complete understanding of how schools, families, and communities must work with students to increase their chances for success.

### How Theory Sounds in Practice

In some schools there are still educators who say, "If the family would just do its job, we could do our job." And there are still families who say, "I raised this child; now it is your job to educate her." These words embody the theory of "separate spheres of influence." Other educators say, "I cannot do my job without the help of my students' families and the support of this community." And some parents say, "I really need to know what is happening in school in order to help my child." These phrases embody the theory of "overlapping spheres of influence."

In a partnership, teachers and administrators create more *family-like* schools. A family-like school recognizes each child's individuality and makes each child feel special and included. Family-like schools welcome all families, not just those who are easy to reach. In a partnership, parents create more *school-like* families. A school-like family recognizes that each child is also a student. Families reinforce the importance of school, homework, and activities that build student skills and feelings of success. Communities, including groups of parents working together, create school-like opportunities, events, and programs that reinforce, recognize, and reward students for good progress, creativity, contributions, and excellence. Communities also create *family-like* settings, services, and events to enable families to better support their children. *Community-minded* families and students help their neighborhoods and other families. The concept of a community school is re-emerging. It refers to a place where programs and services for students, parents, and others are offered before, during, and after the regular school day.

> **Family-like schools welcome all families, not just those that are easy to reach.**

Schools and communities talk about programs and services that are "family-friendly"—meaning that they take into account the needs and realities of family life in the 1990s, are feasible to conduct, and are equitable toward all families. When all these concepts combine, children experience *learning communities* or *caring communities.*[2]

All these terms are consistent with the theory of overlapping spheres of influence, but they are not abstract concepts. You will find them daily in conversations, news stories, and celebrations of many kinds. In a family-like school, a teacher might say, "I know when a student is having a bad day and how to help him along." A student might slip and call a teacher "mom" or "dad" and then laugh with a mixture of embarrassment and glee. In a school-like family, a parent might say, "I make sure my daughter knows that homework comes first." A child might raise his hand to speak at the dinner table and then joke about acting as if he were still in school. When communities reach out to student sand their families,

> **It is possible to have a school that is excellent academically but ignores families.**

youngsters might say, "This program really made my schoolwork make sense!" Parents or educators might comment, "This community really supports its schools."

Once people hear about such concepts as family-like schools or school-like families, they remember positive examples of schools, teachers, and places in the community that were "like a family" to them. They may remember how a teacher paid individual attention to them, recognized their uniqueness, or praised them for real progress, just as a parent might. Or they might recall things at home that were "just like school" and supported their work as a student, or they might remember community activities that made them feel smart or good about themselves and their families. They will recall that parents, siblings, and other family members engaged in and enjoyed educational activities and took pride in the good schoolwork or homework that they did, just as a teacher might.

## How Partnerships Work in Practice

These terms and examples are evidence of the *potential* for schools, families, and communities to create caring educational environments. It is possible to have a school that is excellent academically but ignores families. However, that school will build barriers between teachers, parents, and children—barriers that affect school life and learning. It is possible to have a school that is ineffective academically but involves families in many good ways. With its weak academic program, that school will shortchange students' learning. Neither of these schools exemplifies a caring educational environment that requires academic excellence, good communications, and productive interactions involving school, family, and community.

Some children succeed in school without much family involvement or despite family neglect or distress, particularly if the school has excellent academic and support programs. Teachers, relatives outside of the immediate family, other families, and members of the community can provide important guidance and encouragement to these students. As support from school, family, and community accumulates, significantly more students feel secure and cared for, understand the goals of education, work to achieve to their full potential, build positive attitudes and school behaviors, and stay in school. The shared interests and investments of schools, families, and communities create the conditions of caring that work to "overdetermine" the likelihood of student success.[3]

Any practice can be designed and implemented well or poorly. And even well-implemented partnership practices may not be useful to all families. In a caring school community, participants work continually to improve the nature and effects of partnerships. Although the interactions of educators, parents, students, and community members will not always be smooth or successful, partnership programs establish a base of respect and trust on which to build. Good partnerships withstand questions, conflicts, debates, and disagreements; provide structures and processes to solve problems; and are maintained—even strengthened—after differences have been resolved. Without this firm base, disagreements and problems that are sure to arise about schools and students will be harder to solve.

### What Research Says

In surveys and field studies involving teachers, parents, and students at the elementary, middle, and high school levels, some important patterns relating to partnerships have emerged.[4]

- Partnerships tend to decline across the grades, *unless* schools and teachers work to develop and implement appropriate practices or partnership at each grade level.
- Affluent communities currently have more positive family involvement, on average, *unless* schools and teachers in economically distressed communities work to build positive partnerships with their students' families.
- Schools in more economically depressed communities make more contacts with families about the problems and difficulties their children are having, *unless* they work at developing balanced partnership programs that include contacts about positive accomplishments of students.

- Single parents, parents who are employed outside the home, parents who live far from the school, and fathers are less involved, on average, at the school building, *unless* the school organizes opportunities for families to volunteer at various times and in various places to support the school and their children.

Researchers have also drawn the following conclusions.

- Just about all families care about their children, want them to succeed, and are eager to obtain better information from schools and communities so as to remain good partners in their children's education.

- Just about all teachers and administrators would like to involve families, but many do not know how to go about building positive and productive programs and are consequently fearful about trying. This creates a "rhetoric rut," in which educators are stuck, expressing support for partnerships without taking any action.

- Just about all students at all levels—elementary, middle, and high school—want their families to be more knowledgeable partners about schooling and are willing to take active roles in assisting communications between home and school. However, students need much better information and guidance than most now receive about how their schools view partnerships and about how they can conduct important exchanges with their families about school activities, homework, and school decisions.

The research results are important because they indicate that caring communities can be built, on purpose; that they include families that might not become involved on their own; and that, by their own reports, just about all families, students, and teachers believe that partnerships are important for helping students succeed across the grades.

Good programs will look different in each site, as individual schools tailor their practices to meet the needs and interests, time and talents, ages and grade levels of students and their families. However, there are some commonalties across successful programs at all grade levels. These include a recognition of the overlapping spheres of influence on student development; attention to various types of involvement that promote a variety of opportunities for schools, families, and communities to work together; and an Action Team for School, Family, and Community Partnerships to coordinate each school's work and progress.

## SIX TYPES OF INVOLVEMENT; SIX TYPES OF CARING

A framework of six major types of involvement has evolved from many studies and from many years of work by educators and families in elementary, middle, and high schools. The framework (summarized in the accompanying tables) helps educators develop more comprehensive programs of school and family partnerships and also helps researchers locate their questions and results in ways that inform and improve practice.[5]

**Schools have choices about which practices will help achieve important goals.**

Each type of involvement includes many different *practices* of partnership (see Table 1). Each type presents particular *challenges* that must be met in order to involve all families and needed *redefinitions* of some basic principles of involvement (see Table 2). Finally, each type is likely to lead to different *results* for students, for parents, for teaching practice, and for school climate (see Table 3). Thus schools have choices about which practices will help achieve important goals. The tables provide examples of practices, challenges for successful implementation, redefinitions for up-to-date understanding, and results that have been documented and observed.

### Charting the Course

The entries in the tables are illustrative. The sample practices displayed in Table 1 are only a few of hundreds that may be selected or designed for each type of involvement. Although all schools may use the framework of six types as a guide, each school must chart its own course in choosing practices to meet the needs of its families and students.

The challenges shown (Table 2) are just a few of many that relate to the examples. There are challenges—that is, problems—for every practice of partnership, and they must be resolved in order to reach and engage all families in the best ways. Often, when one challenge is met, a new one will emerge.

The redefinitions (also in Table 2) redirect old notions so that involvement is not viewed solely as or measured only by "bodies in the building." As examples the table calls for redefinitions of workshops, communication, volunteers, homework, decision making, and community. By redefining these familiar terms, it is possible for partnership programs to reach out in new ways to many more families.

The selected results (Table 3) should help correct the widespread misperception that any practice that involves families will raise children's achievement test scores. Instead, in the short term, certain practices are more likely than others to influence students' skills and scores, while other practices are more likely to affect attitudes and behaviors. Although students are the main focus of partnerships, the various types of involvement also promote various kinds of results for parents and for teachers. For example, the expected results for parents include not only leadership in decision making, but also confidence about parenting, productive curriculum-related interactions with children, and many interactions with other parents and the school. The expected results for teachers include not only improved parent/teacher conferences or school/home communications, but also better understanding of families, new approaches to homework, and other connections with families and the community.

Most of the results noted in Table 3 have been measured in at least one research study and observed as schools conduct their work. The entries are listed in positive terms to indicate the results of well-designed and well-implemented practices. It should be fully understood, however, that results may be negative if poorly designed practices exclude families or create greater barriers to communication and exchange. Research is still needed on the results of specific practices of partnership in various schools, at various grade levels, and for diverse populations of students, families, and teachers. It will be important to confirm, extend, or correct the information on results listed in Table 3 if schools are to make purposeful choices among practices that foster various types of involvement.

The tables cannot show the connections that occur when one practice activates several types of involvement simultaneously. For example, volunteers may organize and conduct a food bank (Type 3) that allows parents to pay $15 for $30 worth of food for their families (Type 1). The food may be subsidized by community agencies (Type 6). The recipients might then serve as volunteers for the program or in the community (perpetuating Type 3 and Type 6 activities). Or consider another example. An after-school homework club run by volunteers and the community recreation department combines Type 3 and Type 6 practices. Yet it also serves as a Type 1 activity, because the after-school program assists families with the supervision of their children. This practice may also alter the way homework interactions are conducted between students and parents

**Table 1. Epstein's Framework of Six Types of Involvement and Sample Practices**

| Type 1 Parenting | Type 2 Communicating | Type 3 Volunteering |
|---|---|---|
| Help all families establish home environments to support children as students. | Design effective forms of school-to-home and home-to-school communications about school programs and children's progress. | Recruit and organize parent help and support. |
| **Sample Practices** | **Sample Practices** | **Sample Practices** |
| Suggestions for home conditions that support learning at each grade level. | Conferences with every parent at least once a year, with follow-ups as needed. | School and classroom volunteer program to help teachers, administrators, students, and other parents. |
| Workshops, videotapes, computerized phone messages on parenting and child rearing at each age and grade level. | Language translators to assist families as needed. | Parent room or family center for volunteer work, meetings, resources for families. |
| Parent education and other courses or training for parents (e.g., GED, college credit, family literacy). | Weekly or monthly folders of student work sent home for review and comments. | Annual postcard survey to identify all available talents, times, and locations of volunteers. |
| Family suport programs to assist families with health, nutrition, and other services. | Parent/student pickup of report card, with conferences on improving grades. | Class parent, telephone tree, or other structures to provide all families with needed information. |
| Home visits at transition points to preschool, elementary, middle, and high school. Neighborhood meetings to help families understand schools and to help schools understand families. | Regular schedule of useful notices, memos, phone calls, newsletters, and other communications. | Parent patrols or other activities to aid safety and operation of school programs. |
| | Clear, information on choosing schools or courses, programs, and activities within schools. | |
| | Clear information on all school policies, programs, reforms, and transitions. | |

| Type 4<br>Learning at Home | Type 5<br>Decision Making | Type 6<br>Collaborating with Community |
| --- | --- | --- |
| Provide information and ideas to families about how to help students at home with homework and other curriculum-related activities, decisions, and planning. | Include parents in school decisions, developing parent leaders and representatives. | Identify and integrate resources and services from community to strengthen school programs, family practices, and student learning and development. |
| **Sample Practices**<br><br>Information for families on skills required for students in all subjects at each grade.<br><br>Information on homework policies and how to monitor and discuss schoolwork at home.<br><br>Information on how to assist students to improve skills on various class and school assessments.<br><br>Regular schedule of homework that requires students to discuss and interact with families on what they are learning in class.<br><br>Calendars with activities for parents and students at home.<br><br>Family math, science, and reading activities at school.<br><br>Summer learning packets or activities.<br><br>Family participation in setting student goals each year and in planning for college or work. | **Sample Practices**<br><br>Active PTA/PTO or other parent organizations, advisory councils, or committees (e.g., curriculum, safety, personnel) for parent leadership and participation.<br><br>Independent advocacy groups to lobby and work for school reform and improvements.<br><br>District-level councils and committees for family and community involvement.<br><br>Information on school or local elections for school representatives.<br><br>Networks to link all families with parent representatives. | **Sample Practices**<br><br>Information for students and families on community health, cultural, recreational, social support, and other programs or services.<br><br>Information on community activities that link to learning skills and talents, including summer programs for students.<br><br>Service integration through partnerships involving school; civic, counseling, cultural, health, recreation, and other agencies and organizations; and businesses.<br><br>Service to the community by students, families, and schools (e.g., recycling, art, music, drama, and other activities for seniors or others)<br><br>Participation of alumni in school programs for students. |

## Table 2. Challenges and Redefinitions for the Six Types of Involvement

| Type 1 Parenting | Type 2 Communicating | Type 3 Volunteering |
|---|---|---|
| **Challenges** | **Challenges** | **Challenges** |
| Provide information to *all* families who want it or who need it, not just to the few who can attend workshops or meetings at the school building. | Review the readability, clarity, form, and frequency of all memos, notices, and other print and nonprint communications. | Recruit volunteers widely so that *all* families know that their time and talents are welcome. |
| Enable families to share information with schools about culture, background, children's talents and needs. | Consider parents who do not speak English well, do not read well, or need large type. | Make flexible schedules for volunteers, assemblies, and events to enable parents who work to participate. |
| Make sure that all information for and from families is clear, usable, and linked to children's success in school. | Review the quality of major communications (newsletters, report cards, conference schedules, and so on). | Organize volunteer work; provide training; match time and talent with school, teacher, and student needs; and recognize efforts so that participants are productive. |
| | Establish clear, two-way channels for communications from home to school and from school to home. | |
| **Redefinitions** | **Redefinitions** | **Redefinitions** |
| "Workshop" to mean more than a *meeting* about a topic held at the school building at a particular time. "Workshop" may also mean making information about a topic available in a variety of forms that can be viewed, heard, or read anywhere, any time, in varied forms. | "Communications about school programs and student progress" to mean two-way, three-way, and many-way channels of communication that connect schools, families, students, and the community. | "Volunteer" to mean anyone who supports school goals and children's learning or development in any way, at any place, and at any time—not just during the school day and at the school building. |

| Type 4<br>Learning at Home | Type 5<br>Decision Making | Type 6<br>Collaborating with Community |
|---|---|---|
| **Challenges** | **Challenges** | **Challenges** |
| Design and organize a regular schedule of interactive homework (e.g., weekly or bi-monthly) that gives *students* responsibility for discussing important things they are learning and helps families stay aware of the content of their children's classwork. | Include parent leaders from all racial, ethnic, socioeconomic, and other groups in the school. | Solve turf problems of responsibilities, funds, staff, and locations for collaborative activities. |
| | Offer training to enable leaders to serve as representatives of other families, with input from and return of information to all parents. | Inform families of community programs for students, such as mentoring, tutoring, business partnerships. |
| Coordinate family-linked homework activities, if students have several teachers. | Include students (along with parents) in decision-making groups. | Assure equity of opportunities for students and families to participate in community programs or to obtain services. |
| Involve families and their children in all important curriculum related decisions. | | Match community contributions with school goals; integrate child and family services with education. |
| **Redefinitions** | **Redefinitions** | **Redefinitions** |
| "Homework" to mean not only work done alone, but also interactive activities shared with others at home or in the community, linking schoolwork to real life. | "Decision making" to mean a process of partnership, of shared views and actions toward shared goals, not just a power struggle between conflicting ideas. | "Community" to mean not only the neighborhoods where students' homes and schools are located but also any neighborhoods that influence their learning and development. |
| "Help" at home to mean encouraging, listening, reacting, praising, guiding, monitoring, and discussing—not "teaching" school subjects. | Parent "leader" to mean a real representative, with opportunities and support to hear from and communicate with other families. | "Community" rated not only by low or high social or economic qualities; but by strengths and talents to support students, families, and schools. |
| | | "Community" means all who are interested in and affected by the quality of education, not just those with children in the schools. |

## Table 3. Expected Results of the Six Types of Involvement for Students

| Type 1<br>Parenting | Type 2<br>Communicating | Type 3<br>Volunteering |
|---|---|---|
| **Results for Students** | **Results for Students** | **Results for Students** |
| Awareness of family super-vision; respect for parents.<br><br>Positive personal qualities, habits, beliefs, and values, as taught by family.<br><br>Balance between time spent on chores, on other activi-ties, and on homework.<br><br>Good or improved attendance.<br><br>Awareness of importance of school. | Awareness of own progress of actions needed to main-tain or improve grades.<br><br>Understanding of school policies on behavior, atten-dance, and other areas of student conduct.<br><br>Informed decisions about courses and programs.<br><br>Awareness of own role in partnerships, serving as courier and communicator. | Skill in communicating with adults.<br><br>Increased learning of skills that receive tutoring or targeted attention from volunteers.<br><br>Awareness of many skills, talents, occupations, and contributions of parents and other volunteers. |
| **For Parents** | **For Parents** | **For Parents** |
| Understanding of and confi-dence about parenting, child and adolescent devel-opment, and changes in home conditions for learn-ing as children proceed through school.<br><br>Awareness of own and oth-ers' challenges in parenting.<br><br>Feeling of support from school and other parents. | Understanding school programs and policies.<br><br>Monitoring and awareness of child's progress.<br><br>Responding effectively to students' problems.<br><br>Interactions with teachers and ease of communication with school and teachers. | Understanding teacher's job, increased comfort in school, and carry-over of school activities at home.<br><br>Self-confidence about abil-ity to work in school and with children or to take steps to improve own education.<br><br>Awareness that families are welcome and valued at school.<br><br>Gains in specific skills of volunteer work. |
| **For Teachers** | **For Teachers** | **For Teachers** |
| Understanding families' backgrounds, cultures, concerns, goals, needs, and views of their children.<br><br>Respect for families' strengths and efforts.<br><br>Understanding of student diversity.<br><br>Awareness of own skills to share information on child development. | Increased diversity and use of communications with families and awareness of own ability to communicate clearly.<br><br>Appreciation for and use of parent network for communications.<br><br>Increased ability to elicit and understand family views on children's programs and progress. | Readiness to involve fami-lies in new ways, including those who do not volunteer at school.<br><br>Awarness of parents' tal-ents and interests in school and children.<br><br>Greater individual attention to students, with help from volunteers. |

| Type 4<br>Learning at Home | Type 5<br>Decision Making | Type 6<br>Collaborating with Community |
|---|---|---|
| **Results for Students** | **Results for Students** | **Results for Students** |
| Gains in skills, abilities, and test scores linked to homework and classwork.<br><br>Homework completion.<br><br>Positive attitude toward schoolwork.<br><br>View of parent as more similar to teacher and of home as more similar to school.<br><br>Self-concept of ability as learner. | Awareness of representation of families in school decisions.<br><br>Understanding that student rights are protected.<br><br>Specific benefits linked to policies enacted by parent organizations and experienced by students. | Increased skills and talents through enriched curricular and extracurricular experiences.<br><br>Awareness of careers and of options for future education and work.<br><br>Specific benefits linked to programs, services, resources, and opportunities that connect students with community. |
| **For Parents** | **For Parents** | **For Parents** |
| Know how to support, encourage, and help student at home each year.<br><br>Discussions of school, classwork, and homework.<br><br>Understanding of instructional program each year and of what child is learning in each subject.<br><br>Appreciation of teaching skills.<br><br>Awareness of child as a learner. | Input into policies that affect child's education.<br><br>Feeling of ownership of school.<br><br>Awareness of parents' voices in school decisions.<br><br>Shared experiences and connections with other families.<br><br>Awareness of school, district, and state policies. | Knowledge and use of local resources by family and child to increase skills and talents or to obtain needed services.<br><br>Interactions with other families in community activities.<br><br>Awareness of school's role in the community and of community's contributions to the school. |
| **For Teachers** | **For Teachers** | **For Teachers** |
| Better design of homework assignments.<br><br>Respect of family time.<br><br>Recognition of equal helpfulness of single-parent, dual-income, and less formally educated families in otivating and reinforcing student learning.<br><br>Satisfaction with family involvement and support. | Awareness of parent perspectives as a factor in policy development and decisions.<br><br>View of equal status of family representatives on committees and in leadership roles. | Awareness of community resources to enrich curriculum and instruction.<br><br>Openness to and skill in using mentors, business partners, community volunteers, and others to assist students and augment teaching practice.<br><br>Knowledgeable, helpful referrals of children and families to needed services. |

at home (Type 4). These and other connections are interesting, and research is needed to understand the combined effects of such activities.

The tables also simplify the complex longitudinal influences that produce various results over time. For example, a series of events might play out as follows. The involvement of families in reading at home leads students to give more attention to reading and to be more strongly motivated to read. This in turn may help students remain or improve their daily reading skills and then their reading grades. With the accumulation over time of good classroom reading programs, continued home support, and increased skills and confidence in reading, students may significantly improve their reading achievement test scores. The time between reading aloud at home and increased reading test scores may vary greatly, depending on the quality and quantity of other reading activities in school and out.

> **Achievement test scores were not greatly affected by partnerships at the high school level.**

Or consider another example. A study by Seyong Lee, using longitudinal data and rigorous statistical controls on background and prior influences, found important benefits for high school students' attitudes and grades as a result of continuing several types of family involvement from the middle school into the high school. However, achievement test scores were not greatly affected by partnerships at the high school level. Longitudinal studies and practical experiences that are monitored over time are needed to increase our understanding of the complex patterns of results that can develop from various partnership activities.[6]

The six types of involvement can guide the development of a balanced, comprehensive program of partnerships, including opportunities for family involvement at school and at home, with potentially important results for students, parents, and teachers. The results for students, parents, and teachers will depend on the particular types of involvement that are implemented, as well as on the quality of the implementation.

## ACTION TEAMS FOR SCHOOL, FAMILY, AND COMMUNITY PARTNERSHIPS

Who will work to create caring school communities that are based on the concepts of partnership? How will the necessary work on all six types of involvement get done? Although a principal or a teacher may be a leader in working with some families or with groups in the community, one person cannot create a lasting, comprehensive program that involves all families as their children progress through the grades.

From the hard work of many educators and families in many schools, we have learned that, along with clear policies and strong support from state and district leaders and from school principals, an Action Team for School, Family, and Community Partnerships in each school is a useful structure. The action team guides the development of a comprehensive program of partnership, including all six types of involvement, and the integration of all family and community connections within a single, unified plan and program. The trials and errors, efforts and insights of many schools in our projects have helped to identify five important steps that any school can take to develop more positive school/family/community connections.[7]

**A team approach is an appropriate way to build partnerships.**

### Step 1: Create an Action Team

A team approach is an appropriate way to build partnerships. The Action Team for School, Family, and Community Partnerships can be the "action arm" of a school council, if one exists. The action team takes responsibility for assessing present practices, organizing options for new partnerships, implementing selected activities, evaluating next steps, and continuing to improve and coordinate practices for all six types of involvement. Although the members of the action team lead these activities, they are assisted by other teachers, parents, students, administrators, and community members.

The action team should include at least three teachers from different grade levels, three parents with children in different grade levels, and at least one administrator. Teams may also include at least one member from the community at large and at the middle and high school levels, at least two students from different grade levels. Others who are central to the school's work with families may also be included as members, such as a cafeteria worker, a school social worker, a counselor, or a school psychologist. Such diverse membership ensures that partnership activities will take into account the various needs, interests, and talents of teachers, parents, the school, and students.

The leader of the action team may be any member who has the respect of the other members, as well as good communication skills and understanding of the partnership approach. The leader or at least one member of the action team should also serve on the school council, school improvement team, or other such body, if one exists.

In addition to group planning, members of the action team elect (or are assigned to act as) the chair or co-chair of one of six subcommittees for each type of involvement. A team with at least six members (and perhaps as many as 12) ensures that responsibilities for leadership can be delegated so that one person is not overburdened and so that the work of the action team will continue even if members move or change schools or positions. Members may serve renewable terms of two to three years, with replacement of any who leave in the interim. Other thoughtful variations in assignments and activities may be created by small or large schools using this process.

> **A modest budget is needed to guide and support the work and expenses of each school's action team.**

In the first phase of our work in 1987, projects were led by "project directors" (usually teachers) and were focused on one type of involvement at a time. Some schools succeeded in developing good partnerships over several years, but others were thwarted if the project director moved, if the principal changed, or if the project grew larger than one person could handle. Other schools took a team approach in order to work on many types of involvement simultaneously. Their efforts demonstrated how to structure the program for the next set of schools in our work. Starting in 1990, this second set of schools tested and improved on the structure and work of action teams. Now, all elementary, middle, and high schools in our research and development projects and in other states and districts that are applying this work are given assistance in taking the action team approach.

### Step 2: Obtain Funds and Other Support

A modest budget is needed to guide and support the work and expenses of each school's action team. Funds for state coordinators to assist districts and schools and funds for district coordinators or facilitators to help each school may come from a number of sources. These include federal, state, and local programs that mandate, request, or support family involvement, such as Title I, Title II, Title VII, Goals 2000, and other federal and similar state funding programs. In addition to paying the state and district coordinators, funds from these sources may be applied in creative ways to support staff development in the area of school, family, and community partnerships; to pay for lead teachers at each school; to set up demonstration programs; and for other partnership expenses. In addition, local school business partnerships, school discretionary funds, and separate fund-raising efforts targeted to the schools' partnership programs have been used to support the work of their action teams. At the very least, school's action team requires a small stipend (at least $1,000 per year for three to five years, with summer supplements) for time and materials needed by each subcommittee to plan, implement, and revise practices of partnership that include all six types of involvement.

**Assessments of starting points may be made in a variety of ways.**

The action team must also be given sufficient time and social support to do its work. This requires explicit support from the principal and district leaders to allow time for team members to meet, plan, and conduct the activities that are selected for each type of involvement. Time during the summer is also valuable—and may be essential—for planning new approaches that will start in the new school year.

### Step 3: Identify Starting Points

Most schools have some teachers who conduct some practices of partnership with some families some of the time. How can good practices be organized and extended so that they may be used by all teachers, at all grade levels, with all families? The action team works to improve and systematize the typically haphazard patterns of involvement. It starts by collecting information about the school's present practices of partnership along with the views, experiences, and wishes of teachers, parents, administrators, and students.

Assessments of starting points may be made in a variety of ways, depending on available resources, time, and talents. For example, the action team might use formal questionnaires[8] or telephone interviews to survey teachers, administrators, parents, and students (if resources exist to process, analyze, and report survey data). Or the action team might organize a panel of teachers, parents, and students to speak at a meeting of the parent/teacher organization or at some other school meeting as a way of initiating discussion about the goals and desired activities for partnership. Structured discussions may be conducted through a series of principal's breakfasts for representative groups of teachers, parents, students, and others; random sample phone calls may also be used to collect reactions and ideas, or formal focus groups may be convened to gather ideas about school, family, and community partnerships at the school.

What questions should be addressed? Regardless of how the information is gathered, some areas must be covered in any information gathering.

- *Present strengths.* Which practices of school/family/community partnerships are now working well for the school as a whole? For individual grade levels? For which types of involvement?

- *Needed changes.* Ideally, how do we want school, family, and community partnerships to work at this school three years from now? Which present practices should continue, and which should change? To reach school goals, what new practices are needed for each of the major types of involvement?

- *Expectations.* What do teachers expect of families? What do families expect of teachers and other school personnel? What do students expect their families to do to help them negotiate school life? What do students expect their teachers to do to keep their families informed and involved?

- *Sense of community.* Which families are we now reaching and which are we not yet reaching? Who are the "hard-to-reach" families? What might be done to communicate with and engage these families in their children's education? Are current partnership practices coordinated to include all families as a school community? Or are families whose children receive special services (e.g., Title I, special education, bilingual education) separated from other families?

- *Links to goals.* How are students faring on such measures of academic achievement as report card grades, on measures of attitudes and attendance, and on other indicators of success? How might family and community connections assist the school in helping more students reach higher goals and achieve greater success? Which practices of school, family, and community partnerships would directly connect to particular goals?

### Step 4: Develop a Three-Year Plan

From the ideas and goals for partnerships collected from teachers, parents, and students, the action team can develop a three-year outline of the specific steps that will help the school progress from its starting point on each type of involvement to where it wants to be in three years. This plan outlines how each subcommittee will work over three years to make important, incremental advances to reach more families each year on each type of involvement. The three-year outline also shows how all school/family/community connections will be integrated into one coherent program of partnership that includes activities for the whole school community, activities to meet the special needs of children and families, activities to link to the district committees and councils, and activities conducted in each grade level.

**A detailed one-year plan should be developed for the first year's work.**

In addition to the three-year outline of goals for each type of involvement, a detailed one-year plan should be developed for the first year's work. It should include the specific activities that will be implemented, improved, or maintained for each type of involvement; a time line of monthly actions needed for each activity; identification of the subcommittee chair who will be responsible for each type of involvement; identification of the teachers, parents, students, or others (not necessarily action team members) who will assist with the implementation of each activity; indicators of how the implementation and results of each major activity will be assessed; and other details of importance to the action team.

The three-year outline and one-year detailed plan are shared with the school council and/or parent organization, with all teachers, and with the parents and students. Even if the action team makes only one good step forward each year on each of the six types of involvement, it will take 18 steps forward over three years to develop a more comprehensive and coordinated program of school/family/community partnerships.

In short, based on the input from the parents, teachers, students, and others on the school's starting points and desired partnerships, the action team will address these issues.

- *Details*. What will be done each year, for three years, to implement a program on all six types of involvement? What, specifically, will be accomplished in the first year on each type of involvement?
- *Responsibilities*. Who will be responsible for developing and implementing practices of partnership for each type of involvement? Will staff development be needed? How will teachers, administrators, parents, and students be supported and recognized for their work?
- *Costs*. What costs are associated with the improvement and maintenance of the planned activities? What sources will provide the needed funds? Will small grants or other special budgets be needed?
- *Evaluation*. How will we know how well the practices have been implemented and what their effects are on students, teachers, and families? What indicators will we use that are closely linked to the practices implemented to determine their effects?

## Step 5: Continue Planning and Working

The action team should schedule an annual presentation and celebration of progress at the school so that all teachers, families, and students will know about the work that has been done each year to build partnerships. Or the district coordinator for school, family, and community partnerships might arrange an annual conference for all schools in the district. At the annual school or district meeting, the action team presents and displays the highlights of accomplishments on each type of involvement. Problems are discussed and ideas are shared about improvements, additions, and continuations for the next year.

Each year, the action team updates the school's three-year outline and develops a detailed one-year plan for the coming year's work. It is important for educators, families, students, and the community at large to be aware of annual progress, of new plans, and of how they can help.

In short, the action team addresses the following questions. How can it ensure that the program of school/family/community partnership will continue to improve its structure, processes, and practices in order to increase the number of families who are partners with the school in their children's education? What opportunities will teachers, parents, and students have to share information on successful practices and to strengthen and maintain their efforts?

## CHARACTERISTICS OF SUCCESSFUL PROGRAMS

As schools have implemented partnership programs, their experience has helped to identify some important properties of successful partnerships.

**Incremental progress.** Progress in partnerships is incremental, including more families each year in ways that benefit more students. Like reading or math programs, assessment programs, sports programs, or other school investments, partnership programs take time to develop, must be periodically reviewed, and should be continuously improved. The schools in our projects have shown that three years is the minimum time needed for an action team to complete a number of activities on each type of involvement and to establish its work as a productive and permanent structure in a school.

**Pogress in partnerships is incremental.**

The development of a partnership is a process, not a single event. All teachers, families, students, and community groups do not engage in all activities on all types of involvement all at once. Not all activities implemented will succeed with all families. But with good planning, thoughtful implementation, well-designed activities, and pointed improvements, more and more families and teachers can learn to work with one another on behalf of the children whose interests they share. Similarly, not all students instantly improve their attitudes or achievements when their families become involved in their education. After all, student learning depends mainly on good curricula and instruction and on the work completed by students. However, with a well-implemented program of partnership, more students will receive support from their families, and more will be motivated to work harder.

**Connection to curricular and instructional reform.** A program of school/family/community partnerships that focuses on children's learning and development is an important component of curricular and instructional reform. Aspects of partnerships that aim to help more students succeed in school can be supported by federal, state, and local funds that are targeted for curricular and instructional reform. Helping families understand, monitor, and interact with students on homework, for example, can be a clear and important extension of classroom instruction, as can volunteer programs that bolster and broaden student skills, talents, and interests. Improving the content and conduct of parent/teacher/student conferences and goal-setting activities can be an important step in curricular reform; family support and family understanding of child and adolescent development and school curricula are necessary elements to assist students as learners.

**The action team approach to partnerships guides the work of educators.**

The connection of partnerships to curriculum and instruction in schools and the location of leadership for these partnership programs in district departments of curriculum and instruction are important changes that move partnerships from being peripheral public relations activities about parents to being central programs about student learning and development.

**Redefining staff development.** The action team approach to partnerships guides the work of educators by restructuring "staff development" to mean colleagues working together and with parents to develop, implement, evaluate, and continue to improve practices of partnership. This is less a "dose of in-service education" than it is an active form of developing staff talents and capacities. The teachers, administrators, and others on the action team become the "experts" on this topic for their school. Their work in this area can be supported by various federal, state, and local funding programs as a clear investment in staff development for overall school reform. Indeed, the action team approach as outlined can be applied to any or all important topics on a school improvement agenda. It need not be restricted to the pursuit of successful partnerships.

It is important to note that the development of partnership programs would be easier if educators came to their schools prepared to work productively with families and communities. Courses or classes are needed in pre-service teacher education and in advanced degree programs for teachers and administrators to help them define their professional work in terms of partnerships. Today, most educators enter schools without an understanding of family backgrounds, concepts of caring, the framework of partnerships, or the other "basics" I have discussed here. Thus, most principals and district leaders are not prepared to guide and lead their staffs in developing strong school and classroom practices that inform and involve families.

And most teachers and administrators are not prepared to understand, design, implement, or evaluate good practices of partnership with the families of their students. Colleges and universities that prepare educators and others who work with children and families should identify where in their curricula the theory, research, policy, and practical ideas about partnerships are presented or where in their programs these can be added.[9]

**Underlying all six types of involvement are two defining synonyms of caring: trusting and respecting.**

Even with improved pre-service and advanced coursework, however, each school's action team will have to tailor its menu of practices to the needs and wishes of the teachers, families, and students in the school. The framework and guidelines offered in this article can be used by thoughtful educators to organize this work, school by school.

## THE CORE OF CARING

One school in our Baltimore project named its partnerships the "I Care Program." It developed an I Care parent club that fostered fellowship and leadership of families, an *I Care Newsletter,* and many other events and activities. Other schools also gave catchy, positive names to their programs to indicate to families, students, teachers, and everyone else in the school community that there are important relationships and exchanges that must be developed in order to assist students.

Interestingly, synonyms for "caring" match the six types of involvement: Type 1, parenting: supporting, nurturing, and rearing; Type 2, communicating: relating, reviewing, and overseeing; Type 3, volunteering: supervising and fostering; Type 4, learning at home: managing, recognizing, and rewarding; Type 5, decision making: contributing, considering, and judging; and Type 6, collaborating with the community: sharing and giving.

Underlying all six types of involvement are two defining synonyms of caring: trusting and respecting. Of course, the varied meanings are interconnected, but it is striking that language permits us to call forth various elements of caring associated with activities for the six types of involvement. If all six types of involvement are operating well in a school's program of partnership, then all of these caring behaviors could be activated to assist children's learning and development.

Despite real progress in many states, districts, and schools over the past few years, there are still too many schools in which educators do not understand the families of their students; in which families do not understand their children's schools; and in which communities do not understand or assist the schools, families, or students. There are still too many states and districts without the policies, departments, leadership, staff, and fiscal support needed to enable all their schools to develop good programs of partnership. Yet, relatively small financial investments that support and assist the work of action teams could yield significant returns for all schools, teachers, families, and students. Educators who have led the way with trials, errors, and successes provide evidence that any state, district, or school can create similar programs.[10]

Schools have choices. There are two common approaches to involving families in schools and in their children's education. One approach emphasizes conflict and views the school as a battleground. The conditions and relationships in this kind of environment guarantee power struggles and disharmony. The other approach emphasizes partnership and views the school as a homeland. The conditions and relationships in this kind of environment invite power sharing and mutual respect and allow energies to be directed toward activities that foster student learning and development. Even when conflicts rage, however, peace must be restored sooner or later and the partners in children's education must work together.

## NEXT STEPS: STRENGTHENING PARTNERSHIPS

Collaborative work and thoughtful give-and-take among researchers, policy leaders, educators, and parents are responsible for the progress that has been made over the past decade in understanding and developing school, family, and community partnerships. Similar collaborations will be important for future progress in this and other areas of school reform. To promote these approaches, I am establishing a national network of Partnership-2000 Schools to help link state, district, and other leaders who are responsible for helping their elementary, middle, and high schools implement programs of school, family, and community partnerships by the year 2000. The state and district coordinators must be supported for at least three years by sufficient staff and budgets to enable them to help increasing

numbers of elementary, middle, and high schools in their districts
to plan, implement, and maintain comprehensive programs of
partnership.

Partnership-2000 Schools will be aided in putting the recommendations of this article into practice in ways that are appropriate
to their locations. Implementation will include applying the theory
of overlapping spheres of influence, the framework of six types of
involvement, and the action team approach. Researchers and staff
members at Johns Hopkins will disseminate information and guidelines, send out newsletters, and hold optional annual workshops to
help state and district coordinators learn new strategies and share
successful ideas. Activities for leaders at the state and district levels
will be shared, as will school-level programs and successful partnership practices.

The national network of Partnership-2000 Schools will begin its
activities in the fall of 1995 and will continue until at least the year
2000. The goal is to enable leaders in all states and districts to assist
all their schools in establishing and strengthening programs of
school/family/community partnership.[11]

## NOTES

1. Joyce L. Epstein, "Toward a Theory of Family-School Connections: Teacher
   Practices and Parent Involvement," in Klaus Hurrelmann. Frederick
   Kaufmann, and Frederick Losel, Eds., *Social Intervention: Potential and
   Constraints* (New York: DeGruyter, 1987), pp. 121–36; idem, "School and
   Family Partnerships," in Marvin Alkin, Ed., *Encyclopedia of Educational
   Research,* 6th ed. (New York: Macmillan, 1992), pp. 1139–51; idem, "Theory
   to Practice: School and Family Partnerships Lead to School Improvement and
   Student Success," in Cheryl L. Fagnano and Beverly Z. Werber, Eds., *School,
   Family, and Community Interaction: A View from the Firing Lines* (Boulder,
   Colo.: Westview Press, 1994), pp. 39–52; and idem, *School and Family
   Partnerships: Preparing Educators and Improving Schools* (Boulder, Colo.:
   Westview Press, forthcoming).

2. Ron Brandt, "On Parents and Schools: A Conversation with Joyce Epstein,"
   *Educational Leadership,* October 1989, pp. 24–27; Epstein, "Toward a
   Theory"; Catherine C. Lewis, Eric Schaps, and Marilyn Watson, "Beyond the
   Pendulum: Creating Challenging and Caring Schools," *Phi Delta Kappan,*
   March 1995, pp. 547–54; and Debra Viadero, "Learning to Care," *Education
   Week,* 26 October 1994, pp. 31–33.

3. A. Wade Boykin, "Harvesting Culture and Talent: African American Children
   and Educational Reform," in Robert Rossi, Ed., *Schools and Students at Risk*
   (New York: Teachers College Press, 1994), pp. 116–39.

4. For references to studies by many researchers, see the following literature reviews: Epstein, "School and Family Partnerships"; idem, *School and Family Partnerships*; and idem, "Perspectives and Previews on Research and Policy for School, Family, and Community Partnerships," in Alan Booth and Judith Dunn, Eds., *Family-School Links: How Do They Affect Educational Outcomes?* (Hillsdale, N.J.: Erlbaum, 1996). Research that reports patterns of involvement across the grades, for families with low and high socioeconomic status, for one- and two-parent homes, and on schools' programs of partnership includes: Carol Ames, with Madhab Khoju and Thomas Watkins, "Parents and Schools: The Impact of School-to-Home Communications on Parents' Beliefs and Perceptions," Center on Families, Communities, Schools, and Children's Learning, Center Report 15, Johns Hopkins University, Baltimore, 1993; David P. Baker and David L. Stevenson, "Mothers' Strategies for Children's School Achievement: Managing the Transition to High School," *Sociology of Education,* vol. 59, 1986, pp. 156–66; Patricia A. Bauch, "Is Parent Involvement Different in Private Schools?," *Educational Horizons,* vol. 66, 1988, pp. 78–82; Henry J. Becker and Joyce L. Epstein, "Parent Involvement: A Study of Teacher Practices," *Elementary School Journal,* vol. 83, 1982, pp. 85–102; Reginald M. Clark, *Family Life and School Achievement: Why Poor Black Children Succeed or Fail* (Chicago: University of Chicago Press, 1983); Susan L. Dauber and Joyce L. Epstein, "Parents' Attitudes and Practices of Involvement in Inner-City Elementary and Middle Schools," in Nancy Chavkin, Ed., *Families and Schools in a Pluralistic Society* (Albany: State University of New York Press, 1993), pp. 53–71; Sanford M. Dornbusch and Philip L. Ritter, "Parents of High School Students: A Neglected Resource," *Educational Horizons,* vol. 66, 1988, pp. 75–77; Jacquelynne S. Eccles, "Family Involvement in Children's and Adolescents' Schooling," in Booth and Dunn, op. cit.; Joyce L. Epstein, "Parents' Reactions to Teacher Practices of Parent Involvement," *Elementary School Journal,* vol. 86, 1986, pp. 277–94; idem, "Single Parents and the Schools: Effects of Marital Status on Parent and Teacher Interactions," in Maureen Hallinan, Ed., *Change in Societal Institutions* (New York: Plenum, 1990), pp. 91–121; Joyce L. Epstein and Seyong Lee, "National Patterns of School and Family Connections in the Middle Grades," in Bruce A. Ryan and Gerald R. Adams, Eds., *The Family-School Connection: Theory, Research, and Practice* (Newbury Park, Calif.: Sage, forthcoming); Annette Lareau, *Home Advantage: Social Class and Parental Intervention in Elementary Education* (Philadelphia: Falmer Press, 1989); and Diane Scott-Jones, "Activities in the Home That Support School Learning in the Middle Grades," in Barry Rutherford, ed., *Creating Family/School Partnerships* (Columbus, Ohio: National Middle School Association, 1995), pp. 161–81.

5. The three tables update earlier versions that were based on only five types of involvement. For other discussions of the types, practices, challenges, redefinitions, and results, see Epstein, "School and Family Partnerships"; Lori Connors Tadros and Joyce L. Epstein, "Parents and Schools," in Marc H. Bornstein, Ed., *Handbook of Parenting* (Hillsdale, N.J.: Erlbaum, forthcoming); Joyce L. Epstein and Lori Connors Tadros, "School and Family Partnerships in the Middle Grades," in Rutherford, op. cit.; and idem, "Trust Fund: School,

Family, and Community Partnerships in High Schools," Center on Families, Communities, Schools, and Children's Learning, Center Report 24, Johns Hopkins University, Baltimore, 1994, Schools' activities with various types of involvement are outlined in Don Davies, Patricia Burch, and Vivian Johnson, "A Portrait of Schools Reaching Out: Report of a Survey on Practices and Policies of Family-Community-School Collaboration," Center on Families, Communities, Schools, and Children's Learning, Center Report 1, Johns Hopkins University, Baltimore, 1992.

6. Seyong Lee, "Family-School Connections and Students' Education: Continuity and Change of Family Involvement from the Middle Grades to High School" (Doctoral dissertation, Johns Hopkins University, 1994). For a discussion of issues concerning the results of partnerships, see Eptstein, "Perspectives and Previews." For various resarch reports on results of partnerships for students and for parents, see Joyce L. Epstein, "Effects on Student Achievement of Teacher Practices of Parent Involvement," in Steven Silvern, ed., *Literacy Through Family, Community, and School Interaction* (Greenwich, Conn.: JAI Press, 1991), pp. 261–76; Joyce L. Epstein and Susan L. Dauber, "Effects on Students of an Interdisciplinary Program Linking Social Studies, Art, and Family Volunteers in the Middle Grades," *Journal of Early Adolescence,* vol. 15, 1995, pp. 237–66; Joyce L. Epstein and Jill Jacobsen, "Effects of School Practices to Involve Families in the Middle Grades: Parents' Perspectives," paper presented at the annual meeting of the American Sociological Association, Los Angeles, 1994; Joyce L. Epstein and Seyong Lee, "Effects of School Practices to Involve Families, Parents, and Students in the Middle Grades: A View from the Schools," paper presented at the annual meeting of the American Sociological Association, Miami, 1993; and Anne T. Henderson and Nancy Berla, *A New Generation of Evidence: The Family Is Critical to Student Achievement* (Washington, D.C.: National Committee for Citizens in Education, 1994).

7. Lori Connors Tadros and Joyce L. Epstein, "Taking Stock: The Views of Teachers, Parents, and Students on School, Family, and Community Partnerships in High Schools," Center on Families, Communities, Schools, and Children's Learning, Center Report 25, Johns Hopkins University, Baltimore, 1994; Epstein and Tadros, "Trust Fund"; Joyce L. Epstein and Susan L. Dauber, "School Programs and Teacher Practices of Parent Involvement in Inner-City Elementary and Middle Schools," *Elementary School Journal,* vol. 91, 1991, pp. 289–303; and Joyce L. Epstein, Susan C. Herrick, and Lucretia Coates, "Effects of Summer Home Learning Packets on Student Achievement in Language Arts in the Middle Grades," *School Effectiveness and School Improvement,* in press. For other approaches to the use of action teams for partnerships, see Patricia Burch and Ameetha Palanki, "Action Research on Family-School Community Partnerships," *Journal of Emotional and Behavioral Problems,* vol. 1, 1994, pp. 16–19; Patricia Burch, Ameetha Palanki, and Don Davies, "In Our Hands: A Multi-Site Parent-Teacher Action Research Project," Center on Families, Communities, Schools, and Children's Learning, Center Report 29, Johns Hopkins University, Baltimore, 1995; Don Davies, "Schools Reaching Out: Family, School, and Community Partnerships for Student Success," *Phi Delta Kappan,* January 1991, pp. 376–82;

idem, "A More Distant Mirror: Progress Report on a Cross-National Project to Study Family-School-Community Partnerships," *Equity and Choice,* vol. 19, 1993, pp. 41–46; and Don Davies, Ameetha Palanki, and Patricia D. Palanki, "Getting Started: Action Research in Family-School-Community Partnerships," Center on Families, Communities, Schools, and Children's Learning, Center Report 17, Johns Hopkins University, Baltimore, 1993. For an example of an organizing mechanism for action teams, see Vivian R. Johnson, "Parent Centers in Urban Schools: Four Case Studies," Center on Families, Communities Schools, and Children's Learning, Center Report 23, Johns Hopkins University, Baltimore, 1994.

8. Surveys for teachers and parents in the elementary and middle grades and for teachers, parents, and students in high school, developed and revised in 1993 by Joyce L. Epstein, Karen Clark Salinas, and Lori Connors Tadros, are available from the Center on Families, Communities, Schools, and Children's Learning at Johns Hopkins University.

9. Mary Sue Ammon, "University of California Project on Teacher Preparation for Parent Involvement Report I: April 1989 Conference and Initial Follow-up," mimeo, University of California, Berkeley 1990; Nancy F. Chavkin and David L. Williams "Critical Issues in Teacher Training for Parent Involvement," *Educational Horizons,* vol. 66, 1988, pp. 87–89; and Lisa Hinz, Jessical Clarke, and Joe Nathan, "A Survey of Parent Involvement Course Offerings in Minnesota's Undergraduate Preparation Programs," Center for School Change, Humphrey Institute of Public Affairs, University of Minnesota, Minneapolis, 1992. To correct deficiencies in the education of educators, I have written a course text on supplementary reader based on the theory, framework, and approaches described in this article. See Epstein, *School and Family Partnerships.* Other useful readings for a university course include Sandra L. Christenson and Jane Close Conoley, Eds., *Home-School Collaboration: Enhancing Children's Academic Competence* (Silver Spring, Md.: National Association of School Psychologists, 1992); Fagnano and Werber, op. cit.; Norman Fruchter, Anne Galletta, and J. Lynne White, *New Directions in Parent Involvement* (Washington, D. C.: Academy for Educational Development, 1992); William Rioux and Nancy Berla, Eds., *Innovations in Parent and Family Involvement* (Princeton Junction, N.J.: Eye on Education, 1993); and Susan McAllister Swap, *Developing Home-School Partnerships: From Concepts to Practice* (New York: Teachers College Press, 1993).

10. See, for example, Gary Lloyd, "Research and Practical Application for School, Family, and Community Partnerships," in Booth and Dunn, op. cit. Wisconsin Department of Public Instruction, *Sharesheet: The DPI Family-Community-School Partnership Newsletter,* August/September 1994; and the special section on parent involvement in the January 1991 *Phi Delta Kappan.*

11. For more information about the national network of Partnership-2000 Schools, send the name, position, address, and phone and fax numbers of the contact person/coordinator for partnerships for your state or district to Joyce L. Epstein, Partnership-2000 Schools, CRESPAR/Center on Families, Communities, Schools, and Children's Learning, Johns Hopkins University, 3505 N. Charles St., Baltimore, MD 21218.

# Section 4

# The Future of Change

We have known all along that teaching and reform is a highly passionate and emotional phenomenon. Yet until recently, most analysis was bloodless. Issues of emotion and hope were ignored. There are many legitimate reasons for reformers to get burn-out and give up hope. If this happens, all is lost.

The concepts and cultures described in earlier articles, those associated with success are successful because they foster environments that nurture emotion and hope. If we realize this, we have a chance of going even further in establishing and valuing new professional learning communities. Interestingly, having hope is especially needed when the situation does not call for it. Paradoxically, this may be the best way of working through difficult situations—to maintain hope while working with others to create collaborative work cultures, and to do so under the chaotic conditions of complex change. That is the challenge.

# Emotion and Hope: Constructive Concepts for Complex Times

by Michael Fullan

*Pessimism is a very easy way out when you're considering what life really is because pessimism is a short view of life. If you look at what is happening around us today and what has happened since you were born you can't help but feel that life is a terrible complexity of problems and elusiveness of one sort or another. . . . It is very much easier to be tragic than it is to be comic. I have known people to embrace the tragic view of life, and it is a cop-out. They simply feel rotten about everything, and that is terribly easy.*—Robertson Davies, Canadian Novelist, Csikszentmihalyi, 1996

I t is easy to be pessimistic about educational reform. There are many legitimate reasons to be discouraged. From a rational technical point of view the conclusion that large scale reform is a hopeless proposition seems justified. Like Hargreaves (1997), in the opening chapter of the 1997 ASCD Yearbook, I argue in this chapter that the emotional side of change has been either ignored or miscast. By examining emotions and change from a different perspective, we not only gain insights about the dynamics of change, but we also find new understandings of how to make change work more constructively. The moral and the technical begin to fuse, instead of being two ships passing in the night.

I start with a brief summary of the seemingly intractable problems of change—which could easily lead one to give up. I then rebuild the argument on a different premise starting first with the individual, and then moving to the group and the organization—a premise in which emotion and hope play a prominent but not

From *Rethinking Educational Change with Heart and Mind,* 1997 ASCD Yearbook, pp. 216–233. © 1997 by the Association for Supervision and Curriculum Development (ASCD). Reprinted with permission.

Polyannish role. Wishful thinking or blind hopefulness are no more useful than cynicism.

Technical planning has not worked in educational change. Political pressure has failed to make a difference. Since moral exhortation falls short, is there a way of going deeper that leads to motivating and mobilizing even the most discouraged? I think there is. The question is whether in rethinking the place of emotion and hope in change, we can actually come up with a more effective route to working with complex change.

**Anyone who spends time in public schools can feel the growing and deepening malaise among educators.**

After examining emotion and hope at the individual and group levels, I turn to their implications for understanding and acting on constructive educational change. I will attempt to demonstrate that the more basic concepts of emotion and hope in human affairs provide a more profound explanation of why educational reform works when (in the small number of cases) it does. These deeper understandings, I will argue, are absolutely essential for sustaining and spreading constructive change. Without this all change will falter, as appears to be the case in the late 1990s.

## THE PROBLEMS OF EDUCATIONAL CHANGE

Among the fundamental problems of educational change are: (1) the growing and deepening alienation among teachers, (2) the balkanization and burnout of passionate reform-minded teachers, and (3) the overwhelming multiplicity of unconnected, fragmented change initiatives.

Anyone who spends time in public schools can feel the growing and deepening malaise among educators, whether it stems from a sense on the part of teachers that the public and the government do not care about them, or from an overwhelming sense of despair that the problems are insurmountable and worsening. Ken Dryden spent all year in Kennedy Secondary School outside Metro Toronto sitting in classrooms observing and talking with teachers and students. Dryden writes this about a history teacher whose name is Rick:

> Rick learned a great lesson in humility . . . He has a teacher's need to help kids . . . He has the urge to personalize every kid's success and failure, feel the highs suffer the lows, but by now he knew he is no savior. So much is going on in each kid's life, every story is so complicated. He is just one small brush stroke on a large canvas. (Dryden, 1995:84)

No matter how hard they tried, says Dryden, teachers could not get past the "front row," reaching only a small percentage of the kids. On the opposite side of the world, Bishop and Mulford (1996) subtitle their article on empowerment in four Australian Schools "they don't really care." Teachers talked about the impersonal government as the "they" out there:

> They don't really care. It's purely a numbers and monetary game.

> I wouldn't mind so much if there was a purpose or master plan.

> Pressure and stress are up and I'm not convinced that the government has the best interests of the kids at heart.

By and large the pressure of the job has taken the joy out of teaching for large numbers of the teaching profession.

At the same time a significant minority of teachers has been attracted to specific reform initiatives and networks. There is less documentation on the effects of these heroic efforts, but the signs are not encouraging. Robert Fried (1995)—another author close to front-line teachers—concludes that "passionate teachers" are getting exhausted in the face of "apathy and resistance" (from other teachers as well as from elsewhere). District Superintendent in New York City, Anthony Alvarado reflects on his experience in District 4:

> My strategy there was to make it possible for gifted and energetic people to create schools that represented their best ideas about teaching and learning and to let parents choose the schools that best matched their children's interest. We generated a lot of interest and a lot of good programs. But the main flaw with that strategy was that it never reached every teacher in every classroom; it focused on those who showed energy and commitment to change. So, after a while, improvement slowed down as we ran out of energetic and committed people. Many of the programs became inward-looking instead of trying to find new ways to do things." (Elmore & Burney, 1996:14)

Elmore (1995) discusses the fatal in-built self-defeating nature of going only with the flow of like-minded reformers:

> The first step serious reformers typically take involves gathering up the faithful and concentrating them in one place in order to form a cohesive community of like-minded practitioners. In the case of the progressives, reformers started schools that embodied their ideas; in the case of the curriculum projects, reformers identified early adopters of their new curricula as exemplars of success. This strategy immediately isolates the teachers who are most likely to change from those who are least likely to embrace reform. This dynamic creates a social barrier between the two, virtually guaranteeing that the former will not grow in number and the latter will continue to believe that exemplary teaching requires extraordinary resources in an exceptional environment. (Elmore, 1995: 17)

As satisfying and romantic as this might be in the short view, balkanized reformers eventually burnout, leaving behind more cynicism and even greater gaps between "reformers and resisters." The inevitable long-run result of such a strategy is ironically to reduce the number of teachers committed to reform.

A third counterproductive problem that appears in the guise of reform is the presence of a multiplicity of change initiatives which actually make matters worse. Bryk and his colleagues put it this way:

> A natural concomitant to the multiplicity of the programs, however, is that they are often uncoordinated and may even be counterproductive in terms of student learning. The addition of new programs on top of the old ones may result in a disjointed and fragmented set of experiences for students. . . . Much of school life seems to follow an endless cycle of solicity funds, implementing new initiatives, and then going out to soliciting more funds for even newer initiatives to replace current ones. (Bryk et al, 1993: 26)

Similarly, the increased intrusive scrutiny of the performance of schools and teachers is leaving many teachers emotionally drained with confusion, anxiety, and a sense of professional inadequacy (Jeffrey & Woods, in press). What is a teacher to do? It feels right to be alienated. It seems hopeless to engage in the moral martyrdom of undertaking exhausting reforms against-the-grain. And the presence of a continuous stream of superficial, unconnected innovations justifies the conclusion that the system does not know what it is doing either.

In short, current strategies—top-down, bottom-up, or side-ways—don't work. We need to step back from this conundrum and approach it differently, more basically, and, as usual in postmodern times, more paradoxically.

## EMOTION AND HOPE: THE INDIVIDUAL

What do you do when you are faced with a lost cause that is of great importance? Richard Farson (1996) in *Management of the Absurd* provides a novel entry point in recalling a line from Frank Capra's movie from the thirties, *Mr. Smith Goes to Washington.* James Stewart, who plays a young man just elected to the Senate receives this absurd advice from his father that: "Lost causes are the only ones worth fighting for."

The state of educational reform is a prime candidate for the lost cause category because none of the current strategies being employed result in substantial, widespread change. The first step towards liberation, in my view, is the realization that we are facing a lost cause. Paradoxically as we shall see, this stance offers the only hope of making sustained progress. Moreover, the logic and the emotion of it makes perfect sense.

We all know smart people who do dumb things (Feinberg & Tarrant, 1995), and that many people of modest intelligence are quite successful. The difference, Goleman (1995) argues is the degree to which an individual possesses *emotional intelligence* which includes "self-control, zeal and persistence, and the ability to motivate oneself" (p. xii). Self-control and empathy, says Goleman, are at the heart of emotional intelligence. Moreover, Damasio (1994) presents compelling evidence that emotions are indispensable for rational decisions because they inform and narrow the range of choices in solving problems and making decisions. Cognitive intelligence is an advantage, but it is especially so when it combines with emotional maturity. The combination of heart and head is crucial to effectiveness.

Given the complexity and chaotic conditions of postmodern life, emotional development is crucial to survival:

> Much evidence testifies that people who are emotionally adept—who know and manage their own feelings well, and who read and deal effectively with other people's feelings—are at an advantage in any domain of life, whether romance and intimate relationships or picking up the unspoken rules that govern success in organizational politics.

> People with well-developed emotional skills are also more likely to
> be content and effective in their lives, mastering the habits of mind
> that foster their own productivity; people who cannot marshal some
> control over their emotional life fight inner battles that sabotage their
> ability for focused work and clear thought. (Goleman, 1995: 36)

Remember the metaphorical lost cause, or Czitszentmihalyi's
(1990) observation "frustration is deeply woven into the fabric of
life" (p. 7). This is the lot of teachers. The more they care the more
anxious they get. The more that they become emotionally detached
the poorer the decisions they make. Understanding the intimate two-
way link between emotion and hope is a powerful insight. Hope is
not a naive, sunny view of life. It is the capacity not to panic in tight
situations, to find ways and resources to address difficult problems:

> From the perspective of emotional intelligence, having hope means
> that one will not give in to overwhelming anxiety, a defeatist attitude,
> or depression in the face of difficult challenges or setbacks. Indeed,
> people who are hopeful evidence less depression than others as they
> maneuver through life in pursuit of their goals, are less anxious in
> general, and have fewer emotional distresses. (Goleman, 1995: 87)

It is well known that prolonged stress is unhealthy—deeply
physiologically unhealthy because it undermines the immune system. We think less explicitly that hope or optimism (especially combined with other conditions described in the next section) can lead
to better health. People who are optimistic and hopeful *are* more
resourceful and do better under difficult circumstances (Goleman
1995: 177). Not only do they avoid the costs of perennial pessimism,
they *gain* the benefits of hopefulness. It is important to emphasize
that I am linking hope and purpose. Hopeful people are not unaware
of reality or superficially happier. They are indeed hopeful in the
face of lost causes and other intractable problems.

It would be easy to draw misleading conclusions from this
description. Be happy, no worries, if only more of us could be hopeful, things would be all right. I am instead saying that the situation
of change is profoundly problematic and that we are down to our last
virtue—hope. We stand less of a chance by pursuing the techniques
of innovation than we do by working on a deeper understanding of
the complex interrelationships of emotion, hope, empathy, and
moral purpose.

Let me take two more down-to-earth applications of this line of thought. Both are from the perspective of the individual—one as initiator of change, the other as recipient.

Why does Mintzberg (1994) say, "never adopt a [management] technique by its usual name" (p. 27), and Farson (1996) state: 'once you find a management technique that works, give it up' (p. 35) because there is no silver bullet, no short-cut to reform, and because techniques devalue and disrespect emotions. The initiators of change must learn to put techniques in their place—they are, at best, tools in the service of a more fundamental set of relationships.

> **People who are optimistic and hopeful are more resourceful and do better under difficult circumstances.**

For example, assume you are a principal who is strongly committed to the increased use of technology. You are sincerely convinced that it is in the best interest of students to become technologically proficient. You see yourself as an innovator and change agent. In the old way of thinking—strategically and technically grounded— you might approach the situation along these lines: I am sure that technology is one of the keys to the future for my students; parents support it; I know that some teachers favor it, but others are going to be Luddites; How can I get some teacher leaders to support it? What kind of external resources and expertise can I generate to provide support and pressure to move forward? Maybe I can secure a few transfers and new appointments. My whole approach is advocacy and co-optation into an agenda that I am sure is right.

Now, let us assume that you, as principal are schooled in the deeper insights about complex change. You are equally convinced that technology is critical, but you approach it differently. Cutting the story short, let's say that you are having a staff session in which you are about to show a video segment that portrays a highly successful, technology-based school in action. Instead of showing it to make your case, you present it differently. You randomly ask one half of the staff to view the video with a "positive lens" noting what might be in it for them; you ask the other half of the staff to view it "negatively or critically" by identifying what might be problematic or potentially negative for them. If you are sincere, you have legitimized dissent. You have made it easy for staff to speak up about concerns (which would come out later anyway in more subtle and/or inaccessible ways). You listen carefully, suspending your own advocacy, because you know that some fundamental problems will be identified and that people's fears, real or imagined, will need to be examined carefully. This information may lead you to go back to the drawing board or to work with staff on some preconditions that would have to be addressed; or to proceed into action on a "start small, think big" basis, or to abandon high-profile technology in favor of a different approach.

In other words, with greater emotional intelligence and empathy, initiators of change "learn from resistors." They know that emotion is energy. They know that:

> What is needed is to hear the discontent, not to judge it or deny it, but accept that it is what others perceive. The simple act of listening, of seeking to understand the nature of the discontent, is enough to begin to shift staff's perception. However, many managements refuse to listen because they fear the dissatisfaction is worse than it is or they do not see it as balanced by many positive views of the organization. Once they take the risk of listening they are often surprised by the good news which arrives along with the bad. (Binney & Williams, 1995: 104)

In essence I am saying that the role of enthusiasts has been overestimated, and the value of resistors has been missed. Enthusiasts can be helpful to be sure, but not if in the mid to long run they increase the gap between themselves as small isolated groups of reformers, and the larger numbers of organizational members; and not if they turn out to be wrong because their ideas have not been subjected to critical scrutiny by nay-sayers who have a different point of view. The value of resistors on the other hand has been unappreciated, Resistant acts "often embody a form of good sense" (Gitlin & Margonis, 1995).

Trying to manipulate or otherwise control the change process in order to minimize or eliminate resistance is not only futile, it is exhausting.

> A more successful process is listening to those who seem to be resistors and seeking to understand what lies behind their resistance. (Binney & Williams, 1995: 111–112)

Finding a way to reconcile positive and negative emotion is the key to releasing energy for change. The initiator or leader of change who combines hope and empathy, even in the face of seemingly lost causes has a much greater chance for breakthrough.

It is important to clarify, as is implicit in the above example that hope is not connected only to 'positive' emotion (see the opening chapter by Hargreaves, in this book). Indeed, the opposite is the point in dealing with lost causes. Anger, sadness, frustration, anxiety, loss of control, dissatisfaction, discomfort all inform hopefulness for the emotionally intelligent person. Because the emotionally effective person knows that complexity and diversity is endemic in postmodern society, and always brings disagreement and frustration, he or she approaches the problem with that basic assumption. This is what Patrick Dolan was getting at when he observed:

> In a school, where mistrust between the community and the administration is the major issue, you might begin to deal with it by making sure that parents were present at every major event, every meeting, every challenge. *Within the discomfort of that presence,* the learning and the healing could begin. (Dolan, 1994: 60, emphasis added)

Hopeful people have a greater capacity to deal with interpersonal discomfort, and believe they will get somewhere by staying with it. They know that despair, while sometimes justified is ultimately self-destructive.

Perhaps it is one thing to have hope and empathy if you are in a leadership position, but what if you are the recipient of changes around you (in fact, for the vast majority of changes we experience regardless of our station in life we are recipients much more often than innovators of change). The secret again is the stance toward life. If we try to implement all changes coming our way we are naive and find ourselves in state of constant overload and dependency. If we reject all changes because they are incoherent, we become victimized anyway.

The more effective orientation, which builds on what I have been saying so far, is captured by Howard Gardner (1995) in his incisive study of 11 *Leading Minds.* He summarizes some of the traits in his composite Exemplary Leader (EL):

> Among the markers of the leader's personality, the most telling indication is a willingness to confront individuals in authority. Sometimes

this confrontation is abrasive, but it need not be so. Rather, E. L. stands out in that she identifies with and feels herself to be a peer of an individual in a position of authority. To E. L. it therefore feels natural—or at least possible—to address that person directly. Moreover, E. L. has pondered the issues involved in a specific position of leadership and believes that her own insights are at least as well motivated and perhaps more likely to be effective than those of the person currently at the helm. Perhaps this feeling of confidence stems from the fact that E. L.'s proposed solutions to problems grow out of her own life circumstances and thus are more appropriate than solutions conceived in earlier times or in other places. (p. 286)

Gardner proceeds to identify other traits: "E. L. stands out because of her concerns with moral issues" (p. 286); "another feature is the opportunity for reflection" and "the major reason that reflection is important is that a leader like E. L. must be able to see the big picture" (p. 287).

Similarly Csikszentmihalyi's (1996) study of 91 creative individuals from different fields indicates that creative people do not accept as face value what comes at them:

[They] do not rush to define the nature of problems; they look at the situation from various angles first and leave the formulation undetermined for a long time. They consider different causes and reasons. They test their hunches about what really is going on, first in their own mind and then in reality. They try tentative solutions and check their success—and they are open to reformulating the problem if the evidence suggests they started out on the wrong path. (p. 365)

Farson (1996) echoing Gardner's "willingness to confront others in authority" says that:

Both in school and at home we are taught a reliance on authority, on the opinion of others. We are taught not to trust our emotions, that our emotions are our enemies and will get us into trouble. (p. 150)

The same point, made more powerfully by Binney and Williams (1995) is that:

Intuition is important. Often people know what to do but can't articulate why. they have an instinct, a feeling that they ought to do something or behave in a certain way. So also with change. In our experience managers have a great deal of instinct and intuition about what works and what doesn't. If they feel it is OK to discuss openly what their instincts tells them, there is a huge well of insights to be drawn from. (p. 49)

Suppressing intuition and emotion is a barrier to good judgment, and we need to give them more space in dealing with a complex change circumstances.

Gardner, Csikszentmihalyi and others make it clear that the main purpose of their work is not to identify rarefied individuals, but to provide insights about leadership for everyone. Leadership with a small "l" has to do with how we all can exert greater control in the complexities of everyday experiences. The most important message is "how to find purpose and enjoyment in the chaos of existence" (Csikszentmihalyi, 1996: 20). The answer must start with us as individuals. Being hopeful is a powerful resource in its own right, and it can be amplified tremendously in the group.

## EMOTION AND HOPE: THE GROUP

We know at a common sense and experiential level that relationships matter a great deal, especially during times of intense change. We write about collaborative work attitudes and professional learning communities, but it is too easy for these to become abstract phrases. Once again, I believe that if we dig deeper into roles of emotion and hope in interpersonal relationships, we will gain a lasting understanding of how to deal with change more constructively.

Goleman (1995) provides a basic starting point:

> Studies done over two decades involving more than thirty-seven thousand people show that social isolation—the sense that you have nobody with whom you can share your private feelings, have close contact—doubles the chances of sickness or death." (p. 178)

If we link these findings to the iron law of change, that all change produces fear of the unknown, ambivalence, and anxiety we begin to see what has to be done. Helping ourselves and other people better manage the upsetting feelings of change is the healthiest thing we can do.

Farson (1996) states it this way:

> My experience tells me that people suffer most in their lives from failed or failing relationships—parental rejections, marital strife, difficulties with bosses—or from the lack of relationships—isolation, alienation, erosion of community. It follows, then, that the best way to deal with individuals may be to improve relationships. (p. 91)

Rather than site-based management, rethinking, staff development, assessment systems, and the like, the best way to deal with change may be *to improve relationships.* Because techniques abound (and they don't work), because we have failed to work at the basics—human relationships—and because you cannot really "manage" relationships, many of us have concluded that managing change in a direct sense is a myth (see Binney & Williams, 1995; Farson, 1996; Stacey, 1993). Paradoxically, to know that relationships cannot be managed directly frees us to pursue other approaches that create more powerful situations for dealing with the vicissitudes of complex change.

Change is learning, done under conditions of many real and/or perceived unknowns. In these circumstances prolonged isolation is bad, and interaction is essential, Binney and Williams (1995) observe that "if people work extensively in isolation, from their colleagues or the external environment there is a greater probability that they will find change more difficult to adjust to "because they will be less aware of what is going on inside and outside the organization" (p. 125). They will be more unprepared for change. Interaction on the other hand is vital: "it is as a result of interaction that things can be seen differently, choices appear, and action is supported" (p. 145). This requires individuals "who know and manage their own feelings well, and who read and deal effectively with other people's feelings" (Goleman, 1995: 36).

> **Change is learning, done under conditions of many real and/or perceived unknowns.**

In the same way that crash diets don't work, we must abandon the search for the quick fix. There is a consistent message in the new books on change: have good ideas, but listen with empathy; create time and mechanisms for personal and group reflection; allow intuition and emotion a respected role, work on improving relationships, realize that hope, especially in the face of frustrations is the last healthy virtue.

## CONSTRUCTIVE EDUCATIONAL CHANGE

It is no accident that I have drawn very little up to this point on the educational change literature. I wanted to establish the basic human concepts of emotion and hope as a foundation for a deeper understanding of constructive educational change. I maintain in this section that such a perspective provides us with a more powerful lasting and action-generative basis for interpreting recent research on constructive change.

Despite the consistently and specificity of research findings on the impact of collaborative work cultures and professional learning communities, we do not seem to be gaining ground on educational reform. Understanding these successes as charged with emotion and hope infuses them with more meaning, and may make them more memorable and attractive. Let us first consider briefly, the essence of these findings.

Newmann and Wehlage (1995) provide a concise summary of their studies of "successful school restructuring" in over 1500 schools. Success was defined as school reform efforts that make a positive difference in student learning and performance, measured both by newer standards of performance as well as by traditional achievement test. Successful schools focused on "authentic" pedagogy (teaching that requires students to think, to develop an in depth understanding, and to apply academic learning to important realistic problems) and student learning. They achieved this in two main ways:

1. *Greater Organizational Capacity*

   The most successful schools were those that used restructuring tools to help them function as professional communities. That is, they found a way to channel staff and student efforts toward a clear, commonly shared purpose for student learning. (Newmann & Wehlage, 1995: 3)

2. *Greater External Support*

   We found that external agencies helped schools to focus on student learning and to enhance organizational capacity through three strategies: setting standards for learning of high intellectual quality; providing sustained, school wide staff development; and using deregulation to increase school autonomy. (p. 4)

In short, vibrant internal learning communities dynamically plugged into two-way relationships with external networks made the difference. Corroborating evidence on the critical combination of internal and external learning is mounting (see for example, Elmore & Burney, 1996; Louis & Kruse, 1995; and Spillane & Thompson, 1996).

However, it takes a careful, I would say deeper, reading of these studies to grasp their full meaning. Collaborative work of the kind described in these studies embodies socio-emotional support as well as technical assistance. It creates a culture as Joe MacDonald (in press) observes of "lateral accountability" which "puts more peer pressure and accountability on staff who may not have carried out their fair share, but it can also ease the burden on teachers who have worked hard in isolation but who felt unable to help some students" (Newmann & Wehlage, 1995: 31)

These studies show the folly of searching for quick managerial fixes. Elmore and Burney (1996) talk about Superintendent Anthony Alvarado's in District 2 in New York City:

> Alvarado worries that District 2's approach to instructional improvement will be seen by outsiders as a collection of management principles, rather than as a culture based on norms of commitment, mutual care, and concern. Implementing the principles without the culture, he argues, will not work, because management alone cannot affect peoples' deeply-held values. (p. 22)

The strategies used in District 2 consist of a highly interactive and interpersonal network of learning and assessing progress.

Griffin's (1996) study of teachers in 13 restructuring schools also describes the personal and interpersonal nature of emotion and hope at work. The teachers in Griffin's research were characterized by:

- A sense of obligation/urgency "this urgency is rooted in the teachers' belief that schools can make a difference in students' lives, present and future, and that this belief must be played out against the complex tapestry of the larger society" (p. 3)
- An eagerness to recognize and act upon the 'problems' they encountered
- Retreat from beliefs that others can solve one's personal/professional problems
- Redesigned the use of time to understand, decide, act, reflect together
- A greater sense of future possibility
- A concern for everyday life and the schools relation to it
- A commitment and understanding of the interdependence of people, events, ideas and agencies (Griffin, 1996)

In their investigation of "local capacity" to implement mathematics and science reforms in nine schools districts, Spillane and Thompson (1996) found that, on the surface, all nine districts appeared to be aligning their curriculum with state policy, but on closer examination only three were engaged in substantive reform.

The now familiar list of differences in these three districts was different conceptions and use of: time, staffing, materials, knowledge, commitment and disposition, professional networks, and trust and collaboration. In turn, Spillane and Thompson organize these characteristics into three main categories:

- Physical capital (material resources)
- Human capital (commitment to reform and disposition to learn by administrators and teacher leaders)
- Social capital (relationships and networks internally and externally to the district)

Once again, we see the centrality of individual motivation and social relationships. We are now in a position to be more explicit about the main argument that connects emotion and hope to sustained reform in a way that provides a deeper explanation and a more powerful reform agenda. First, in many respects, the experience of teachers with reform is generating deep negative emotions and a sense of hopelessness, either because they are on the defensive from external attack and/or because they have been part of small groups of reformers who have burned themselves out. What makes this situation so serious is that it is so fundamentally flawed and self-defeating.

Second, the first step toward liberation is the recognition, on the one hand, that persistent negative emotions lead to ever greater individual and organizational illness and diminution of capacity and, on the other hand, that being hopeful is a critical resource, especially in the face of seeming lost causes. This realization contains a powerful insight for breaking free of a vicious cycle of despair.

Third, the research findings of successful reform just reviewed should be understood as providing, at least temporarily, the very conditions that enable hope to be experienced—again in the face of daunting problems.

The point is not that these conditions represent the elusive solutions that we have been seeking, but rather that hope is to be especially prized when it is fragile. Put another way, it is easy to be hopeful when things are rosy, it is *essential* to be hopeful when they are not. Holding onto hope in difficult situations is a necessary (although not a sufficient condition for longer term survival).

Fourth, reformers are ill-advised to work only within the balkanized cocoons of like-minded individuals. We stand more of a chance of getting somewhere if we confront differences earlier in the process, working through the discomfort of diversity than we do if we attempt to work in sealed-off cultures.

Fifth, and this is crucial, to stay hopeful under conditions is not to be politically quiescent. It is not only possible, but indeed essential to work on the connection between hopefulness and the structural conditions that promote it. The hopeful change agent that I am talking about is painfully aware that the current working conditions of teachers work against reform. The development of collaborative work cultures under very different internal structural conditions (more grouping of students, and teachers; more time for teaches to work together; close collaboration with parents and communities; redistribution of resources) and very different external relationships (standards of performance and accountability, access to networks of ideas and professional learning) must become part and parcel of the working agenda of hopeful reformers. This stance includes pushing for, demanding and expecting new policy frameworks to alter the incentives and structural conditions that currently frustrate reform.

In short, hope has a dual interconnected track—working with students, parents, and other educators, even when it seems like a lost cause; and participating in the politics of altering the structural conditions of schools so that reform and quality have a greater chance of being built into the daily experiences of the majority of educators and students.

## CONCLUSION

Society is more complex, more chaotic, more non-linear than ever before. The demands on schools are ever more multiple and fragmented. The boundaries between schools, their communities and society are more porous and permeable (see Hargreaves & Fullan, 1996).

To survive in these circumstances requires a greater individual and group capacity. This capacity at it's core is to be able to handle emotions and hope differently. Frustration, disagreement, intractable problems are common fare. Working together under these circumstances takes on radically different meaning and urgency. It's not matter of having trusting relationships with like-minded people. As Elmore (1995) puts it "small groups of self-selected reformers apparently seldom influence their peers" (p. 20). If we are to get anywhere on a larger scale we have to take on the "negative" emotions. Hope is not blind. It recognizes that disagreement and matters of power are central to working through the discomfort of diversity (see also, Henry, 1996).

The successful school restructuring efforts described earlier may not be enduring and/or may not spread (and that, indeed, is the problem). The argument in this chapter is that we have a greater chance of capitalizing on these findings if we understand the roles of emotion and hope that underlie successful individuals and groups, and if we strive to create the structural conditions that challenge and help create hopefulness. It is my contention that these successes occurred precisely because emotion and hope were channeled in promising directions, and that, if we fail this more basic understanding, we will not be able to sustain such efforts let alone go beyond them.

Being hopeful and taking action in the face of important lost causes (improving education being the one in question) may be less emotionally draining than being in a permanent state of despair. There is also evidence that it may be one of the few routes to success still available to us. To be hopeful is not to be naive, but to struggle to move ahead. Judge Rosalie Abella born in a refugee camp in Stuttgart Germany, on July 14, 1946, may have said it best "there was nothing expected and everything hoped for."

## REFERENCES

Binney, G. & Williams, C. (1995). *Learning into the Future*. London: Nicholas Brealey.

Bishop, P. & Mulford, W. (1996). Empowerment in four Australian primary schools. *International Journal of Educational Reform* V5, No. 2, pp. 193–204.

Csikszentmihalyi, M. (1990). *Flow the Psychology of Optimal Experience*. New York: Harper & Collins.

———. (1996). *Creativity*. New York: Harper & Collins.

Damasio, A. (1994). *Descartes' Error*. New York: Grosset Putnam.

Dolan, P. (1994). *Restructuring our Schools*. Kansas City, MO: Systems & Organizations.

Dryden, K. (1995). *In School.* Toronto: McClelland.

Elmore (1995). Getting to scale with good educational practice. *Harvard Educational Review* V66, No 1, pp. 1–26.

Elmore, R. & Burney, D. (1996). Staff development and instructional improvement: Community District 2. New York City, paper prepared for the National Commission of Teaching and America's Future.

Farson, R. (1996). *Management of the Absurd.* New York: Simon & Schuster.

Feinberg, M. & Tarrant, J. (1995). *Why Smart People do Dumb Things.* New York: Fireside.

Fried, R. (1995). *The Passionate Teacher.* Boston, MA: Beacon Press.

Gardner, H. (1995). *Leading Minds.* New York: Basic Books.

Gitlrrin, A. & Margonis, F. (1995). The political aspects of reform. *American Journal of Education* V103, pp. 377–405.

Goleman, D. (1995). *Emotional Intelligence.* New York: Bantam Books.

Griffin, G. (1996). Restructuring Schools: Implications for teacher education. Paper presented at the Annual Meeting of the American Educational Research Association, New York.

Hargreaves, A. ed. (1997). *Rethinking educational change with heart and mind: The 1997 ASCD Yearbook.* Alexandria, VA: Association for Supervision and Curriculum Development.

Hargreaves, A. & Fullan, M. (1996). *What's worth fighting for out there?* Toronto: Ontario Public School Teachers' Federation and New York: Teachers College Press.

Henry, M. (1996). *Parent-School Collaboration.* Albany: State University of New York Press.

Jeffrey, B., & Woods, P. (in press). Feeling deprofessionalized. *The Cambridge Journal of Education.*

Louis, K. & Kruse, S. (1995). *Professionalism & Community.* Thousand Oakes, CA: Corwin Publishers.

MacDonald, J. (in press). *Redesigning School.* New York: Teachers College Press.

Mintzberg, H. (1994). *The Rise and Fall of Strategic Planning.* New York: Free Press.

Newmann, F. & Wehlage, G. (1995). *Successful School Restructuring.* Madison, WI: Center on Organization and Restructuring of Schools.

Spillane, J. & Thompson, C. (1996). Restructuring conceptions of local capacity. Paper presented at the annual meeting of the American Educational Research Association, New York, San Francisco: Jossey-Bass.

# Authors

**Tom Donahoe,** former president of Pacific Telesis Foundation, Tom Donahoe serves on the boards of several educational, civic, and arts organizations, including WestEd, the public agency uniting Far West Laboratory for Educational Research and Development and Southwest Regional Laboratory.

**Richard F. Elmore** is a Professor of Education at Harvard Graduate School of Education in Cambridge, Massachusetts. His specialization is public policy.

**Joyce Epstein** is Director of the Center on School, Family, and Community Partnerships and Principal Research Scientist in the Center for Research on the Education of Students Placed at Risk (CRESPAR) at John Hopkins University. Dr. Epstein is co-author of *School, Family, and Community Partnerships: Your Handbook for Action* published by Corwin Press.

**Michael Fullan** is Dean of Education at the Ontario Institute for Studies in Education of the University of Toronto. He has written extensively about educational reform and the management of change including *The New Meaning of Educational Change* (Teachers College Press), the *What's Worth Fighting For?* trilogy with Andy Hargreaves (Teachers College Press) and *Change Forces* (Falmer Press).

**Helen Gunter** is a lecturer in the Department of Education at Keele University, U.K., and is currently working on an intellectual history of the field of education management in the United Kingdom from the 1960s.

**Andy Hargreaves** is Director of the International Centre for Educational Change at the Ontario Institute for Studies in Education of the University of Toronto in Canada. He is the author and co-author of many books including *Changing Teachers, Changing Times,* and *Schooling for Change.*

**Judith Warren Little** is professor of education at the University of California, Berkeley, where her research centers on teachers' work and on policies and practices of professional development.

**Sarah J. McCarthey** is an Associate Professor in the Department of Curriculum and Instruction, University of Texas at Austin. Her specializations are literacy and classroom discourse.

**Penelope Peterson** is University Distinguished Professor of Education at Michigan State University and co-author with Richard Elmore and Sarah McCarthey of *Restructuring in the Classroom: Teaching, Learning, and School Organization.* She is also co-editor with Anna Neumann of *Learning from Our Lives: Women, Research, and Autobiography in Education* and past-president of the American Educational Research Association.

**Priscilla Wohlstetter** is associate professor of education and director of the Center on Educational Governance at the University of Southern California. She has published extensively in both research and practitioner journals, and is co-author of *School-Based Management: Organizing for High Performance.*

# Acknowledgments

Grateful acknowledgment is made to the following authors and agents for their permission to reprint copyrighted materials.

## SECTION 1

Association for Supervision and Curriculum Development (ASCD) for "Rethinking Educational Change" by Andy Hargreaves from *Rethinking Educational Change with Heart and Mind,* 1997 ASCD Yearbook, edited by Andy Hargreaves, pp. 1–26. Copyright 1997 by ASCD. Reprinted with permission. All rights reserved.

Taylor and Francis International Publishers for "The Complexity of the Change Process" by Michael Fullan. From *Change Forces,* 1993, pp. 19–41. Copyright 1993 by Taylor and Francis. Reprinted with permission. All rights reserved.

Kluwer Academic Publishers for "Cultures of Teaching and Educational Change" by Andy Hargreaves. From *International Handbook of Teachers and Teaching,* by B. Biddle, T. Good, and I. Goodson. Copyright pending by Kluwer Academic Publishers. Reprinted with permission. All rights reserved.

## SECTION 2

Cassell and Helen Gunter for "Chaotic Reflexivity" by Helen Gunter. From *Rethinking Education: The Consequences of Jurassic Management,* by Helen Gunter, 1997, pp. 83–103. Copyright 1997 by Helen Gunter. Reprinted with permission. All rights reserved.

Kluwer Academic Publishers for "Leadership for Change" by Michael Fullan. From *International Handbook of Educational Leadership and Administration,* edited by K. Leithwood et al., 1996, pp. 701–722. Copyright 1996 by Kluwer Academic Publishers. Reprinted with permission. All rights reserved.

American Educational Research Association (AERA) for "Teacher's Professional Development in a Climate of Educational Reform" by Judith Warren Little. From *Educational Evaluation and Policy Analysis,* 1993, vol. 15, no. 2, pp. 129–155. Copyright 1993 by the American Educational Research Association. Reprinted with permission. All rights reserved.

## SECTION 3

Phi Delta Kappa for "Getting School-Based Management Right: What Works and What Doesn't" by Priscilla Wohlstetter. From *Phi Delta Kappan,* September 1995, pp. 22–26. Copyright by Phi Delta Kappa. Reprinted with permission. All rights reserved.

American Educational Research Association (AERA) for "Learning from School Restructuring" by Penelope L. Peterson, Sarah J. McCarthey, and Richard F. Elmore. From *American Educational Research Journal,* 1996, vol. 33, no. 1, pp. 119–153. Copyright 1996 by the American Educational Research Association. Reprinted with permission. All rights reserved.

Phi Delta Kappa for "Finding the Way: Structure, Time, and Culture in School Improvement" by Tom Donahoe. From *Phi Delta Kappan,* December 1993, pp. 298–305. Copyright 1993 by Phi Delta Kappa. Reprinted with permission. All rights reserved.

Phi Delta Kappa for "School/Family/Community Partnerships: Caring for the Children We Share" by Joyce L. Epstein. From *Phi Delta Kappan,* May 1995, pp. 701–712. Copyright 1995 by Phi Delta Kappa. Reprinted with permission. All rights reserved.

## SECTION 4

Association for Supervision and Curriculum Development (ASCD) and Michael Fullan for "Emotion and Hope: Constructive Concepts for Complex Times" by Michael Fullan. From *Rethinking Educational Change with Heart and Mind,* 1997 ASCD Yearbook, edited by Andy Hargreaves, pp. 216–233. Copyright 1997 by Michael Fullan. Reprinted with permission. All rights reserved.

# Index

**CORWIN
PRESS**

The Corwin Press logo—a raven striding across an open book—represents the union of courage and learning. Corwin Press is committed to improving education for all learners by publishing books and other professional development resources for those serving the field of PreK–12 education. By providing practical, hands-on materials, Corwin Press continues to carry out the promise of its motto: **"Helping Educators Do Their Work Better."**